Praise for *As One*

The Great Commission of making disciples of all nations has been one of the greatest challenges for the church and for followers of Jesus. Where to begin and what is the goal has eluded disciples for so long. *As One Discipleship and Mind Renewal* is exemplary in that it brings one to a relationship of knowing Who God is, knowing who you are in Him and a relationship with others. *As One* brings us to the culmination of our faith and salvation of becoming One with God, reconciled with God through Christ as a new creation. *As One* utilizes the mind renewal and visualization which is an awesome tool in receiving and walking in the Truth and the yet unseen reality of our identity and purpose in Christ. Caprice did an awesome job of this gift that will bring the Body of Christ into the supernatural realm of healing and wholeness.
— **Jennifer Najem**, Pastor, Abbalove Church

***

Caprice has revelation about the heart of God that will transform anyone who will allow their spirit and soul to be touched by these words. Being a pastor for 36 years and an author of many books myself, I know revelation knowledge when I hear it. As you read this book, you will realize it is not a mental book only. The words written here are obviously a result of seeking God and wanting to help people. Her explanation of the character of God and personal relationship with God will help pull anyone up and out of any bondage, sickness or crisis who is screaming, "No hope!" I found myself very touched as I was reading through the manuscript while the Holy Spirit was ministering to me personally. A book for everyone and anyone, as well as Bible studies, church classes, etc.
— **John Cappetto**, Founding Pastor, Faith Heights Church

***

Get ready for your life to change for the better! If you apply the tools outlined in the *As One* program every day, you are going to see the manifestation of your healing! Your relationship with the Lord will grow into an intimate and personal relationship with Jesus, far exceeding the one you may already have with Him. Your true identity is in knowing you are the righteousness of Christ and *As One* will teach you how to cultivate that relationship on a step-by-step basis! You will better understand His love for you and the price He has already paid for your healing!

Caprice Scott and I both started our healing journey in 2019, however, we were working with different groups that focused more on neuroplasticity and retraining the brain. The missing link was the major role Jesus Christ plays in this transformation. I can honestly say I believe with all my heart we ended up in the same group by divine intervention and that is where I came to know the depth of her love for Him. I came to deeply love and respect Caprice during this time. The most obvious connection was that we both KNEW Jesus was the central solution yet wasn't being taught enough about the crucial role He plays, in our opinions.

It was during this time that Holy Spirit gave Caprice the creative idea to write the curriculum for *As One* that could reach many more people. She was already leading an incredible group that began to grow exponentially called Healing Is for You while also writing As One. She was also conducting interviews, making teaching videos, having Bible study, conducting individual as well as group coaching ... all while writing *As One*! She has such a heart for God and I have nothing but admiration, not only for that, but also for her intelligence, work ethic and burden for souls. Her work had already impacted so many lives and her own testimony is proof that *As One* "works!"

Caprice is not only an awesome Certified Life Coach Minister, but her heart is to see others grow in their relationship with Jesus as well as to see them have their healing manifest in their lives as well. From day one after she shared with me the idea to write *As One*, I was her greatest cheerleader and encouraged her every opportunity I had. I knew in my spirit this was part of her destiny and what she was called to do!

Working with Caprice changed my life for the better and I am not only healed but closer to Jesus than I have ever been in my walk with Him! If you approach the following pages by using the tools provided, it will transform your life as well as deepen your relationship with Jesus. Keep your mind open and your hands lifted to the Lord and listen for that still, small voice. Holy Spirit abides in you as a believer. He will help to guide, teach, and encourage you! He will be with you every step of the way on your healing journey that I can attest to works! I cannot emphasize enough how valuable this book will become to you! It is written in a clear, precise, step-by-step method that will direct you across the "finish line" and your life, both physically and spiritually, will be deeply enhanced. You will come to understand that YOU ARE the

righteousness of Christ! That understanding is the key to the success of *As One*! Get ready for your new life and enjoy the journey!
Be blessed and highly favored!
— **Pastor Mary Jo Glenn**, Raleigh, NC

***

This course has been such a blessing to me. It came to me at a time when I really, really needed it. My relationship with God is so much deeper. And it has so much more meaning and understanding of how much He loves me. Thank you for using your gift, Caprice, to help others deepen their relationship and understanding with God. You are a true blessing, and I am thankful that a woman I did not even know told me about the *As One* program. May you continue to be blessed and bless others!
— **Michele Hughes**

***

The *As One* program was a tremendous blessing in my life! It helped me on a daily basis to reinforce the truth of who I am in Jesus, who He is in me, and the reality that we are inseparable; we do this life together, and we are victorious together. The content was laid out in a way that was clear and easy to understand and follow. Caprice's teaching style really helped me absorb the information. The way Caprice communicates is clear and passionate, and her visualizations not only calmed me, but helped me to connect with God tangibly as my loving Father. In addition, the written exercises are thorough yet not overwhelming, and they helped me to absorb the truth more deeply into my heart and apply the knowledge in my personal life. I highly recommend this course to any person--a young believer, a more mature believer, or even someone who is unsure of their beliefs and is searching for their identity and purpose, and the truth about God.
— **Stacey Woodward**

***

Life's traumas can cripple a person for life, bringing them into a state of fear, anxiety, depression, and physical illness. What Caprice teaches is how overcoming trauma can bring forth healing, without being dismissive of one's journey. Her teachings can help guide you into a relationship with God, leaving behind self-works and victim mentality, bringing you into true self-identity, your identity in Christ. As Christians we know GOD is our Healer, and that Christ came to heal the broken hearted and bind up our wounds. Learning how to walk life's journey through Christ is where our true healing journey begins. This book brings that journey to life, giving us the full visual of our journey with Christ "Our Healer"!

***

What Caprice brings to life in this book is the truest answers to mental, physical and spiritual healing available today. I have personally practiced what she teaches to receive my own healing. I was able to easily navigate these principles and apply them to my daily life. Caprice's delivery is shared by experience and love, her heart is very evident in her writings.

— **Janice Wegner,** Discipleship Team Leader and Charis Bible College Student

***

Looking forward to sharing this beautiful *As One* teaching with friends. How blessed I truly am. Thank you Caprice and everyone that was involved in making this available for me & everyone that will come.

—**Darlene Moree**

***

Wow! Caprice's messages are packed with so much beautiful knowledge! I am blown away and usually go over each one multiple times. I am praying I can begin to memorize scripture and be able to recite it. I often struggle with hearing the Spirit and realize if messages don't line up with scripture, then it is not from Him.

As One is a program I'd been in search of for so long, and when I was blessed to participate in it, I knew the Holy Spirit brought me to Caprice and her program. *As One* is a program every person can benefit from. A newcomer all the way to lifelong believers in Christ. I actually can't wait to go through her program again, as it is packed with lessons, allowing for new learning to occur each time you participate!

—**Jennifer Corey**

***

I never imagined how much this course would help me. The teachings are jam-packed with wonderful truths that are foundational for our relationships with Christ. This program has taught me more about Christ than I've ever known. Important subjects were written by Caprice in an extremely understandable manner. Her experiences of walking with the Lord in such a close relationship would make you envious of her childlike faith and her ability to know the Lord so intimately.

She covers the basics of our pursuit to encounter God on a deeper level as well as to experience who He truly is. The anointing of God is evident in each and every syllable she wrote, it's evident she has a profound relationship with the Lord. The visualizations are incredibly moving and comforting, bringing tears of joy as one delves into them. It's clear they are divinely inspired. I've come to understand the depth of His love, not just intellectually but in the core of my being. Realizing that my wonderful Heavenly Father, who crafted the heavens and the universe, knows me personally, designed me as a masterpiece before the world's creation, recognized me before my conception, and created me with a unique purpose, fills me with immense joy and peace. It's truly amazing to learn and be reminded that God has always known me, sees me, and cares for me. My desire for a relationship with Him is stronger now than ever before. Understanding your identity in Christ and the authority you possess in Him can transform how you navigate daily life, moving from a place of victory rather than striving to attain it. God views us as perfect as Jesus. Indeed, this is the greatest news.

—Lidya Djuhana

AS ONE

The Biblically Based Discipleship
& Mind Renewal Program

Caprice Scott

Published by KHARIS PUBLISHING, an imprint of
KHARIS MEDIA LLC.

Copyright © 2025 Caprice Scott

ISBN: 978-1-63746-347-5

ISBN: 1-63746-347-2

Library of Congress Control Number: 2025946238

All KHARIS PUBLISHING products are available at special quantity discounts for bulk purchase for sales promotions, premiums, fund-raising, and educational needs. For details, contact:

Kharis Media LLC
Tel: 1-630-909-3405
support@kharispublishing.com
www.kharispublishing.com

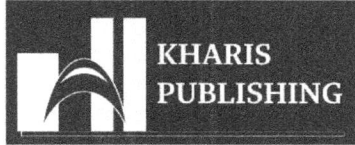

Your Guide to the As One Program

As One is about *discipleship*. Jesus in The Great Commission, before He returned to heaven, told his followers that they were to "Go therefore and make disciples of all the nations, baptizing them in the name of the Father and of the Son and of the Holy Spirit." Matthew 28:19 (NKJV) Whether you are exploring a bit about God out of curiosity, are a new believer, or have been a life-long Christian, this program will bring to light the truths in the Word of God in a fresh, new way.

As One is about *mind renewal*. The Apostle Paul tells us in Romans 12:2 (NKJV) "And do not be conformed to this world, but be transformed by the renewing of your mind, that you may prove what is that good and acceptable and perfect will of God." Mind renewal is about learning to see things through God's perspective. As you read through the program, utilizing the applications and meditations, you will be actively renewing your mind. Learning about the character of God, your identity in Christ, and what this union with Him looks like is part of that renewal process. Mind renewal is something we must choose to make a daily habit. As you apply what you learn in your day-to-day life, you will begin this incredible transformation.

How the Program Works:

There are three sections to the *As One Program*. Throughout this program but specifically in the first section, *Who God Is*, you will learn about the loving character and goodness of God and His feelings toward you. In the second section, *Who You Are in Him*, you will learn about your true identity and authority in Christ including your union with His Spirit. In section three, *Your Relationship Together*, you'll learn what this relationship entails.

Chapters & Truths: Each chapter is broken down into smaller bite-sized "Truths." Some chapters will consist of two or three Truths while others may have up to six, depending on the amount of content covered. Pray each time you sit down to read and do the applications and ask the Holy Spirit to guide your heart. Take time to work through each Truth, choosing to meditate on and contemplate anything that stands out to you. Ask the Holy Spirit to open your understanding for a deeper revelation as you do so. This will allow Him to speak to your heart and help you in the process of mind renewal. If it works for you to do so, plan to work through one lesson per week or two but do what works best for you to remain consistent. Most importantly, don't give up.

Applications: Helpful applications including some occasional scripture meditations and visualizations, are included after each Truth. Take time to listen to the meditations, answer questions, and talk with Papa God about the things you discover. These meditations and visualizations may be accessed by scanning the QR code with your phone.

Toolkit: The Toolkit is a quick reference you can find in the appendix. You may want to refer to it at the end of each chapter. It expands on some of the applications and other things you'll be learning. The Toolkit will be helpful for you to refer to often as you continue in your mind renewal process, especially after completing the program.

You'll find additional resources in the Appendix:

Glossary: Throughout the program you may come across terms that are unfamiliar to you. Please check the glossary in the appendix for the meaning and explanation behind these terms.

Toolkit Sources for Deepening Your Walk with God: Suggested reading and YouTube videos.

Acknowledgements

To Anne Whitaker, Donna Rasmussen, Dee Smith - thank you ladies for your time and selfless dedication to going through *As One* with a fine-tooth comb and making sure the many scriptures were correct. You are gems!

Lezli Urlacher, you especially took on the massive, daunting task of helping me organize this work. You and Stacey Woodward accomplished an amazing feat through the initial editing. There's no possible way I could have done this without your help and attention to detail. Stacey, I am still amazed that you mentioned editing at just the right time - absolutely God's leading. Lezli, thank you for reaching out to me when you did through the prompting of the Holy Spirit, also. I not only received timely, much needed help in answer to prayer, but also a friend and sister in Christ because of your obedience to Him. Your calm, level-headed suggestions have helped anchor me. I am forever grateful to and for you!

Leigh-Ann Evans, Kimberly Maus, and Sabrina Se - thank you, dear sisters, for your suggestions, your willingness to read through and share your thoughts. Kimberly - you are my resource lady and my Joshua! Thank you for taking on so much in the ministry as I worked on this program and to you and Leigh-Ann for praying me through it. Leigh-Ann - I appreciate your creativity and ability to hear the Lord so clearly and your gift in creating incredible content that others may also experience the love and goodness of our Papa. Thank you for being my Aaron and always holding up my arms in victory. Janice Wegner, I am also grateful to you for helping "hold down the fort" as I was working to get this program created.

Mary Jo Glenn - there's no way I could have done this without your love and encouragement through one of my most difficult years. You reminded me of my true identity, which I hope shines through this book. Sheri Wahl - when I thought everything was lost in 2023, you told me to get back up and start dreaming with Papa again. This book would not exist if it weren't for your encouragement and honesty (and a little kick in the pants). You reminded me I wasn't going to have to do any of this "alone" because it was Papa's project anyway.

As One Activated ladies - thank you Tanda Archer, Lidya Djuhana, Julie Burns, and Gina Bosick, for being "boots on the ground", willing to take the Gospel message and disciple others in the body of Christ through loving guidance. I am truly grateful for each of you, not only in the way you disciple and lead others, but for your encouragement, love, and friendship to me. You ladies are the real deal.

Richard Scott, you probably had no idea what you were signing up for when you said, "I do", but I'm so blessed and grateful to not only call you my husband but also my bestie. Thank you for your grace, patience, and love for me, and for always knowing how to help when I'm feeling like I've jumped into the deep end and have forgotten how to swim.

Mom and Bob, thank you for your love, support, and understanding while I've been so busy these last 2 years. I'm truly thankful for you. Dad, remember when I told you I wanted to do something big to make a lasting change in the world? You said, "You will" like you had no doubt. I wish you could have been here to see it happen.

My loving Papa, You reminded me when I had lost my vision and dream that YOU were and are my Partner, and I never have to do anything alone. Papa God - this book is for You. Thank You for radically saving my life, putting me on a new trajectory full of purpose, healing, and love.

CONTENTS

My Testimony

As I lay in bed on a mid-February day in 2019, my heart broke at the thought of never seeing my family again, never returning to the Southwest desert that I loved so much, never again being able to travel and explore new places with my husband. My health problems which had begun nearly ten years earlier had escalated to the point that I was certain I wouldn't last another week, much less survive until summer. Not only did I not see myself surviving much longer, I didn't even want to continue trying, given the way I felt.

Every part of my body was sick. At that point, I had been diagnosed with seven autoimmune diseases, including rheumatoid arthritis and Celiac disease, along with many other debilitating issues: heart problems, skin and other connective tissue problems, gut and digestive issues including motility disorder, parasites, SIBO, candidiasis which had spread to my blood, allergies, food sensitivities, EMF sensitivities, POTS, Lyme and coinfections, mold illness, migraines, carpal tunnel syndrome, tendonitis, four genetic mutations that didn't allow my body to detox properly, chronic fatigue syndrome, chronic sinus infections, depression, anxiety, panic attacks, and even skin cancer. These things made day-to-day living a nightmare, and most of my days were spent just trying to do common things that most people take for granted. There were days I couldn't stand and had to crawl through my house to get from my bedroom to the bathroom or kitchen.

Over the past decade, I had seen just about every kind of doctor and specialist imaginable from naturopaths to rheumatologists, hoping to get answers. It was discouraging to chase these endless rabbit trails that brought no relief. At one point, I was on 13 different medications and only seemed to be getting worse. A friend with similar motility issues had endured surgery to remove most of her intestines, and I began to fear this would happen to me as well. I was losing hope.

The latest doctor I had been seeing for the past several months had also suffered through an autoimmune disease which led him to study integrative medicine. I was hopeful, but exhausted, as he ran every kind of test imaginable to try to find the root cause, gave me weekly glutathione IVs and several other treatments, and sent me home with a long list of expensive supplements. As time seemed to be running out, I still wasn't getting better.

"Heavenly Father," I prayed, "if I'm not going to survive this and You're going to take me, please give me peace about it and let it happen quickly . . . preferably in my sleep. But Lord, if You're going to pull me out of this, I need a sign of hope from You that this isn't the end. Lord, remember the dove You sent me years ago? Would You somehow let me see a dove as the answer that You're going to pull me out of this? I just need hope, Father."

As I lay there, the memory surfaced of the dove that God sent me 20 years earlier. I remembered how gracious He was to comfort me with this dove after I had made a bad decision. Back then, my husband at the time and I were very poor. We struggled to make ends meet and put food on the table. People from church often dropped off food on our front porch, or we'd receive gift cards for groceries. My husband worked for an ophthalmologist as an eye technician while I worked at the local church school as an art teacher as well as occasionally painted murals for a general contractor.

At that time, my husband and I had a Christmas party to attend. It was going to be far more formal than anything I had attended before, and I wanted a nice dress to wear. I had gone shopping that day and purchased a dress on clearance. Guilt began to overwhelm me—the kind of guilt that sets in so deeply that you fear God won't forgive you because you ignored His Spirit. I couldn't take the dress back because of an "all sales are final" policy. I began praying and then pleading that God would forgive me for buying a dress that really wasn't necessary when we were so poor that we were depending on the generosity of others just to buy food.

Psalm 51 played over and over in my mind, specifically verse 11 where David said: "Do not cast me from your presence or take your Holy Spirit from me."(NIV) I struggled with this fear until it had grown to the point that I was terrified God wouldn't forgive me and I would be lost for buying a dress. Although that may seem like irrational thinking, it wasn't an uncommon way of thinking for me, due to some very incorrect theology I had learned.

After praying and pleading for a while, I was impressed to look outside on our front porch. I was shocked to see a pure white dove sitting on the porch railing. It was beautiful! I'd never seen one in person before. I recalled the prayer and scripture I had been praying, specifically "please don't take Your Holy Spirit from me," and I was sobered by the realization that the Holy Spirit is often symbolized as a white dove.

I prayed, "Lord, if this is Your answer to me, if You've sent this dove as a sign that You're not taking Your Spirit from me, then please let it stay on my porch for 24 hours." Incredibly, the dove stayed right there for 24 hours. When we went outside, it would hop down the railing but never flew away. It even allowed me to get close enough to take a photo.

Back to that day in February 2019 as I lay sick in bed, the memory of the white dove 20 years before brought me comfort. God brought another memory to mind of a prayer He had answered several years before. A friend and I had been discussing how, in the Bible, God would do miraculous things for people, and in response, they would give Him a name reflecting who He is and what He had done for them—or sometimes, God Himself provided a name for them to call Him. An example of this is found in Genesis 22 when Abraham climbs Mount Moriah with his son Isaac after the Lord has asked Abraham to sacrifice his son. Isaac asks, "…but where is the lamb for the burnt offering?" Abraham answers, "God Himself will provide the lamb for the burnt offering, my son." As we know, sure enough, a ram is caught in the thicket nearby and Abraham sacrifices the ram instead of Isaac. Abraham names the place, "The Lord will provide," or in Hebrew, Jehovah Jireh. A similar story is found in Exodus 15:26, where God reveals Himself as Jehovah-Rapha— "The Lord who heals you." In Psalm 23, we find Jehovah-Raah— "The Lord is my Shepherd." There are many other examples in the Scriptures of names God's people have called Him because of what He did for them.

I had spent time praying and asking God to reveal to me what He'd like for me to call Him. At the time, I was a potter, creating pottery to sell in galleries in the Pacific Northwest and Colorado. One day as I was praying about this, I was impressed to read Isaiah chapter 64, and I stopped at verse 8: "And yet, O LORD, you are our Father. We are the clay, and you are the potter. We all are formed by your hand." This was my verse. I heard the Spirit speak to my heart, saying, "You are my daughter the potter, Caprice, and I am your Father the Potter."

As I reflected back to the times I had experienced God speaking or revealing Himself to me, these two stood out. Because I was too sick and weak to do anything else, I scrolled through Instagram® to take my mind off my current misery. As I had been praying, asking God to give me hope, I scrolled to a photo of a white ceramic dove in its creator's hand. I knew immediately that this was my answer. God had a fellow potter create a small ceramic dove and post it just when I needed it to see it. Here was my Hope. To my knowledge, this potter had never created sculptures like this before. It seemed to be just for me.

Several days later, I was in bed praying and bravely asked the Lord, "Father God, if You aren't just going to pull me out of this, but are going to heal me fully, then I need to see at least one dove every day until I'm completely healed." From that day on, I continued to see doves every single day. I wasn't searching the internet for them. I wasn't using hashtags to find them online. Doves would just show up in my newsfeed on Facebook® or Instagram® or even in cards or flyers in the mail.

About that time, a dear friend of mine sent me a couple of books: *HOPE – A Practical Guide to Praying for Healing*© by Rebecca Ribnick (Rebecca Ribnick, 2018) and *Tell Your Heart to Beat Again*© by Dutch Sheets (Regal Books, 2002) As I was reading these two books, I started to believe that God was going to heal me instantaneously the way He had healed Rebecca Ribnick of her autoimmune disease. I thought maybe I just needed the right prayer and once I figured out the "formula," I would be healed. God gently began revealing to me that it wasn't that there was a special way of praying the correct words or a checklist of things that I had to do in order to *get* Him to heal me. He began opening my understanding to His love and compassion, and to my need to change my beliefs about Him, and myself.

In March of 2019, my doctor realized that because of four genetic mutations, my body was not able to detoxify. The glutathione IVs were not helping my liver or anything else as we had hoped. As my husband and I were sitting in the exam room with my doctor, he put his head in his hands and began rocking back and forth. He had just looked at some of my newest test results that had come in and he told us that he had no idea what else to do for me because my latest test results were "off the charts bad." Thankfully, I had a little glimmer of hope because of the promise God had given me about my healing the month prior. Then it was like the doctor had a light bulb moment and said there might be one thing that could help my motility issue that he hadn't thought of previously.

"Dr. Johnson" asked me if I had experienced any emotional trauma in my childhood. Indeed, I had. My entire childhood was filled with emotional trauma—from an unhealthy, dysfunctional family life, to years of being bullied in elementary school. In high school I made some poor choices that culminated in me becoming pregnant at 16. I married my son's father, and our 18-year relationship was toxic.

The doctor told us about a brain retraining course[1] that was scientifically based in neuroplasticity, the brain's ability to adapt and change. He believed that this might be an answer for at least some of my gut issues.[2]

I went home from the doctor's that day curious if brain retraining might be at least part of the answer to my health problems. I began praying about it. "Father God, is this your answer? Do you want me to do this?" I looked online and read through the list of all the conditions brain retraining allegedly had been known to help or cure. Only a few of the problems that I had were listed. My heart sank a little, but I decided I would give it a try if this was where God was leading me. The program wasn't terribly expensive, but I just didn't have the money for it; I wanted to be certain that this was what God wanted me to do. I prayed, "Father God, if you want me to do this program, I need You to cover the entire cost of it." Within 48 hours, my now husband, a church musician, was asked to play at two memorial services. The pay from the second service was triple the usual amount. It wasn't typical for him to be asked to play for two memorial services back-to-back, and he had never been paid as much as he was for the second service that week. I took that as God's answer, a confirmation that He wanted me to do the brain retraining program. I ordered the program and eagerly got started.

After learning the brain retraining steps, I did this program religiously, every day for a year. While I saw some improvement in many areas, I still had symptoms and knew I was missing something. God began revealing that He wanted me to pursue Him the way He was pursuing me. God became my life and my focus, not just to be healed, but because He was wooing me into a deep love relationship with Him.

---

[1] for information about brain retraining and neuroplasticity:
https://positivepsychology.com/neuroplasticity/

[2] Editor's note: Although the concept and process of brain neuroplasticity is documented and has valid and reliable research support, there is very seldom any scientific support for "brain retraining" programs such as this. The reader is advised to thoroughly investigate any such program, consider the cost that may be involved, and proceed with caution.

I stripped away distractions—no news, minimal social media, and no secular music or TV. I immersed myself in studying neuroplasticity, the way God created my brain, and God's healing. I made these drastic changes to pursue God and discover His purpose for my life. If my relationship with God had not changed, I honestly don't believe I would have experienced all the healing that I did, and I probably wouldn't be here today.

During the first few months of my journey, a friend of a friend reached out to me and told me God woke her in the middle of the night with a message for me. God said to her, "Tell Caprice that her healing will come in the bridal chamber with Me. Also, tell her to read Song of Solomon so that she will know how I feel about her." I believe that changed *everything* and illuminated God's love for me.

Yes, I believe God used brain retraining to teach me that healing was possible and to give me the tools to begin changing my "stinking thinking", but it was His *love* for me that brought me complete healing. God used this program to reveal to me where I needed to begin making changes. He knew that in my very isolated life I wouldn't have learned these things otherwise.

Forgiveness was a vital element God revealed to me for my healing. There is a connection between forgiveness and healing - not only the forgiveness that God gives to us, but our willingness to forgive others. I had heard stories of people forgiving and then experiencing healing. God also opened my understanding to this through such scriptures as James 5:16 and 1 Corinthians 11:18-30.

After years of emotional trauma I experienced from numerous individuals, I understood that choosing to forgive them would be a daunting challenge. Guided by the Holy Spirit on how to forgive, I progressed through journaling and using my imagination in a step-by-step approach (which you will find in this program). It took several months as I worked through the list of those who had hurt me, but the emotional relief and the decision to embrace love and forgiveness transformed my heart and accelerated my healing.

This new direction that God had given me for my life began to lead me to more resources and truth. At the end of 2019, I learned of Andrew Wommack[3],

---

[3] Leader of Andrew Wommack Ministries (https://www.awmi.net/) and Charis Bible College (https://www.charisbiblecollege.org/) in Woodland Park, CO

and I discovered similar ministries which taught truths that were completely new to me—my true identity and authority in Christ, the fact that God wants everyone well, and that Jesus paid for our complete healing at the whipping post. I learned that I was a brand-new creation in Christ and that sickness and disease did not belong to me. This was the most important revelation! God took me above and beyond any course of study. He taught me who I am in Him. This understanding brought true and lasting healing, and that is why I've created *As One: The Biblically-based Discipleship and Mind Renewal Program.*

Symptoms began to disappear as I changed my thoughts, words, and imaginations to line up with Scripture. The Holy Spirit led me to a discovery of deeply-rooted core beliefs that He and I began changing through the study and application of His Word. Within a few months, I was hiking again—from being bedridden to hiking 9 miles on a mountain trail with elevation! Within 2 years I had added all foods back into my diet and had experienced complete healing! No more pain, no more diets, no more medications! I was *free.*[4]

In 2021 God spoke to my heart about creating a ministry and coaching others who were struggling with their health. My life is now dedicated to teaching others what I learned through my experience. Most of all, I've dedicated my life to help others discover the extraordinary love God has for them and His great desire for them to know that He wants them well.

Any healing is good, but healing and becoming the person with a purpose God created you to be, is so much more! That's true healing—body, mind, and spirit. It's my greatest desire for you, dear reader, to experience the freedom that I have found as you walk through this program: Freedom from emotional and physical pain, freedom to know how deeply Your Father God loves you, and freedom to know that as you experience His amazing love, you will understand what being *As One* with Him is all about.

"The Spirit of the Lord is upon me, because he has anointed me to proclaim good news to the poor. He has sent me to proclaim liberty to the captives and recovering of sight to the blind, to set at liberty those who are oppressed, to proclaim the year of the Lord's favor." (Luke 4:18-19 ESV)

---

[4] This was a process, however. I did not stop all medications until I knew my body was healed enough to do so. There are certain medications that should not be stopped "cold turkey" but must be tapered under a doctor's supervision. We need to be led by the Holy Spirit as we make these changes, and as mentioned, with a doctor's help where necessary.

Chapter 1

WHO GOD IS:

The Truth About God's Character

———— ✕ ⌗⌗⌗ ✕ ————

We've all heard variations on the idea that you can't trust something that seems too good to be true. Consider this—our entire Christian faith is built upon a too-good-to-be-true story. But that's who God is. The devil wants us to think we've been conned, but the truth is, God is so much better than we can imagine.

Truth 1.1

The Trinity

The Godhead, also known as the Trinity, is a three-person Being, or even a family, I believe. While there is only One God, He exists as three Persons. The word Trinity is not found in the Bible, but the Hebrew plural noun *Elohim* is used in Genesis 1:1. We find in Genesis 1:26, 11:7, and Isaiah 6:8 that God refers to Himself as "us."

In Isaiah 48:16, the Son (Jesus) speaks of the Father and the Spirit. Matthew 3:16-17 reveals that all three members of the Godhead were present at the baptism of Jesus. While Jesus came to John the Baptist at the River Jordan in human form, the Father's voice was heard, and the Holy Spirit took the form of a dove as He rested upon Jesus.

While each member of the Godhead has a different role, they do not operate independently from each other, but rather they always operate in unity with one another. Jesus tells us in John 5:19 that He could only do what He saw His Father doing. He saw and understood what His Father was doing and where His Father was leading through the spiritual vision, direction, and guidance of the Holy Spirit.

God the Father is the ultimate source of power and authority, gives divine revelation, and is the Author of salvation, but works these things through the Son (1 Corinthians 8:6; Revelation 4:11; Revelation 1:1; John 3:16-17). The Son, Jesus, is the One through whom the Father works to bring about Creation, His divine revelation, salvation, and to reveal His works (John 1:1-3, 16:12-15; Matthew 11:27; 2 Corinthians 5:19; John 4:42). The Holy Spirit was also involved in Creation, as well as giving divine revelation and salvation. It is the Spirit's power by which these things are done (Genesis 1:2; Psalm 104:30; John 16:12-15; Ephesians 3:5; 2 Peter 1:21; John 3:6; 1 Peter 1:2; Isaiah 61:1; Acts 10:38).

So, while we see that God is a three-person Being, and each person is unique and distinguished, He is One God in purpose, unity, and heart and has always existed. To help us better understand that God is a three-person Being, it's helpful to know that we also are three-part beings. We *are* a spirit, we *have* a soul, and we *live in* a body. We are created in the image of God in this manner (Matthew 10:28; 1 Thessalonians 5:23; Hebrews 4:12).

It's also important for us to note that the Word of God uses mind, soul, and heart interchangeably (Matthew 22:37; Mark 12:30; Luke 10:27). "Our heart includes the inward self where our feelings, emotions, and even thinking occurs. The soul is the entire inner person, and the mind is the part of us where thinking occurs."[5]

Now that we've discussed a bit about the Trinity, let's delve into our study on the character of God. The best place to begin is the subject of love.

---

[5] https://faithalone.org/blog/is-there-a-difference-between-heart-soul-and-mind/

God is LOVE

1 John 4:7-10,16 tells us that God is love. Love wouldn't exist without Him, but it's important for us to understand that love isn't just something God DOES. Love is who God IS. It's His character. It's His Being. Love and God are inseparable. Many of us may have heard this before, but let's take a closer look at 1 Corinthians 13:4-8. I'm going to put God's name in place of the word "love" because love only exists as part of His character.

> God is patient, God is kind. He does not envy, He does not boast, He is not proud. God does not dishonor others, He is not self-seeking, He is not easily angered, He keeps no record of wrongs. God does not delight in evil but rejoices with the truth. He always protects, always trusts, always hopes, always perseveres. God never fails.

God is Love, but the truth is, we can't even limit Him to our human understanding of love. God isn't Love in the way that we love our pets or even our spouses. God is *agape*—the most self-sacrificial Being in the universe—and as such, He was prepared to go to incredible lengths to save and redeem us. This kind of love—this being of "Love—cannot be compelled, manipulated, or predetermined if it is to be genuine love. It has to be freely given and freely received. God did not have to love a world full of self-centered and sinful human beings, but He chose to do this—and this accorded with God's very nature."[6]

God's agape love is a kind of love that sees the object of its affection and is overwhelmed with adoration, admiration, wonder, and care. God stands in awe of His creation, and His love is not based on the idea that it must be reciprocated (though once we are able to grasp the incredible goodness of it, how could we not reciprocate?) The agape of God moves toward us. It chases after its objects of affection (you and me) with the desire to protect, provide, and bless. Agape love is benevolent, kind, generous, and charitable. Through His love, God sees us as irresistible. He holds mankind in highest appreciation. We have been so precious to Him, His love compelled Him to go to the greatest lengths to save and redeem us, whatever that might cost Him. Agape love knows no limits.

To quote Kyle Winkler in his book, *Shut Up, Devil! Silencing the 10 Lies Behind Every Battle You Face©*, because of His agape love, God "is not weighing your good works against your mess-ups to see if the scale tips in favor of you being worthy of love today."[7] God embodied Himself, the God of love, in flesh, in

---

[6] https://www.biblicalarchaeology.org/daily/what-god-is-love-actually-means/
[7] Winkler, Kyle, *Shut Up, Devil! Silencing the 10 Lies Behind Every Battle You Face©* (2022, Chosen Books) p. 105

order to touch the untouchables, to speak to the unspeakable, to forgive the unforgivable, to use the unusable (my paraphrase).[8] Not only does God love those whom no one else deems worthy, but He goes out of His way to pursue them and draw them into His family. This is what agape love does. It wraps itself in flesh and reaches out to the most unworthy of us all and embraces us. That is the nature of God.

Truth 1.1 Application:

God Is Love: *John 16:27; Psalm 36:7; Romans 5:8; 1 John 4:9-10*
How have you personally experienced God is Love?

_____

_____

_____

_____

    Jehovah-Nissi: *Exodus 17:15*
    says God is: _____
    El-Elyon: *Genesis 14:17-20; Deuteronomy 26:19; Isaiah 14:13-14*
    El-Elyon means "The _____ _____ God."
    El-Gibhor: According to *Isaiah 9:6*, the Lord God is _____.

Truth 1.2
God is El-Chuwl

The God who gave birth. Have you ever considered that you were conceived in God's heart and imagination? He saw you long before you were born. I'm not talking about the way we see a human baby in the womb through an ultrasound. God *saw you* and all of your potential before you even existed! He saw you in His heart! God is our Creator and our Father. He saw us and He loved us even before we were born.

Did you catch that? God created you out of the love of His heart, and knew you before He even created the world. This gives a whole new meaning to the term "love child" because God knew what He was getting when He created you (and most of us pretty much have no clue what we're getting when we have kids, right?), but God knew what He was creating and He said it/each of us was good.

---

[8] Winkler, op cit., p. 113

Caprice Scott

Ephesians 1:4-5 ESV: "... even as he chose us in him before the foundation of the world, that we should be holy and blameless before him. In love He predestined us for adoption to Himself as sons through Jesus Christ, according to the purpose of His will."

Psalm 139:13-18 ESV:

> 13) For you formed my inward parts; you knitted me together in my mother's womb.
>
> *Imagine that! God knitted you together in your mother's womb.*
>
> 14) I praise you, for I am fearfully and wonderfully made. Wonderful are your works; my soul knows it very well.
>
> *Verse 14 reminds us that there are times when we look at ourselves and we don't like what we see. We might be tempted to criticize ourselves, but according to this passage, we're not criticizing something we created—we were knitted by the very hand of God.*
>
> 15) My frame was not hidden from you, when I was being made in secret, intricately woven in the depths of the earth. 16) Your eyes saw my unformed substance; in your book were written, every one of them, the days that were formed for me, when as yet there was none of them. 17) How precious to me are your thoughts, O God! How vast is the sum of them! 18) If I would count them, they are more than the sand. I awake, and I am still with you.

These last verses show that God has more thoughts of you than every single grain of sand on this planet. You are always on His mind. He's your Creator. He gave birth to you. Not only did God know all about you long before He made you, but also He knew all the ways you would fall short and all of the messes that you'd make in this life. Still, He chose to bring you into existence because He longed to introduce Himself to you. You were *always* God's idea.

He is your Papa God, and just like any good parent, what touches His heart most is to share His love with His child —with *you*. There are few things that bring a parent more joy than to be close to their children, and Papa God is no different.

Isaiah 49:15-16 ESV: "Can a woman forget her nursing child, that she should have no compassion on the son of her womb? Even these may forget, yet I will not forget you. Behold, I have engraved you on the palms of my hands;"

Notice all the lines in your palms. Imagine that each one of those lines represents a stripe from the whip that Jesus took for you. And while we're on that subject:

God is Yahweh/Jehovah-Rapha

The Lord our Healer. "… by His stripes we are healed," declares Isaiah 53:5. Jesus Christ died to give life to you. Not only was God the Healer in the Old Testament, but Jesus Christ revealed the healing heart of God for all of us, more than ever, in the New Testament.

John 10:10 ESV: "The thief comes only to steal and kill and destroy" But Jesus said, "I came that they may have life and have it abundantly."

We'll talk more about that later. There's nothing in this verse that says God puts sickness on anyone. On the contrary, that's what the devil does. God is *good* and wants us to have abundant life. That word *abundant* means *more, greater, excessive, beyond what is anticipated, exceeding expectation, going past the limit, advantage.*[9] When we belong to God and receive the love and care He has for us, we live with an advantage that others don't have.

Healing is a manifestation of God's love and character as Jehovah Rapha. It's what happens when His Kingdom reality supersedes our current physical reality. Healing is literally heaven coming to earth. When we lack revelation about His nature of goodness, we often fail to have hope that it's His desire to heal. This makes it very difficult to pray and expect Him to act out of His love and goodness toward us.[10]

But you see, God concerns Himself with our pain and every detail of our lives. In this program, I will bring up Isaiah 53:4-5 quite a bit, because it truly reveals the nature and goodness of God. Let's look at these verses:

"Surely he has borne our griefs…" (*griefs* in Strong's Concordance is #2483 *choli* ("khol-ee") which means pain and sickness)

"and carried our sorrows…" (*sorrows* is Strong's #4341 *makob* ("mak-obe") which means both physical and mental suffering)

"…yet we esteemed him stricken, smitten by God, and afflicted. But he was pierced for our transgressions; he was crushed for our iniquities; upon him was the chastisement that brought us peace, and with his wounds we are healed."

---

[9] (Strong's G4053) (All Hebrew and Greek definitions, unless otherwise noted, are taken from *Strong's New Exhaustive Concordance of the Bible*, James Strong, S.T.D., LL.D. World Bible Publishers, Inc. 1986.)

[10] My belief regarding healing is based on much personal Bible study which has revealed God desires our healing so much so that He included this as part of the Salvation package through Jesus. (The word Salvation itself, soteria in the Greek, Strong's 4991, includes "health" as one of its benefits.). Both Isaiah 53:1-8 and 1 Peter 2:24 reveal that Jesus took stripes upon His back for our physical healing. It is my opinion that as 3-part beings, Christ covered our emotional/mental healing (soul) in the Garden of Gethsemane when He sweated drops of blood. He bore our emotional griefs there. Our physical healing was paid for at the whipping post, and our spiritual healing was purchased by Jesus upon the Cross.

I've heard many pastors in churches I have attended in the past state that when Jesus bore our griefs and sorrows, our pain and sickness and suffering, that Isaiah was only talking about Jesus purchasing our salvation and doing this to secure eternal life, healing, and peace for us in heaven - *not* here on earth. But we know that there won't be any pain, suffering, or sickness in heaven. So what is Isaiah talking about here? Let's go back to the word "borne" in verse 4, which is Strong's #5375 *nasa* ("naw-saw"). *Nasa* means to lift, bear up, carry, endure, forgive, to be taken away, be carried off, etc. Jesus took upon Himself, carried, and took away pain, sickness, and suffering.

God isn't just some God who heals. His very nature is healer. His very name, Jehovah-Rapha, means The Lord Our Healer. And guess what? If you have given your life to Jesus, the Healer lives inside of you. He can't do anything contrary to His nature. Since He lives in us, would He want or put sickness in us when it's contrary to who He is?

1 Corinthians 6:19-20 ESV says, "Do you not know that your body is a temple of the Holy Spirit within you, whom you have from God? You are not your own, for you were bought with a price."

The Healer is in you, so why wouldn't His nature as Healer be revealed in and through you?

Jesus Christ showed that He is the Great Physician who heals the sick. In Galilee, Jesus went from town to town "…healing every disease and sickness among the people" (Matthew 4:23 NIV). In Judea, "large crowds followed him, and he healed them there" (Matthew 19:2 NIV). In fact, "…wherever he went—into villages, towns or countryside—they placed the sick in the marketplaces. They begged him to let them touch even the edge of his cloak, and all who touched it were healed" (Mark 6:56 NIV).

Not only did Jesus heal people physically (and by the way, He never put stipulations on anyone who asked for healing), but He also healed them spiritually by forgiving their sins (Luke 5:20). Every day, in every way, when Jesus walked this earth He proved Himself to be Jehovah-Rapha in the flesh. Healing is who God is. And healing is absolutely 100% His desire for you.

Truth 1.2 Application:

El-Chuwl: *Psalm 139*

If you were to write a letter from God based on Psalm 139 through the lens of the *God Who Gave Birth to You*, what might it say? (Use an additional piece of paper if necessary.) I'll use the first two verses from the NKJV "O Lord, You have searched me and known me. You know my sitting down and my rising up; You understand my thought afar off" as an example:

> *My dear child, how I love you. You are so very special to Me. I*
>
> *know you better than anyone else does, even better than you know yourself. I*
>
> *know all your thoughts, your actions, and even why you speak and think the*
>
> *way you do.*
>
> *I know your good days and bad days. I see your every smile (which*
>
> *delights My heart), and I see when you are struggling with painful realities*
>
> *that happen in life. You may not feel it physically, but I wrap my arms*
>
> *around you when you cry. That's how well I know you, dear one.*

_____

_____

_____

_____

_____

Yahweh/Jehovah-Rapha: *Exodus 15:26; 2 Chronicles 7:14; Psalm 6:2, 41:4, 103:3, 147:3; Isaiah 19:22, 57:18-19; Jeremiah 3:22, 17:14, 30:17*
After looking at a few of these verses, what would you say Jehovah-Rapha means?

_____

El-Olam: *Isaiah 40:28-31*
God is Everlasting. In what ways does this/doesn't this bring you comfort?

_____

Truth 1.3

Yahweh/Jehovah-Jireh

The Lord will provide. Jesus Christ said that God cares for us and we never need to worry about provision. He is our Source of life in every way. Not only will He provide what we need, He *is* what we need. God is not only the Provider, but He also is Provision. Not only is He Provision, but also He desires to be *your* Provision.

As Abraham and Isaac learned in Genesis 22:13-14, the Lord will provide for all our needs.

Abraham was told to take his son Isaac up to Mt. Moriah to sacrifice him. Isaac had been God's promised son to Abraham, who was supposed to be the father of many nations. When Isaac asked where the sacrifice was, Abraham told his son that the Lord would provide the sacrifice. Abraham believed that God could provide a sacrifice, or would give Isaac his life back if Abraham had to go through with the act.

Genesis 22:13-14 ESV: "And Abraham lifted up his eyes and looked, and behold, behind him was a ram, caught in a thicket by his horns. And Abraham went and took the ram and offered it up as a burnt offering instead of his son. So Abraham called the name of that place, 'The LORD will provide'; as it is said to this day, 'On the mount of the LORD it shall be provided.'"

This is one of the most poignant stories in the Old Testament foreshadowing Jesus becoming our Sacrifice and Provision. God revealed to Abraham that He would supply the sacrifice (ram). He is faithful to provide when we trust Him.

Jeremiah 29:11 says that He has only good plans for us, to prosper us and give us hope. He has a plan for your life, and if you walk with Him, He will fulfill His dreams over your life and amaze you (my paraphrase). Jesus shares with us in the Gospel of Matthew that our Heavenly Father knows all of our needs and will meet all of them through His loving provision:
Matthew 6:25-33 NLT:

> "That is why I tell you not to worry about everyday life—whether you have enough food and drink, or enough clothes to wear. Isn't life more than food, and your body more than clothing? Look at the birds. They don't plant or harvest or store food in barns, for your heavenly Father feeds them. And aren't you far more valuable to him than they are? Can all your worries add a single moment to your life?

> "And why worry about your clothing? Look at the lilies of the field and how they grow. They don't work or make their clothing, yet Solomon in all his glory was not dressed as beautifully as they are. And if God cares so wonderfully for wildflowers that are here today and thrown into the fire tomorrow, he will certainly care for you. Why do you have so little faith?

> "So don't worry about these things, saying, 'What will we eat? What will we drink? What will we wear?' These things dominate the thoughts of unbelievers, but your heavenly Father already knows all your needs. Seek the Kingdom of God above all else, and live righteously, and he will give you everything you need."

Yahweh/Jehovah-Tsidkenu

The Lord our righteousness. When we believe in Jesus Christ, His righteousness is imputed to us. He forgives our sins and washes us with His blood. (Genesis 15:6, Jeremiah 23:6, Psalm 4:1, 5:8, 24:5, 31:1, 36:10, 71:15, 89:16)

2 Corinthians 5:21 ESV: "For our sake he made him to be sin who knew no sin, so that in him we might become the righteousness of God." We'll talk more about righteousness and why it's a big deal later on.

Yahweh-Shalom

The Lord is peace. Whenever there are storms in your life, hide in Him. He is your shelter in the storm. He gives peace beyond understanding, even when circumstances are chaotic. He is our shelter and our shield (Judges 6:24). When we put our trust in Him, He gives and keeps us in His own peace.

Isaiah 26:3 NKJV: "You will keep him in perfect peace, Whose mind is stayed on You, Because he trusts in You."

John 14:27 ESV: "Peace I leave with you; my peace I give to you. Not as the world gives do I give to you. Let not your hearts be troubled, neither let them be afraid."

Philippians 4:7 NKJV: "And the peace of God, which surpasses all understanding, will guard your hearts and minds through Christ Jesus."

And remember what we read in Isaiah 53:5? Jesus purchased that peace for us through those stripes He took—and when He lives in us, His peace becomes ours. It's important to note that the Hebrew word *shalom* (peace) has many meanings: Strong's Concordance #7965 says among those meanings are: completeness, welfare, peace, safety, soundness (in body), health, prosperity, quiet, tranquility, contentment, friendship, peace [with God, especially in covenant relationship], peace (from war). The peace of God has the ability and power to change every aspect of our lives when we allow it to do so—from emotional peace, to safety, soundness and health, prosperity and contentment. God's peace provides everything we need.

El Nose

The Lord is forgiving. Remember at the beginning when we learned that God is love? Love keeps no record of wrongs. When Jesus went to the cross, He became sin for us, that we should become His righteousness. It's important to understand that being righteous means we are forgiven and God sees us in the same way that He sees Jesus—spotless, holy, blameless.

Ephesians 5:26-27 ESV: "... that he might sanctify her, having cleansed her by the washing of water with the word, so that he might present the church to himself in splendor, without spot or wrinkle or any such thing, that she might be holy and without blemish."

Nehemiah 9:17 (NIV) says, "... But you are a forgiving God, gracious and compassionate, slow to anger and abounding in love ..."

Romans 8:1 (NIV) tells us, "There is therefore now no condemnation for those who are in Christ Jesus."

Truth 1.3 Application:

Jehovah-M'Kaddesh: *Exodus 31:13; Leviticus 20:8; Ezekiel 37:28*
What do these verses tell us of the character of God?

_____

_____

_____

_____

Jehovah-Rohi: *Psalm 23, 80:1, 95:7, Isaiah 40:11, Jeremiah 31:10, Ezekiel 34:12,23*
What does Jehovah-Rohi mean according to these verses?

_____

_____

_____

_____

Jehovah-Shammah: *Genesis 28:15; Ezekiel 48:35; Psalm 23:4, 46:1, 139:7-12; Jeremiah 23:23-24; Amos 5:14*
What do these verses reveal about this specific characteristic of God?

_____

_____

_____

_____

El-Roi: *Genesis 16:13* Hagar said He is the God who _____ _____.
El-Shaddai-Rohi: *Genesis 17:1; 49:24; Psalm 91:1, 132:2,5*
What feminine quality does this name of God reveal about His character?

_____

_____

_____

_____

Truth 1.4

Ha'El hanne'eman

The faithful God. The root word behind this name is *'aman.* The meaning of the root here is the concept of certainty. Deuteronomy 7:9 (ESV) states, "Know therefore that the LORD your God is God, the faithful God who keeps covenant and steadfast love with those who love him and keep his commandments, to a thousand generations." Isaiah referred to "the LORD, who is faithful, the Holy One of Israel, who has chosen you" (Isaiah 49:7 ESV).

Hosea called God, "...the Holy One who is faithful" (Hosea 11:12 NASB).

In the New Testament, specifically the book of Revelation, we find three similar names that refer to Jesus as being "the faithful and true witness." Revelation also calls Jesus the "Amen" (Revelation 3:14). This brings us back to where we started, because the Greek word *amen* is adapted from the Hebrew word *'aman.*

1 Corinthians 1:8-9 (ESV) assures us that God "... will sustain you to the end, guiltless in the day of our Lord Jesus Christ. God is faithful, by whom you were called into the fellowship of his Son, Jesus Christ our Lord."

We have no reason to fear as we put our trust in Jesus. He's going to sustain us because He keeps His promises to do so.

Hebrews 10:23 says, "Let us hold fast the confession of our hope without wavering, for he who promised is faithful."

Once again, we are told that God is faithful to keep His promises to us:

1 Thessalonians 5:23-24 NKJV: "Now may the God of peace Himself sanctify you completely; and may your whole spirit, soul, and body be preserved blameless at the coming of our Lord Jesus Christ. He who calls you is faithful, who also will do it."

We find even more beautiful promises of God's faithfulness in keeping us safe from pestilence—being our shield, our place of shelter, and our refuge from the enemy. Psalm 91:3-6 (NKJV) states:

> Surely He shall deliver you from the snare of the fowler and from the perilous pestilence. He shall cover you with His feathers, and under His wings you shall take refuge; His truth shall be your shield and buckler. You shall not be afraid of the terror by night, nor of the arrow that flies

by day, nor of the pestilence that walks in darkness, nor of the destruction that lays waste at noonday.

There are so many references to promises of healing—both physical and emotional—in the Word of God, and these are also related to His faithfulness. Let's look at a few:

Jeremiah 33:6 NKJV: "Behold, I will bring it health and healing; I will heal them and reveal to them the abundance of peace and truth."

1 Peter 2:24 ESV: "He himself bore our sins in his body on the tree, that we might die to sin and live to righteousness. By His wounds you have been healed."

Psalm 41:3 ESV: "The Lord sustains him on his sickbed; in his illness you restore him to full health."

Psalm 147:3 ESV: "He heals the brokenhearted and binds up their wounds."

James 5:15 ESV: "And the prayer of faith will save the one who is sick, and the Lord will raise him up. And if he has committed sins, he will be forgiven."

Along with these promises, Paul tells the Philippians in the first chapter, sixth verse: "And I am sure of this, that he who began a good work in you will bring it to completion at the day of Jesus Christ." I love how the Amplified version states this verse: "I am convinced and confident of this very thing, that He who has begun a good work in you will [continue to] perfect and complete it until the day of Christ Jesus [the time of His return]."

God isn't going to stop doing any of the good things He has promised until they are perfected and complete in us, and He's going to continue doing this until Jesus returns. God's faithfulness toward us never stops!

Truth 1.4 Application:

The "I Am": *Exodus 3:14; John 8:58; Revelation 1:7-9*
When God says that He is the "I Am," consider the power in those words. When you use the words, "I am" before making a statement, consider what it means. "I am" statements speak to who and what you are. Might you need to rethink some of your "I am" statements so that they line up with what God says about you? Can you think of an example?

Ask the Holy Spirit to reveal to you any "I am" statements that you may have spoken over yourself that He wants you to change. Re-write those statements below. I've given you several examples:

"I am sick" → "I am healed, whole, and well because of Jesus!"

"I am a failure" → "I am an overcomer and have victory in Jesus!"

_____

_____

_____

Adonai: *Genesis 15:2; Judges 6:15; Malachi 1:6; Deuteronomy 10:17; Psalm 2:4, 8:1, 97:5, 136:3; Isaiah 1:24, 6:1; Romans 10:9*
Adonai means:

_____

Yahweh-Sabbaoth: *Isaiah 6:1-3; 1 Samuel 1:3, 17:45; 2 Samuel 6:2, 7:26-27; 1 Chronicles 11:9; Haggai 1:5*
When the Word speaks of Yahweh-Sabbaoth, it is calling God the:

_____

_____

_____

_____

Yahweh-Ghmolah: *Jeremiah 51:6*
Is there a time that this characteristic of God has been something you've needed? Why?

_____

_____

_____

Elohim: *Genesis 1:1, 17:7; Psalm 19:1; Jeremiah 31:33*
What does this characteristic teach us about the nature of God?

_____

_____

_____

El-Deah: *1 Samuel 2:3; Romans 11:33-36; 1 Corinthians 1:18-31*
Because God is El-Deah and lives inside of you, what might this mean you have access to?

_____

Attiyq Youm: *Daniel 7:9,13-14*
Attiyq Youm means that God is the _____ of _____.

Truth 1.5

There are many other names of God in the Bible. We've only looked at a handful of them, but I hope that through this study you have a clearer picture of the beautiful true character of God.

You see, the goal of the enemy is to cause you to be confused about who God is, to misunderstand the heart of God toward you, and to live in fear. God reveals His character through His name(s) and the Word. He speaks out of who He is. God wants to do immeasurably above all that you could ask or think "…according to His power at work within you" (Ephesians 3:20). Think about that; His power at work within you. He put Himself within you and all the power of the universe comes with God. These paraphrases emphasize this important point:

As we saw in Jeremiah 29:11, He thinks and wants good things for you.

Numbers 23:19: God never lies. We can trust He always keeps His Word. The devil is the liar.

Ezekiel 36:25-28: Cleanses us, gives us new hearts, gives us His Spirit, causes us to walk in His ways, makes us His.

Psalm 34:8: David encourages us to taste and see that God is good—through personal encounter.

Matthew 7:11: God is even better than the very best earthly father.

Luke 15:20: Always waiting on the horizon to welcome His wayward kids home.

Exodus 33:19: Moses wanted to see His glory. It's impossible to encounter God apart from His goodness. His goodness leads Him to always act on our behalf and is constant and consistent.

God and His love never fail. Imagine with me . . . as you experience these words about your Papa God, as they penetrate your heart and mind, that the very presence of the Lord surrounds you. Every cell in your body experiences the goodness and love of God. His saving power—the power that heals, restores, creates peace in your soul—is your abundant provision. Nothing is lacking; He is all, and because you are in Him and He is in you, there is now no lack in you. You are His utmost delight.

God, the Holy One, the Creator of all life, *your* Creator, is rejoicing over you. Rejoicing includes making mirth. God is gleeful! He is dancing, laughing, and celebrating that you are on this journey to experience Him—to know Him and to be known by Him. It fills His heart with joy beyond the joy of every human parent—because His love is deeper and is more extravagant than is humanly possible. This is His greatest wish—this is what His Spirit has longed for since before the foundation of the world—that you would come to know and experience how much He loves you and that you would desire this relationship as well.

The God of all Creation is so overjoyed that you have an interest in knowing Him that His heart could burst. He is a parent whose greatest longing is to be loved by His child. As the Lover of your soul, His happiness exceeds that of a husband whose beautiful bride is walking down the aisle to be joined to him forever. God's cup is running over because of you right now. This is the point in time He has looked forward to—the very day that you would seek and find Him.

He quiets all other voices around you in order for you to hear His sweetness speaking to your soul. *Hush, hush*, He says. *Listen to My voice, My child. Experience and know My deep longing to share My love with you, little one. How I've looked forward to this day since before time began and the first time I conceived you by love in My heart.* From the depths of His heart, a song crafted just for you pours from His lips—His voice like an entire angelic choir fills the air and every fiber of your being. The voice of God singing over you is more beautiful, more perfect, and more lovely than anything you've ever heard. This experience feels as though it is what you were created for. It floods you with wonder, amazement, peace. You experience a belonging, a knowing and being known that leave you undone, yet whole.

This day that you are choosing Him has been the day He has prepared for. This is the greatest fulfillment of all. He has gone through from the beginning of earth's time—waiting, longing to hear that you are ready to receive His love and embrace. Ready to begin your new life together as one with Him. Knowing who God is and experiencing His love and goodness requires personally encountering Him on a regular basis. These encounters will lead you to an existential understanding of who He is, how good He is, and how all of that goodness is meant for you to experience and receive in and through Him. You are His beloved child, His creation. He adores you. He wants to provide for you. He is trustworthy. His peace is yours. His righteousness is yours. And His healing is yours. Zephaniah 3:17 (ESV) states: "The LORD your God is in your midst, a mighty one who will save; he will rejoice over you with gladness; he will quiet you by his love; he will exult over you with loud singing."

Truth 1.5 Application:

Psalm 139:13-14 ESV: "For you formed my inward parts; you knitted me together in my mother's womb. I praise you, for I am fearfully and wonderfully made. Wonderful are your works; my soul knows it very well."

Author Mark DeJesus asks in his book, *God Loves Me and I Love Myself!: Overcoming the Resistance to Loving Yourself*©, if you have considered God's Presence and involvement in your conception? Psalm 139:13 says He formed you in your mother's womb. Before God even created the world, He knew you. "Before you were ever conceived, God had an identity and calling in store for you. He was and is personally and directly involved in your creation as a human being. The word 'covered' means to knit and to weave. God covered you and intricately formed each thread of your biology."[11] DeJesus goes on to say that the devil knows you were created in God's image—that's why he hates you. He's the enemy. You and your body are not the enemy. You are God's masterpiece. What does God say to your heart about this? What about the desires of your heart that God has given you?

Speak out loud once a day:

- ➢ I was created *for a* purpose.
- ➢ I was created *on* purpose.
- ➢ I am at the forefront of God's mind.
- ➢ God created me.
- ➢ I am significant.
- ➢ I was created to overcome and live in victory!
- ➢ I am special in His eyes.
- ➢ God is aware of every part of my being.
- ➢ Thank You, God, for overseeing and directing my conception and birth.
- ➢ Thank You, God, for creating me and re-creating me into a brand new person today.

Notes:

_____

_____

_____

_____

---

[11] DeJesus, Mark, *God Loves Me and I Love Myself!: Overcoming the Resistance to Loving Yourself*© Turning Hearts Ministries, 2016) p. 141

Chapter 2

WHO GOD IS:

The Truth About Jesus and Salvation

❧ ⟞⟝⟞⟝ ❧

Truth 2.1

In his article, *God With Skin On*, Pastor Greg Laurie tells the story of a little boy who was frightened one night during a big thunderstorm. Terrified, he called out from his room, "Daddy, I am scared!" His father, not wanting to get out of bed, called back, "Don't worry, son. God loves you and will take care of you." There was a moment of silence. The little boy said, "I know God loves me, but right now, I need somebody who has skin on."[12]

Somebody who has skin on. I feel this in the depth of my being, don't you? John 1:14 (ESV) gives us some of the best news possible: "And the Word became flesh and dwelt among us, and we have seen his glory, glory as of the only Son from the Father, full of grace and truth." I love the way the NLT states John 1:14: "So the Word became human and made his home among us. He was full

---

[12] *(https://www.christianpost.com/news/god-with-skin-on.html) pastor, author, podcaster, and speaker Greg Laurie (1952-)*

of unfailing love and faithfulness. And we have seen his glory, the glory of the Father's one and only Son."

The meaning of this verse? *He pitched His tent among us.* Pitched His tent. What a great visual. God clothes Himself with humanity and pitches His tent with us, getting down into the muck, yuck, and grime with us—God with skin on. We aren't alone anymore. We don't have to deal with the scary things of life by ourselves. God is with us. He came with skin on. He pitched His tent next to ours.

Strong's Concordance #6005 tells us that "God with skin on" has a name: "Immanuel." — "with us is God," or more simply, "God with us." As Isaiah 7:14 says, "Therefore the Lord himself will give you a sign. Behold, the virgin shall conceive and bear a son, and shall call his name Immanuel."

Christ the Lord. Immanuel. Jesus. In Strong's #2424 we find how to pronounce His name in Greek (New Testament) *Iésous* (ee-ay-sooce). This is the transliteration of the Hebrew (Old Testament) term, found in: *Yehoshua,* meaning: "the LORD is salvation." Let's take this a step farther and look at the word, "salvation," beginning with one of the specific Hebrew translations (Old Testament) found in Psalm 118:14: "The LORD is my strength and my song; he has become my *salvation*" (Strong's #3444: Yeshuah).

He has become my Yeshuah. The word "salvation" here means: *deliverance, victory, health, helping, save, saving health, welfare, prosperity.* If you've ever wondered where all of those "prosperity gospel" preachers get the idea that God wants us to be prosperous, here it is. Jesus Himself is our salvation—providing deliverance, victory, health, help, welfare, and prosperity.

Strong's #4991 tells us that "salvation" in the New Testament is *sótéria,* and means: *welfare, prosperity, deliverance, preservation, salvation, safety, rescue or safety (physically or morally), and health.*

Our study of the original Hebrew and Greek words here wouldn't be complete without looking at the word "save" to help us better understand the rich meanings of each word that our English language fails to capture.

Matthew 1:21 NKJV: "And she will bring forth a Son, and you shall call His name JESUS, for He will save His people from their sins." The word "save" here means: to save, heal, preserve, rescue from destruction, cure, ensure salvation, to make well, to recover, restore, and make whole. Jesus came to save us. He came to recover what the enemy had stolen from us… Peace. Health. Prosperity. Relationship with God. Life.

In Isaiah 53 we find the incredible prophecy of what Jesus would experience in order to provide all that salvation includes for us. Let's look at verses 3-6 (ESV):

He was despised and rejected by men,
a man of sorrows and acquainted with grief;
and as one from whom men hide their faces
he was despised, and we esteemed him not.
Surely he has borne our griefs
and carried our sorrows;
yet we esteemed him stricken,
smitten by God, and afflicted.
But he was pierced for our transgressions;
he was crushed for our iniquities;
upon him was the chastisement that brought us peace,
and with his wounds we are healed.
All we like sheep have gone astray;
we have turned—every one—to his own way;
and the LORD has laid on him
the iniquity of us all.

Take a deeper look at several of the words in these verses. You'll notice a few words we've seen before.

> Borne: took on. The Hebrew word is *nasa* (naw-saw), meaning to lift, bear up, carry, take, to be taken away, be carried off.
> Griefs: infirmities. The Hebrew word is *choli* (khol-ee), meaning sickness.
> Carried: *sabal* (saw-bal) in Hebrew, meaning to take on a heavy burden.
> Sorrows: The Hebrew word is *makob* (mak-obe'), meaning every kind of pain—sorrow, physical, and mental.
> Peace: *shalom* in Hebrew, as we saw before, is more than just a relaxed feeling. Look once again at all that shalom means—completeness, soundness, welfare, safety, soundness (in body), health, prosperity, quiet, tranquility, contentment.

Spend a moment meditating on the significance of each word. How does knowing that Jesus bore and carried away your sickness help (and possibly change) your understanding of how God views sickness? Based on this verse and these definitions in Hebrew, do you see that He wants you free from physical and mental illnesses? That He purchased your wholeness, welfare, and healing through the trials He experienced in His own body?

1 Peter 2:24 echoes Isaiah 53 (ESV): "He himself bore our sins in his body on the tree, that we might die to sin and live to righteousness. By his wounds

you have been healed." Friends, Jesus truly paid it all. Salvation includes everything we could ever need.

Truth 2.1 Application:

1. God came "with skin on". What was His corresponding name and what does it mean? (Isaiah 7:14)

_____

_____

2. The word "save" in Matthew 1:21 means:

_____

_____

_____

Truth 2.2

My husband and I have a feral cat that adopted us. She showed up two winters ago, living under one of the sheds in the backyard. She was terrified of humans. She didn't trust us for anything. We noticed one of her ears was clipped off about halfway down, and we realized she had most likely been trapped, spayed, given some shots, and released. That was the extent of her experience with humans.

I started feeling sorry for her because it was so cold in the freezing weather and she'd often go out and sit in the sun to get warm. I wondered where she was getting her food and water. She appeared to be an older cat. We decided to start putting cat food and fresh water out for her daily, and gradually, after about 6 months, she allowed me to pet her a little. I named her Zoe (which in Greek means "life").

Over the next two years, we created several different sheltering spaces for Zoe. The second year, I created a little bed for her by putting some blankets in a plastic litter box that was set up underneath a table covered with a shower curtain. This was her place to stay next to the house and she took to that immediately. We then tried making a shelter out of a large plastic bin with Styrofoam® lining the inside. She wouldn't go near it, so we cut the sides out of the bin and she stayed in that, but it couldn't have been much better than her spot under the shed; in the winter and rain storms, she wasn't protected from the elements.

This year, with the help of my brother, we built a Zoe house. We used pallets filled with housing insulation, put a roof with hinges, and even straw and a quilt for warmth. My husband and I stained it a lovely warm gray because, as an artist, I have a need for my patio and its furniture to be aesthetically appealing. I was sure she'd appreciate the gesture, too. My brother remarked, "This is a lot of work for a stray cat." (He wasn't wrong.)

Guess what Zoe did? She avoided the back patio. She was so afraid of the "Zoe house" that she didn't even want to come to the patio to eat. We spent an entire day building this house for her and she was terrified of it.

While I was praying about Zoe's resistance to our generous gift, the Holy Spirit reminded my heart that many of us have felt the same way about God and His generous gifts to us. Many of us have been terrified of Him because of wrong religious teachings—teachings that made us feel like He was angry with us, just waiting for us to mess up so He could punish us. Some of us may have wanted nothing to do with Him because of how some people who claimed to be Christians treated us in the past. Like Zoe, we may have experienced pain from people even if they didn't realize the harm they did to our hearts. We might have assumed that God would be just like them.

Then there were others who may have treated us as though we were worthless, so we assumed God would feel that way about us, too. If people cast us off, wouldn't He? Some of us may have had abusive parents and may have assumed God had similar traits. Many of us were taught that God is a God of vengeance who expects perfection from us. We may have believed the lie that we'd never be good enough for God, so why try? Or, we could have learned that God is the One behind all the evil in the world; He's the One who makes us sick or "allows" child trafficking or molestations, or any other horrific event. Someone may have taught us that because God is sovereign, He controls everything, even the bad things happening in the world.

Those teachers may have taken scripture verses out of context and twisted them into lies about Him. Many of us were told that God uses the conviction of guilt, shame, and condemnation to get us to see the error of our ways. Maybe there were fear tactics like, "You're going to hell if you don't accept Jesus and beg for forgiveness." We've been persuaded to believe that somehow the Holy Spirit's voice sounds just like the Accuser of the Brethren (that's satan, by the way). So. Many. Wrong. Teachings. It's no wonder we have struggled to know God and His goodness amid so many wrong teachings.

Strong's #1228 tells us that the devil or *diabolos* in Greek, is the Slanderer. He uses false accusations, unjustly criticizing to hurt (malign) and condemn, to sever a relationship. He's a backbiter, making charges that bring down and destroy, yet somehow we have believed, instead, that these characteristics belonging to satan are attributes of God. What lies! No wonder so many are terrified of God when they think He behaves like the devil.

Like Zoe, we may be resisting the goodness of God without understanding that He has done everything possible for our well-being. How could I convince a cat that doesn't speak my language that I love and care for her, and that we created a space for her to keep her safe from the elements? How do I convince her I want to provide for her and not harm her, so she can live a happy, peaceful life?

And how does a God, whose language is love and trust, which is entirely foreign to selfish and self-centered humans, teach us that He only desires our good? He desires to provide for all our needs, to give us food and shelter, to heal us, to love us, and to fill us with His wonderful characteristics so we can live in and experience His joy, His peace, and have a purpose, a God who wants us to join His family and become one with Him. How could He reveal this to a world that doesn't speak His language or understand His beautiful, selfless character, about which the lying slanderer has told entirely wrong things.

So where did all this start? For us humans, it started in the Garden of Eden. The slanderer took the beautiful truth of what God said and twisted it. We find the story in Genesis 3:1-13 (NKJV)

> Now the serpent was more cunning than any beast of the field which the LORD God had made. And he said to the woman, "Has God indeed said, 'You shall not eat of every tree of the garden'?"

> And the woman said to the serpent, "We may eat the fruit of the trees of the garden; but of the fruit of the tree which is in the midst of the garden, God has said, 'You shall not eat it, nor shall you touch it, lest you die.'"

> Then the serpent said to the woman, "You will not surely die. For God knows that in the day you eat of it your eyes will be opened, and you will be like God, knowing good and evil."

> So when the woman saw that the tree was good for food, that it was pleasant to the eyes, and a tree desirable to make one wise, she took of its fruit and ate. She also gave to her husband with her, and he ate. Then the eyes of both of them were opened, and they knew that they were naked; and they sewed fig leaves together and made themselves coverings.

> And they heard the sound of the LORD God walking in the garden in the cool of the day, and Adam and his wife hid themselves from the presence of the LORD God among the trees of the garden.
>
> Then the LORD God called to Adam and said to him, "Where are You?"
>
> So he said, "I heard Your voice in the garden, and I was afraid because I was naked; and I hid myself."
>
> And He said, "Who told you that you were naked? Have you eaten from the tree of which I commanded you that you should not eat?"
>
> Then the man said, "The woman whom You gave to be with me, she gave me of the tree, and I ate."
>
> And the LORD God said to the woman, "What is this you have done?"

Our first parents went from being in the most beautiful place that ever existed on the planet, having absolute trust in God, who met all of their needs, lacking nothing, being in perfect health, joy, love, bliss, and smelling like roses… to blaming God for *their* massive screw-up. I realize that word may make you cringe, but what they did was really, really dumb. It was the worst possible choice they could have made. And all civilization has paid the price ever since.

Truth 2.2 Application:

Have you felt fearful of God in such a way that Zoe cat's story resonates with you? Spend some time talking with Him about this. He is tender-hearted and loving toward you. Yes, God is holy, but He doesn't want you to avoid Him out of fear. He longs for you to know His lovingkindness toward you.

_____

_____

Truth 2.3

So let's talk about what happened here and how all of this ties into Jesus and salvation. If you're like me, you might question why God put the tree of the knowledge of good and evil in the Garden in the first place. I didn't understand that for the longest time. Then I realized this very important part of the story: The devil wanted to destroy their trust in God because the devil knows that if we don't trust God we're going to self-destruct. God is a God of love, and His Kingdom is based on love and trust. And God created Adam and Eve (and all of us) in His image—as free-will beings. But there had to be a way for them to express their free will, and that came down to the question of trust. Would they choose to eat from the tree of the knowledge of good and evil, which, as God told them would be death, or would they choose to trust God and live?

Besides God Himself, do you know what the most powerful force in the universe is? No, neither Einstein nor *Star Wars*® had it correct. The power of *choice* is the most powerful force in the universe. That power gives us the ability to choose life or death. It gives us the ability to choose the direction of our lives, the words we speak, the thoughts we think. It gives us the power to heal or remain sick, to be kind or be a jerk. It gives us the power to choose to doubt God or to trust Him, and that last option is the choice that lasts for eternity.

Consider this: It's impossible for us to exist without God. We simply wouldn't be here if He hadn't decided to create us. But continuing to live our lives apart from God, apart from His love, would be like expecting the earth to continue being a safe place to live if somehow it could be hurled through space away from its sun. What would happen to the earth without the sun? We wouldn't last long. We cannot exist apart from God, "for 'in Him we live and move and have our being' ..." (Acts 17:28 NIV). We don't survive without the Lifegiver. The deceiver of our souls knows this. So does Jesus.

Let's go back to my feral outdoor cat, Zoe. You can imagine my thinking that once we'd built her little luxury kitty castle on the back patio she'd run straight to it, but she didn't. She didn't trust it and she wasn't trusting us. I considered trying to catch her and shove her inside to show her how magnificent it was. After thinking about that for a minute, I realized that would do more harm than good. Zoe had to choose to go into her little castle on her own. It had to be her choice. Why? Because if I forced her, she would have been even more terrified of the Zoe house and of me. She had to experience it herself. She couldn't take my word for it, however much I tried to sell her on the idea.

So, after Adam and Eve decided to make their fatal choice, God had to step in and make a way for them to be redeemed. That word redeemed? *To be delivered from death.* And death is anything that is contrary to the Lifegiver.

In Deuteronomy 30:19, God practically begs us to choose life. He knows that through the power of choice, if we decide not to trust Him, it will mean our destruction—not because He wants that for us, but because that's what happens when we live contrary to who He is. It's like assuming we can live without air. We were created to breathe; if we stop breathing, our lives stop. If we are determined to live without God, we won't live. The creation can't survive without the Creator. We are living in a time of grace in which we get to choose, and God desperately wants us to choose life. That's why He came "with skin on". He came through Jesus to teach us what He is like—every bit of warmth and kindness, joy and peace.

He's better than chocolate chip cookies fresh out of the oven, or a Hawaiian sunset. He's more beautiful than Acadia National Park in autumn, or enjoying a cup of hot cocoa next to a warm fire in a mountain cabin while watching the snow fall. He's better than every Christmas gift you've ever opened. He's better than all the good we can imagine—because He *is* Good. He is the author of Good (James 1:17). He embodies the very existence of Love. Just as we must trust that Goodness and Love; we also must trust Him.

You see, without faith (also known as trust) "it is impossible to please God …" (Hebrews 11:6 NIV). Here's why: If we don't have faith and trust in God, we will function out of fear and selfishness. Fear and selfishness lead to our destruction. We see it all over the planet. 1 John 4:18 tells us: "There is no fear in love; but perfect love casts out fear, because fear involves torment. But he who fears has not been made perfect in love." (NKJV)

Fear involves torment. Fear involves misery. Fear makes us do stupid things. Adam and Eve thought God was holding out on them, but He had been telling them the truth all along. Not trusting Him meant their choice would bring separation and death. So He, because He is Goodness and Love, determined to pay that death penalty for every one of us who has come (or will come) under the curse of the deceiver. In order to give us the choice to choose life, Jesus came and died once for all of humanity. So every person on the planet has the option to choose life. Every person on the planet has the option to trust Jesus.

Jesus revealed to us what God is. Through His life here on earth, He did miracles, signs, and wonders. Every one of those was to reveal the Father's love for humanity. Not enough food? Jesus took those small elements and multiplied them into abundance. Blind, deaf, sick, infirm? Jesus healed every single disease. Being tormented by the enemy? Jesus set them free. Jesus revealed in the most powerful, meaningful way possible that God is Trustworthy. He put forth the most extensive effort, and that sent Him to His death, in order to give us the choice to choose life. And the most incredible part about this? He knew that many still would not choose life. Yet He chose to give the extravagant gift of

Himself regardless. That's how much He values free will and the power of choice. That's how much He loves us.

The Word of God, from Genesis to Revelation, is His story of redeeming humanity, wooing and loving through the most scandalous (seemingly improper for the Creator of the universe) decision to actually become one of His creations in order to give us the choice to choose Life. He's done this by showing us He is more loving and good than we can possibly imagine, and He is absolutely trustworthy. Jesus is Salvation. He is our Life. He's the One we get to choose because He absolutely, wholeheartedly has chosen us. He did so with His life and through His death.

You'll be happy to know that after a few days of avoiding her kitty castle on the patio, Zoe has settled in and is enjoying the nice, warm, blissful gift we've given her. She's going to have a warm winter—my wild little kitty, whose name means "Life."

Truth 2.3 Application:

1. Why did God put the tree of knowledge of good and evil in the Garden of Eden?

_____

_____

_____

_____

2. Other than God Himself, what is the most powerful force in the universe and why?

_____

_____

_____

_____

3. What must we have in order to please God?

_____

_____

_____

_____

Truth 2.4

Why the Plan of Salvation was Necessary
You may still be wondering why the plan of salvation was entirely necessary. Why did Jesus have to come and die in order to save us, other than revealing that He can be trusted? When Adam and Eve chose to eat the forbidden fruit, many changes occurred physiologically, emotionally, and spiritually. (I'll share more about this subject in the lesson *Spirit, Soul, and Body*.)

Possible Changes After the Fall
Consider that before the fall, Adam and Eve had no reason to fear. After the fall, however, something changed in them. We know that they experienced a spiritual death (falling out of relationship with God), but it seems mentally/emotionally, and even physically they were also changed. As Genesis 3:17-19 reveals, there were physical changes that happened to the earth based on their decision. Knowing good and evil would now affect them in every part of their being as well. Notice that Genesis 3:7 states "their eyes were opened." What were their eyes opened to? This is not only referring to the fact that they noticed they had no clothing - it seems to be speaking of a new kind of awareness, and in their case, this new awareness was not to their benefit. This event which happened to our first parents left them feeling extreme fear - possibly at the realization that they would need to begin fending for themselves (guilt and shame isolate us and make us feel we must do things without the help of God because we fear He does not accept us). They no longer trusted God based on the fact that they no longer trusted themselves. Their own hearts' deceitfulness led to a severed relationship with their Creator and Friend.

Enter – Fear, Shame, Guilt, Condemnation
God created Adam and Eve in His image and likeness in glory, similar to how Christ appeared on the Mount of Transfiguration (Luke 9:28-36). Before Adam and Eve sinned, they were *naked and without shame* (Genesis 2:25) and upon sinning, their *eyes were opened, and they saw they were naked*. Christ appeared in a glorified body which Adam and Eve most likely possessed before the fall. This glorified body may have been similar to the brightness of Moses' face after communing with the Lord face to face. The face of Moses was so radiant it

required a veil in order for him to speak to the children of Israel because they were terrified of him (Exodus 34:29-35).

Genesis 3:10 reveals Adam and Eve hid from God because they were *afraid*. God then had to clothe them with physical coverings (Genesis 3:21). We lost that glory once Adam and Eve ate the fruit out of disobedience when they decided to stop trusting God. Not only that, because they were changed, all who were born from Adam's seed would be changed as well. (Consider how every seed reproduces its own kind.) They lost their glory and took on characteristics belonging to the adversary, also known as satan. Jesus came in order to buy us back from the enemy—to "redeem" us because someone had to pay the penalty for sin.

Romans 6:23 (NKJV) tells us, "For the wages of sin is death, but the gift of God is eternal life in Christ Jesus our Lord." Jesus had to pay the death penalty in order to redeem us.

Someone had to die, because one who is living contrary to God and who He is, simply cannot exist. (Remember how I mentioned that life on earth couldn't survive without the sun? Not to mention gravity and other atmospheric physical phenomena.) Consider the fact that anyone who is opposed to who and what God is would ultimately bring destruction, misery, and eternal death upon themselves. Life and death cannot coexist, just as darkness and light cannot. Where there is light, darkness abates or even flees. Darkness is the absence of light. Sin is the absence of Life. Jesus came to remedy that.

Spiritual Death Remedied

Adam and Eve experienced a spiritual death the day they decided to eat the fruit of the tree of the knowledge of good and evil. This meant that they were separated from God at that point. Separation from God is spiritual death.

As Pastor Chad Gonzales shares in his book, *Never Be Sick Again; Access Supernatural Health Through Jesus' Resurrection Power©*, "When God created man, He made man in His image and according to His likeness. When God made man, it was good; man was righteous, spiritually alive, and filled with God's life and nature. Man was perfect just like God and, as a result, was able to contain His abundant life; however, when Adam sinned, he died spiritually and lost the life and nature of God."[13]

1 Corinthians 15:45 ESV: "Thus it is written, 'The first man Adam became a living being'; the last Adam became a life-giving spirit."

---

[13] Gonzales, Chad, *Never Be Sick Again; Access Supernatural Health Through Jesus' Resurrection Power©* (Harrison House, 2024) p. 69

Adam was a living being but when he sinned, he experienced spiritual death. But as Pastor Gonzales states, "Jesus came to be a life-giving spirit; He came to put in us what the first Adam lost."[14]

Jesus became the firstborn among many brothers and sisters. Romans 8:29 (ESV) states, "For those God foreknew he also predestined to be conformed to the image of his Son, that he might be the firstborn among many brothers and sisters." We became new creations conformed to the image of Jesus.

Our spirits had to be saved. Our spirit man is dead until we receive Jesus, which means we won't survive after this period of grace if we don't receive the gift of *zoe life* - the kind of life which God, who is innately life, intimately shares with us. Receiving His gift of life is the only way that we can live because if we don't choose life, what's the alternative?

Our first parents not only lost their faith and trust in God, but they also lost the faith of God. When their spirits died, that benefit died with them. As Andrew Wommack states in His article, "Faith of God"[15] "Romans 4:17 says, 'God … calleth those things which be not as though they were.' God's faith goes beyond sight. God's faith operates supernaturally, beyond the limitations of our natural faith." Faith functions in a way that doesn't make much sense in the natural/carnal realm because before we learn about faith, seeing is believing. However, with faith, believing is seeing. When we receive Jesus and trust Him, we learn to believe that: "… with God all things are possible." (Matthew 19:26)

"… faith is the substance of things hoped for, the evidence of things not seen." (Hebrews 11:1 NKJV)

They lost their authority. Genesis 1:28 tells us that Adam had full authority and dominion over everything on earth. When he decided to trust the enemy rather than God, he surrendered that authority to satan. Jesus had to legally purchase that authority back for us.

Luke 10:19 ESV: "Behold, I have given you authority to tread on serpents and scorpions, and over all the power of the enemy, and nothing shall hurt you."

Because authority was given to man (that man being Adam), a man had to take it back. No man could have possibly lived a sin-free life and been a perfect sacrifice unless he didn't have a sin nature; therefore, God had to become the sinless man Himself. He came to redeem us and purchase that authority back, as a man, in order to delegate it once again to mankind.

Because we lost our ability to walk in the spirit (due to the fall of Adam and Eve), we now have to learn how to walk by the power of the Holy Spirit

---

[14] Gonzales, op cit., p. 69

[15] https://www.awmi.net/reading/teaching-articles/faith_god/

(through our spiritual new birth united with Him) teaching us to operate in faith. That isn't natural to us in our physically fallen states because our spiritual eyes, ears, and understanding were lost at the fall. As we learn how to hear the Holy Spirit through the Word of the Lord, and as He indwells us, we find out how to, "... walk by faith, not by sight." (2 Corinthians 5:7 ESV)

We must do our part to learn who we are in Christ. Romans 12:2 ESV: "Do not be conformed to this world, but be transformed by the renewal of your mind, that by testing you may discern what is the will of God, what is good and acceptable and perfect." We learn how to live and behave according to who God says we are as the new creations we became when we were saved. That new creation is something that never existed before Jesus made a way for us to become one with Him.

2 Corinthians 5:17 ESV: "Therefore, if anyone is in Christ, he is a new creation. The old has passed away; behold, the new has come." We become something brand new. Adam and Eve didn't even have the Spirit of God inside of them, so this is truly extraordinary!

Truth 2.4 Application

1. What were some of the changes that occurred to Adam and Eve after the fall?

_____

_____

_____

_____

2. "_____" is the "absence of light."

3. What kind of death happened to Adam and Eve the day they decided to eat from the tree of knowledge of good and evil?

_____

_____

_____

_____

Truth 2.5

Jesus purchased our peace and righteousness. As mentioned previously regarding the words "saved" and "salvation", part of the gift was peace. Isaiah 53:5 NKJV: "But He was wounded for our transgressions, He was bruised for our iniquities; The chastisement for our peace was upon Him, And by His stripes we are healed." Not only did He purchase our peace and healing, but He also, through His death, granted us the right to be righteous before God. That means that God sees us as being just as perfect as Jesus.

Pastor Gonzales says it this way, "Because of your union with Christ, you are forever perfect. When God sees you, He sees you through the Blood of Jesus. He sees you as perfect."[16]

2 Corinthians 5:21 ESV: "For our sake he made him to be sin who knew no sin, so that in him we might become the righteousness of God." It was necessary that One who had never sinned take our place so that His perfect life might become a substitute for ours. This is what Jesus did so we might live. He paid for everything we could ever need through His own life and death, freely given for us.

In the Old Testament, God set up the sacrificial system as a symbolic foreshadowing of what Jesus would come to do to take away the sins of the world. It was necessary for people to understand the devastating consequences of sin. When a person brought their spotless, perfect lamb to be sacrificed, it was with the understanding that this lamb was paying the penalty for the sins of the individual. The sacrificial lamb represented atonement for the sinner, allowing them to be forgiven. Atonement means we agree to be reconciled by our reparation to make things right after wrongdoing. God, however, gave His people the sacrificial system so that they wouldn't have to die immediately for their sins. That sacrificial lamb represented Jesus' death to pay the ultimate price for sin, redeeming our eternal salvation, our healing, our peace--everything we had lost as a result of sin. When Jesus came to offer Himself as the final sacrifice, He made full and complete restitution for all sin, which removed the separation and rift between us and God and restored us to right standing before Him. We can now approach God with nothing separating us.

---

[16] Gonzales, op cit., p. 68

Leviticus 17:11 (NIV) states, "For the life of a creature is in the blood, and I have given it to you to make atonement for yourselves on the altar; it is the blood that makes atonement for one's life." Hebrews 10:1-10 (NKJV) states:

> For the law, having a shadow of the good things to come, and not the very image of the things, can never with these same sacrifices, which they offer continually year by year, make those who approach perfect. For then would they not have ceased to be offered? For the worshipers, once purified, would have had no more consciousness of sins. But in those sacrifices there is a reminder of sins every year. For it is not possible that the blood of bulls and goats could take away sins.
>
> Therefore, when He came into the world, He said:
>
> "Sacrifice and offering You did not desire,
>
> But a body You have prepared for Me.
>
> In burnt offerings and sacrifices for sin
>
> You had no pleasure.
>
> Then I said, 'Behold, I have come—
>
> In the volume of the book it is written of Me—
>
> To do Your will, O God.'"
>
> Previously saying, "Sacrifice and offering, burnt offerings, and offerings for sin You did not desire, nor had pleasure in them" (which are offered according to the law), then He said, "Behold, I have come to do Your will, O God." He takes away the first that He may establish the second. By that will we have been sanctified through the offering of the body of Jesus Christ once for all.

Because we believe and accept what Jesus has done through His atoning sacrifice for us, God now sees us in the same way that He sees Jesus—perfect, holy, righteous, and without sin!

Truth 2.5 Application

Listen to "The Divine Exchange" meditation:
https://drive.google.com/file/d/1DbbrUOOXbo2qhgLwRn2C1uwmq9zdtru
Z/view?usp=sharing

After listening to this meditation, what was your experience? Write about it in a letter from Jesus to you. Pray: *Holy Spirit, please speak to my heart and write a letter from You to me about the divine exchange that took place where Jesus took all my sin upon Himself so that I could be forgiven and made clean. In Jesus' name I pray, Amen.*

_____

_____

_____

_____

_____

_____

_____

_____

_____

_____

_____

_____

_____

_____

_____

_____

_____

_____

_____

_____

Decision to Receive Salvation

Acts 2:21 tells us, "And it shall come to pass that everyone who calls upon the name of the Lord shall be saved." We're told in Romans 10:9-10, "... if you confess with your mouth that Jesus is Lord and believe in your heart that God raised him from the dead, you will be saved. For with the heart one believes and is justified, and with the mouth one confesses and is saved."

Justification is the act of God which declares a sinner righteous in His sight. This was done through the sacrifice Jesus made upon the cross. The reason this is important for us today is that it gives us the opportunity and right to experience a relationship with our Creator once again. This relationship, when we truly understand and receive the love of God and the God of love, will transform every part of our being. As we've discovered in this lesson, the love of God has compelled Him to do everything possible to be reunited with His children. Many times, our experiences in the world have affected us in such ways that we have felt God isn't that good or He doesn't really love us. I want to encourage you today to give God a chance (if you've not yet experienced Him) or to give Him another chance (if for some reason you've lost your first love). God doesn't "need" us human-beings - but by His love, He desires to be united with us, to share and do life with us.

If you have not personally received the gift of salvation that Jesus purchased for you on the cross, I'd like to invite you to make this decision today. God is trustworthy. He adores you and longs for you to have a personal relationship with Him. He longs for you to know and experience Him and desires that you receive eternal life. When we make a decision for Jesus, receiving His gift of salvation, eternal life begins at that moment.

If you would like to receive Jesus into your heart and life, pray this prayer with me:

> *Papa God, I know I have sinned, and I need a Savior. I believe with my heart and confess with my mouth that Jesus is Your Son and that He died upon the cross for my sin. I believe that He rose from the dead so that I may experience a relationship with You. Jesus, I ask that You come into my heart and life and be my Lord. Thank You so much for loving me, dying for me, and saving me! It's in Jesus' name I pray. Amen.*

If you prayed this prayer for the first time, welcome to the family of God! You may now want to choose to be baptized as a public declaration of your faith. Similar to a wedding, water baptism is a display of giving your life to Jesus and is symbolic of dying to self (going under the water) and coming alive as a new creation in Christ. (See Luke 3:21-22; Mark 1:9-11.)

Truth 2.6 Application:

If you chose to give your life to Jesus for the first time today, talk with Him about this choice. Read Luke 3:21-22; Mark 1:9-11 and consider making a public confession through water baptism. (If you would like to know more about baptism, you may want to discuss this with a pastor or other church member.) Write your thoughts about Luke 3:21-22; Mark 1:9-11 here:

_____

_____

_____

_____

_____

_____

_____

_____

_____

If you aren't already part of a church, I encourage you to find a local church to join. By giving your life to the Lord, you are now part of a huge family of believers! The church is the body of Christ. It was His plan that we join together and connect with other believers as this strengthens our faith and walk with the Lord. We find accountability; receive instruction and teaching; grow and develop our spiritual gifts; have opportunities to join in ministry and outreach, and enjoy fellowshipping with the family of God. When looking for a church to attend, keep in mind that no church will be perfect; every church is filled with people who are still learning and growing. You can consider these criteria as you decide:

- Members are grace-filled and submitted to God
- Biblically based, teaching the FULL Gospel message
- Believes in the suffering, death and resurrection of Jesus
- Believes in healing as part of salvation and the atonement
- Not conformed to the world
- Believes in the Trinity
- Walks in the fruit of the Spirit
- Believes in and flow in the gifts of the Spirit
- Has a healthy outreach program
- Includes loving, caring people who express God's unconditional love to you

Chapter 3

WHO GOD IS:

The Truth About the Holy Spirit

❦ ∞∞∞ ❦

Truth 3.1

The Victorian Era Baptist preacher Charles Spurgeon (1834-1892) once said, "Without the Spirit of God, we can do nothing. We are as ships without wind. We are useless."[17] That's a pretty heavy statement: We can do *nothing?* This statement from Spurgeon reminds me of the statement Jesus made in John 5:19: "Truly, truly, I say to you, the Son can do nothing of his own accord, but only what he sees the Father doing. For whatever the Father does, that the Son does likewise." How did Jesus know what His Father was doing and how His Father was leading Him? Luke 3:22 tells us that the Holy Spirit rested upon Jesus in the form of a dove at His baptism. *Jesus was being led by the Holy Spirit.*

---

[17] https://wisdomtrove.com/author_quotes/charles-spurgeon-quotes/

Caprice Scott

In John chapter 16, before Jesus left this earth, He told His disciples that it was actually for their benefit that He return to the Father, because He was sending His Spirit for them. This promise is for us, as well, and for all who receive Jesus as Savior and Lord. While Jesus could be here to speak with us and guide us as a Friend, the Holy Spirit lives in (indwells) the believer, making it possible to be joined with Him and transformed by His very power! This union we have with the Holy Spirit makes Him part of us! Consider that for a moment. God is part of us when we have His Spirit in us. Let's take a look at those verses in John 16:7-15 (ESV):

> Nevertheless, I tell you the truth: it is to your advantage that I go away, for if I do not go away, the Helper will not come to you. But if I go, I will send him to you. And when he comes, he will convict the world concerning sin and righteousness and judgment: concerning sin, because they do not believe in me; concerning righteousness, because I go to the Father, and you will see me no longer; concerning judgment, because the ruler of this world is judged. I still have many things to say to you, but you cannot bear them now. When the Spirit of truth comes, he will guide you into all the truth, for he will not speak on his own authority, but whatever he hears he will speak, and he will declare to you the things that are to come. He will glorify me, for he will take what is mine and declare it to you. All that the Father has is mine; therefore I said that he will take what is mine and declare it to you.

In these verses, we find many of the reasons Jesus wanted us to receive His Spirit: He's our Helper, yet how does He help us? Based on these verses, He guides us into all truth. What He hears from the Father, He declares to us. Just as Jesus did what the Father revealed to Him, the Holy Spirit declares what Jesus established.

He convicts Believers of Righteousness

God wants us to understand that when we are in Him and He is in us, He sees us as perfect and as righteous as His Son. We find this truth in Romans 3:21-22 where Paul tells us, "But now the righteousness of God has been manifested apart from the law, although the Law and the Prophets bear witness to it—the righteousness of God through faith in Jesus Christ for all who believe." The Spirit wants to convict our hearts that we are seen and found right and righteous in God's sight. Why does this matter? Because He doesn't see us as sinful any longer! He sees us as perfect and holy and worthy of all of the things the enemy tries to tell us we are unworthy of. A righteous standing before God changes everything.

Let's see what the Word of God says about any other roles the Holy Spirit has and plays in a believer's life. The Holy Spirit speaks God's Word and helps bring it to remembrance, and He is our Friend and our Comforter. In John 14:26 (AMP), Jesus says: "But the Helper (Comforter, Advocate, Intercessor—Counselor, Strengthener, Standby), the Holy Spirit, whom the Father will send in My name [in My place, to represent Me and act on My behalf], He will teach you all things. And He will help you remember everything that I have told you." The Holy Spirit empowers us to spread the Gospel, to cast out demons, to speak in new tongues, and to heal. Acts 1:8: "But you will receive power when the Holy Spirit has come upon you, and you will be my witnesses in Jerusalem and in all Judea and Samaria, and to the end of the earth."

In Mark 16:17-18 we find: "These signs will accompany those who have believed: in My name they will cast out demons, they will speak in new tongues; they will pick up serpents, and if they drink anything deadly, it will not hurt them; they will lay hands on the sick, and they will get well." (AMP)

2 Corinthians 13:14 speaks of the fellowship of the Holy Spirit. Think of this as companionship. What a beautiful gift! God our Companion. He prays through us: Romans 8:26 (AMP) states: "In the same way the Spirit [comes to us and] helps us in our weakness. We do not know what prayer to offer *or* how to offer it as we should, but the Spirit Himself [knows our need and at the right time] intercedes on our behalf with sighs and groanings too deep for words."

He gives us victory and power to overcome, directs us, and gives us resurrection life. In Romans 8:9-11 (AMP) we learn:

> However, you are not [living] in the flesh [controlled by the sinful nature] but in the Spirit, if in fact the Spirit of God lives in you [directing and guiding you]. But if anyone does not have the Spirit of Christ, he does not belong to Him [and is not a child of God]. If Christ lives in you, though your [natural] body is dead because of sin, your spirit is alive because of righteousness [which He provides]. And if the Spirit of Him who raised Jesus from the dead lives in you, He who raised Christ Jesus from the dead will also give life to your mortal bodies through His Spirit, who lives in you.

He is able to help us do things beyond all that we could ask, think, or imagine.

Ephesians 3:20 (NKJV): "Now to Him who is able to do exceedingly abundantly above all that we ask or think, according to the power that works in us."

He gives visions and dreams: Joel 2:28 (AMP): "It shall come about after this that I shall pour out My Spirit on all mankind; And your sons and your daughters will prophesy, your old men will dream dreams, your young men will see visions."

He fills us with abundant hope: Romans 15:13 (NKJV): "Now may the God of hope fill you with all joy and peace in believing, that you may abound in hope by the power of the Holy Spirit."

He influences, directs, and teaches: 2 Peter 1:20-21 (NKJV): "... knowing this first, that no prophecy of Scripture is of any private interpretation, for prophecy never came by the will of man, but holy men of God spoke as they were moved by the Holy Spirit."

1 Corinthians 2:9-10 (NKJV): "But as it is written: 'Eye has not seen, nor ear heard, Nor have entered into the heart of man the things which God has prepared for those who love Him.' But God has revealed them to us through His Spirit. For the Spirit searches all things, yes, the deep things of God." So now you might be asking: How can we know that we are being led by the Spirit? What does the voice of the Holy Spirit sound like compared to any other "voices" we might hear? (You'll learn more about that in Truth 3.2.)

Truth 3.1 Application:

Become aware of your thoughts. Try setting a timer and catching your thoughts every 15, 30, or 60 minutes to be aware of what you are thinking. Start tracking the kinds of negative or intrusive thoughts you're catching and write some of them below. (We will discuss how to deal with these in the next few "Truth" sections):

_____
_____
_____
_____
_____
_____
_____
_____
_____
_____
_____
_____
_____

Truth 3.2

Let's discuss how to recognize the voice of the Holy Spirit—how to distinguish that voice from the voice of the enemy.

Where Do Our Thoughts Come From?
Our thoughts come from one of three sources: Our mind, the Holy Spirit, or the enemy. How do we know who is speaking? When *God* speaks, He says such things as: "'For I know the plans I have for you,' declares the LORD, 'plans for welfare and not for evil, to give you a future and a hope.'" (Jeremiah 29:11 ESV)

He has good thoughts for us. Peaceful thoughts, never evil thoughts. He desires that we have a positive future and hope. Jeremiah 29:11 gives us a clue about thoughts the Holy Spirit might give us: *God* says . . .

You are beloved:
"But because of his great love for us, God, who is rich in mercy, made us alive with Christ even when we were dead in transgressions—it is by grace you have been saved" (Ephesians 2:4-5 NIV).

You are a masterpiece:
"For we are God's workmanship, created in Christ Jesus to do good works, which God prepared in advance for us to do" (Ephesians 2:10 NIV). You were created for a purpose. God has good work for you to do, and He custom-made you for that work.

You are healed:
1 Peter 2:24: "He himself bore our sins in his body on the tree, that we might die to sin and live to righteousness. By his wounds you have been healed."

You are righteous:
2 Corinthians 5:21 (NKJV): "For He made Him who knew no sin to be sin for us, that we might become the righteousness of God in Him."

God tells us *not* to fear. I've heard that the Bible says, "Don't fear," or "Don't worry," in some way or another 365 times.[18] That's enough for every single day of the year. "Fear not" is the most repeated command in the New Testament! Let's look at a few in both the Old and New Testaments: For example, Isaiah states:

---

[18] https://believersportal.com/list-365-fear-not-bible-verses/

Isaiah 41:10 (NASB): "Do not fear, for I am with you; Do not anxiously look about you, for I am your God. I will strengthen you, surely I will help you, surely I will uphold you with My righteous right hand."

Isaiah 41:13 (NASB): "For I am the Lord your God, who upholds your right hand, Who says to you, 'Do not fear, I will help you.'"

Isaiah 43:1 (NASB): "But now, thus says the Lord, your Creator, O Jacob, And He who formed you, O Israel, 'Do not fear, for I have redeemed you; I have called you by name; you are Mine!'"

Matthew 6:30-32 (NKJV) says: "Now if God so clothes the grass of the field, which today is, and tomorrow is thrown into the oven, will He not much more clothe you, O you of little faith? Therefore do not worry, saying, 'What shall we eat?' or 'What shall we drink?' or 'What shall we wear?' For after all these things the Gentiles seek. For your heavenly Father knows that you need all these things."

1 Peter 5:7 (NIV): "Cast all your anxiety on him because he cares for you." Those are just a few out of 365. God doesn't want you to be fearful, worried, anxious, or guilt-ridden.

Guilt and shame don't come from God. They come from the enemy. Revelation 12:10 says satan is the accuser of the brethren (God's kids). The Holy Spirit convicts (1 Thessalonians 1:5) and gently urges us to stay on the right track, but guilt and shame never come from God. As a matter of fact, the conviction of the Holy Spirit is actually to reveal our true natures of righteousness.

"And when He [the Holy Spirit] has come, He will convict the world of sin, and of righteousness, and of judgment: of sin, because they do not believe in Me; of righteousness, because I go to My Father and you see Me no more; of judgment, because the ruler of this world is judged." (John 16:8–11 NKJV, Emphasis added)

He convicts *unbelievers of their sin.*

He convicts *believers of their righteousness,* and

He convicts *the ruler of this world (satan) of the judgment he will face, which is the judgment of God.*

Another interesting thing to note is the Holy Spirit's voice comes from our belly, as John 7:38 (KJV) tells us: "He that believeth on me, as the scripture hath said, out of his belly shall flow rivers of living water." When the enemy speaks, he is going to say the opposite of what God says about you. However, keep in mind that he will try to make it sound like your voice, or he will try to make you assume it's God voice because of wrong religious beliefs you may have been taught in the past. Thoughts you might hear from the enemy:

You're sick. You're gonna die.

You've gone too far this time - you won't be forgiven for this!

You're gonna lose your job.

God doesn't like you.

You should be afraid because this won't end well.

You don't have a purpose.

You're a complete failure.

No one likes you.

You're not even lovable.

God needs to punish you in order to save you.

God isn't listening to your prayers.

You're going to be poor and stay poor.

You will never have peace or joy in this life.

Nothing ever works out for you.

You'll never heal.

Even calling a sickness "my sickness" and owning it is a thought from the enemy. When we understand God's incredible love for us and the healing that He purchased for us through Christ, we begin to realize God would never want us to be sick. We will continue to explore this further in the coming chapters.

Notice how these thoughts are accusatory (coming from the accuser of the brethren) and notice they all address "you." "You will never heal," "no one likes you," etc. These are from a voice *outside* of you speaking lies to you. This can be a clue that the voice is not yours but the enemy's, because we don't think of ourselves this way in our minds. We also would never *choose* to say these things to ourselves. I certainly wouldn't want to claim any of these as my truth. Would you?

Just as God, through the Holy Spirit, desires to make Himself manifest in and through us (the fruit of the Spirit—Galatians 5:22-23), the devil also desires to manifest himself in and through us. He gives us thoughts and feelings that he himself has. Consider some of the statements on the list above and others like them such as, "You're a horrible sinner. You're not even lovable. You should be afraid!" Why would the devil think those things? Because they are absolutely true about him, but not about God's kids!

Truth 3.2 Application

Download the "Shut Up, Devil!" app (available from either the Apple Store or Google Play) to your phone and use it when you're dealing with negative thoughts and emotions. Write out some of the truths that you are finding in the app to help combat your negative thoughts:

_____

_____

_____

_____

_____

_____

_____

Truth 3.3

The enemy loves to take facts from the Word of God and our lives and twist them to fit his lies. 2 Corinthians 10:4-5 says that the enemy comes against us with arguments and every high thing (other versions say presumption, pretension, or lofty opinions) attempting to exalt itself against the knowledge of God. The knowledge of God includes the truth about who He actually is, your identity in Him as a believer and son of God, and how He feels about you.

The devil will try to destroy your confidence and trust in what God's Word says about you. He always aims at our identity. He will remind you of sins you committed in your past, and because of those sins he will tell you that you will never be loved, accepted, or even saved by God. He will even go as far as to condemn you, suggesting you have no hope where God is concerned and He has stopped loving you because you're not living up to God's perfect standards.

The truth is, when you gave your life to Jesus, none of the past regrets or even current struggles define you. Your only truth is the Word of God and what He says about you. Jesus made you a brand-new creation—righteous, whole, holy, and accepted in the Beloved.

Our own brain will usually echo whatever programming it receives. We may hear things we've learned from the Holy Spirit, the Word of God, or from the enemy. Our worldviews will also affect how and what we hear and believe, the experiences we've had in our past, and what we have allowed to influence us.

Once we recognize where certain thoughts may be coming from, we can choose what to do with those thoughts. When I realize I'm dealing with a thought from the enemy, I remind myself that negative thoughts are not my thoughts. I have the mind of Christ (which is in your spirit as discussed in Chapter 1: *The Truth About God's Character*). Why would I want negative thoughts? Why would I choose to think so poorly of myself or assume that God isn't for me? Would any of us purposefully choose thoughts like this?

Filter your thoughts through this, and ask yourself the following question: Does this thought line up with Philippians 4:8? This is an excellent filter for our thoughts: "Finally, brothers and sisters, whatever is true, whatever is noble, whatever is right, whatever is pure, whatever is lovely, whatever is admirable— if anything is excellent or praiseworthy—think about such things." (NIV)

> ➢ Is this thought one that would glorify God?
> ➢ Is this thought one that I would want to think or choose to believe about myself?
> ➢ Does it line up with Scripture and what I know about God's thoughts toward me?

John 10:10 is another excellent filter for our thoughts: "The thief comes only to steal and kill and destroy. I came that they may have life and have it abundantly." If this thought would steal your peace, kill your joy, or destroy your hope in the promises of God, it's not a thought from the Holy Spirit. However, if this thought is life-giving and lines up with the promises in the Word, it's a great indication that the Holy Spirit is speaking.

Allowing and accepting negative thoughts from the enemy is like allowing your next-door neighbor to dump toxic waste into your garden. Your brain doesn't have to be the enemy's dumping ground! Tell him to take his trash elsewhere because your brain and body belong to Christ. You are the temple of the Holy Spirit. That garbage from the devil isn't yours. It doesn't belong to you, and you are not his trash receptacle.

God is good. His thoughts toward us are always good. Satan is bad. His thoughts toward us are always bad. If you're dealing with any kind of thoughts that speak contrary to the goodness of God and His love for you, you can know where those thoughts are coming from and choose to rebuke the enemy and replace those thoughts with the truth that you know from God's Word.

Truth 3.3 Application:

What is the Holy Spirit speaking to you? How are you discerning His voice differently than what the enemy may be speaking to you? Go back and look at some of the thoughts that you wrote about in Truth 3.1. Knowing what you know now about where those negative thoughts are coming from, what might be a way to filter those thoughts through the truth of God's Word?

_____

_____

_____

_____

_____

_____

_____

_____

_____

Truth 3.4

Baptism of the Holy Spirit

One of the greatest blessings that we as Christians can receive is the baptism of the Holy Spirit. When we become Christians, we are *born of the Spirit*, but that is not the same as being *baptized in and filled with the Spirit*. Being born of the Spirit means that we receive eternal life. We become the new creations in our spirit that 2 Corinthians 5:17 (NIV) speaks of, "…Therefore, if anyone is in Christ, the new creation has come: The old has gone, the new is here!" Only born-again believers can then be filled with the Holy Spirit. Receiving the baptism of the Holy Spirit comes after receiving salvation.

In Acts chapter 8, we find Philip going down to Samaria, a region of Israel, to share the Gospel—the good news of Christ. In verse 12, we read that they believed Philip concerning the Kingdom of God and the name of Jesus Christ and they were baptized. However, verses 14-17 (ESV) reveal there's more to just being baptized into Christ:

> Now when the apostles at Jerusalem heard that Samaria had received the word of God, they sent to them Peter and John, who came down and prayed for them that they might receive the Holy Spirit, for he had not yet fallen on any of them, but they had only been baptized in the name of the Lord Jesus. Then they laid their hands on them and they received the Holy Spirit.

We see here that while it's possible to be saved in Jesus for eternal life, that doesn't necessarily mean we've received the *baptism of the Spirit* and *have become Spirit-filled*. These Samaritans were already saved but had not received the Holy Spirit. Peter and John prayed they would receive the Holy Spirit.

The baptism of the Holy Spirit is a gift. When someone gives you a gift, what do you have to do when you get it? *Receive it.* It's that easy. God desires you to receive the gift of the Holy Spirit even more than you desire to receive it. As Luke 11:10-13 states, "For everyone who asks receives, and the one who seeks finds, and to the one who knocks it will be opened. What father among you, if his son asks for a fish, will instead of a fish give him a serpent; or if he asks for an egg, will give him a scorpion? If you then, who are evil, know how to give good gifts to your children, how much more will the heavenly Father give the Holy Spirit to those who ask him!"

The Holy Spirit was given on the day of Pentecost. Although He had always been active in the world, He did not indwell believers until Jesus made the way for us to become new creations. We find this pouring out of the Spirit in Acts chapter 2, and He has been indwelling believers ever since. We don't need to beg or plead with God to give us His Spirit.

As I mentioned before, those who have already accepted Jesus as their Lord and Savior can receive the Holy Spirit. All that is necessary on our part is to ask, believe, and receive. Pray this with me right now:

> *Father God, I recognize and desire for Your power to live this new life as a new creation. Please fill me with Your Holy Spirit. I receive it right now by faith! Thank You for baptizing me. Holy Spirit, You are welcome in my life and I'm so thankful You are a part of me! In Jesus' name. Amen.*

"Therefore I tell you, whatever you ask in prayer, believe that you have received it, and it will be yours" (Mark 11:24).

That's it! Congratulations! You are now Spirit-filled!

When we receive the gift of the Holy Spirit, we are filled with supernatural power, the same power that raised Jesus from the dead. The Spirit also gives us the ability to pray in our heavenly prayer language. You may begin opening your mouth and expecting the Holy Spirit will give you words. He will begin speaking through you, but the words won't be anything you understand. This language will be entirely new, just between you and the Lord. Begin making sounds and syllables as the Spirit prays through you. These syllables and words will not make sense to your mind:

"For if I pray in a tongue, my spirit prays but my mind is unfruitful" (1 Corinthians 14:14). This means that your spirit communes with the Holy Spirit in a language that your mind won't understand. However, when we ask for understanding, God will give us revelations on what we are praying for. Now that you have received the gift of the Spirit, here are some of the benefits:

1. Building up spirit man—1 Corinthians 14:4: This means that our spirit grows stronger and helps our hearts to become focused on the things of the Spirit.

2. Declares mysteries of God—1 Corinthians 14:2: Praying in tongues is a tool the Holy Spirit has given us to access hidden truths and divine revelations. Andrew Sharpe says it this way, "The Spirit of wisdom and revelation is released when we pray in tongues. Our minds are illuminated to understand things that would otherwise be hidden, enabling us to tap into the mind of Christ and understand things that our natural minds could never comprehend."[19]

3. Greater intimacy and communion—1 Corinthians 14:14: When we pray in tongues, our spirit communes with the Holy Spirit on an intimate level that our human minds can't understand.

4. Helps in intercession—Romans 8:26: Oftentimes, we don't even know what or how to pray about a circumstance or need. We can spend time praying in tongues, and answers may begin coming to us. When we pray in tongues, while it may be a mystery to us, it is praying God's will because He helps our spirits to pray according to His perfect will.

5. Glorifies God—Acts 10:46: When we pray in tongues, we glorify and exalt God beyond what we could in our natural language.

6. Helps in spiritual warfare—Ephesians 6:18: Praying in the Spirit is listed in the same chapter as the armor of God. It is a powerful spiritual weapon along with the sword of the Spirit (the Word) and the shield of faith! When we pray in the Spirit, things are changing on our behalf in the spirit realm.[20]

7. Releases a supernatural peace and rest in the believer's spirit—1 Corinthians 14:14-15; Romans 8:6: Praying in the Spirit, having our minds set upon the Spirit, brings life and peace. When we pray through the Spirit, we will have peace that guards our hearts and minds through Christ (Philippians 4:7).

8. Releases wisdom and revelation—Ephesians 1:17-18: When we pray in the Spirit, God's mysteries are revealed to us, and our spiritual eyes are enlightened.

---

[19] https://andrewsharpe.org/benefits-of-praying-in-tongues-explained/

[20] *The spirit realm is the invisible realm inhabited by heavenly angels who actively serve God by ministering to the believers (Hebrews 1:14). It is also occupied by satan's demonic forces who oppose God and continuously wage war against God's people (Ephesians 6:12). We humans can only see and experience the natural realm, but the spirit realm exists all around us.

From an Instagram post by *Living Christian*:

God's voice:	satan's voice:
Stills you	Rushes you
Leads you	Pushes you
Reassures you	Frightens you
Enlightens you	Confuses you
Encourages you	Discourages you
Comforts you	Worries you
Calms you	Obsesses you
Convicts you	Condemns you

Truth 3.4 Application:

Pray in tongues at least half an hour a day: Some suggestions:

- Pray in tongues before studying the Word and ask for further revelation.
- When you are uncertain of what to pray for someone, pray in tongues.
- When you need wisdom and guidance from the Holy Spirit, pray in tongues.
- When you are in need of supernatural peace, spend some time praying in your prayer language.

Chapter 4

WHO YOU ARE IN HIM:

The Truth About Your

True Identity— in Christ

Have you seen the episode of *The Office*© where Jim impersonates Dwight for a day? He talks like him, behaves like him, and dresses like him, right down to the wire-rimmed glasses and mustard-colored short-sleeved dress shirt. Dwight is furious and tells him, "Identity theft is not a joke, Jim! Millions of families suffer every year!" While the episode is hilarious, Dwight isn't wrong. Identity theft is no joke, as you've no doubt learned from the media, and it has even become a major epidemic in the church today. Many Christians identify more with the world and their unbelieving counterparts than they do with who the Word tells them they are – simply because they haven't learned differently.

Truth 4.1

I think it is not uncommon for Christians to be wrapped up in trying to figure out who they are, based on the world's definitions of identity: their education, career, job title, income level, what they've accomplished, their looks, what they drive, where they live, who their friends are, nationality, political leanings, church denomination, and so on. These beliefs tend to be stored in the subconscious, even if we don't realize they are impacting the way we think, speak, and behave. I see this as a problem because, as believers in Christ, not one of these things represents our true identity, not even the church or denomination we may belong to.

What kinds of messages have we heard from the church about our identities? I can tell you that for the majority of my Christian walk (and I grew up attending church), I was terrified of God. Terrified that He wouldn't accept me. Terrified that He would send me to Hell because of my bad behavior. I never could figure out how to overcome sin. The harder I tried, the worse I'd fail. It was a vicious, unhealthy cycle from which I couldn't break free. It seemed hopeless. I heard teachings that I had to straighten up and clean up my behavior in order to be saved, or that because I was saved I should be walking out of sin…But no one could tell me how to stop sinning. Everything seemed to be based on my own efforts. Try harder. Use self-control. Confess every single sin, or you won't be forgiven.

Our greatest enemy would love to keep us in spiritual bondage through the belief that we share his identity; that we are guilty, hopeless sinners who are unwanted, unloved, rejected, destined to be sick and miserable. We see ourselves as never having enough, but instead lacking financially, physically, and emotionally; never measuring up and always subject to whatever the enemy chooses to do to us. Satan wants us to believe that we can't overcome, that we must strive to be loved and accepted by our Papa God, and that we need to constantly beg God to forgive us, and even then, who knows if we really are forgiven? These are the things that may be circulating through the church, and they are the lies the enemy has woven into religion.

When you consider the deeper message, these lies are works-based. They are based on human effort. Why does that matter? Because if we receive anything from the Lord based on our efforts—eternal life, healing, provision, peace, etc., then there was no reason for Jesus to come to earth to take our sickness and sin upon Himself. If we could accomplish anything to save ourselves, then the sacrifice of Jesus was completely unnecessary. And we know that's not the case. It is impossible for us to be righteous without God, but through Christ, we are made righteous if we receive what He has done for us. It has never been about our righteousness. It's always been about us believing God for righteousness, since the very beginning. What was Adam and Eve's greatest sin in the Garden of Eden? They stopped trusting God. Righteousness is about trusting God.

Even Abraham was considered righteous. He passed his wife off as his sister, twice. He lied and put her in harm's way. How can someone like that be considered righteous? Genesis 15:6 tells us how—he believed the LORD, and He counted it to him as righteousness. His righteousness was not based on his behavior but his belief and trust in the Lord.

God's Word has incredibly wonderful promises about our true identity in Christ Jesus. God wants us to know all the benefits and blessings that come with being His child. He desires for us to understand the things that He has in store for those of us who love Him, who have been chosen by Him from the foundation of the world. But, just as it's impossible to cash a $1,000,000 inheritance check unless we know about it, we also won't be able to step into our true identity in Christ unless we understand who He says we are. 2 Corinthians 5:17 (ESV) tells us, "Therefore, if anyone is in Christ, he is a new creation. The old has passed away; behold, the new has come."

In my opinion, another problem is that some Christians don't see themselves in their new identity. They're stuck believing they are still those old sinful people; they are stuck in a pre-Cross mentality. When we don't see ourselves in our true identity in Christ, we won't live and behave as we should.

If you're like me, you may have gone to a church that taught, based on Isaiah 64:6, that your righteousness is as filthy rags and that it's necessary to beg and plead for forgiveness for every single sin. You may even worry or wonder if you're ever going to be right with God. While it's true that without Christ we were completely unrighteous, 2 Corinthians 5:21 (ESV) states, "For our sake he (God the Father) made him (Jesus) to be sin who knew no sin, so that in him we might become the righteousness of God" (emphasis added).

Isaiah was under the Old Covenant—before the Cross. Jesus came to change this—*He took on our sin* so that *we might take on His righteousness*. Romans 3:21-26 (NLT) states:

> But now God has shown us a way to be made right with him without keeping the requirements of the law, as was promised in the writings of Moses and the prophets long ago. We are made right with God by placing our faith in Jesus Christ. And this is true for everyone who

believes, no matter who we are. For everyone has sinned; we all fall short of God's glorious standard. Yet God, in his grace, freely makes us right in his sight. He did this through Christ Jesus when he freed us from the penalty for our sins. For God presented Jesus as the sacrifice for sin. People are made right with God when they believe that Jesus sacrificed his life, shedding his blood... and he makes sinners right in his sight when they believe in Jesus.

While God does tell us to confess our sins to Him (1 John 1:9), He is more concerned with our repentance. We can say how wrong we are until we're blue in the face, but that doesn't change us. God desires that we have a change of heart and agree with Him. This is what repentance is; it is having a change of mind, choosing to think differently; doing an about-face and changing directions. According to Strong's (#3341) the Greek word is *metanoia*, which means "repentance; a change of mind, change in the inner man". It means to "be changed after being with." You can imagine, when we spend time with the Lord, we are being changed into His image. 2 Corinthians 3:18 (NLT) states, "So all of us who have had that veil removed can see and reflect the glory of the Lord. And the Lord—who is the Spirit—makes us more and more like him as we are changed into his glorious image."

Truth 4.1 Application

Each morning, read at least 10 of these declarations over yourself. Say them out loud and offer prayers of gratitude and praise to the Lord that you are truly a new creation in Christ. You may also want to record yourself reading these declarations so you can listen to them often. Research has revealed that we believe our own voice more than we believe anyone else's.[21]

God's Declarations— (amended to say in the first person):

- I am overtaken and chased down by the blessings of God (Deuteronomy 28:1-2; Luke 6:38).
- I will prosper in whatever I put my hand to (Joshua 1:8; Psalm 1:3; Psalm 35:27; 3 John 2).
- I live under God's blessing (Galatians 3:13-14).
- I am blessed and cannot be cursed. I am the head and not the tail, above and not beneath. I will lend and not borrow (Deuteronomy 28:3-14; Proverbs 10:6).

---

[21] https://www.medicalnewstoday.com/articles/recognizing-your-own-voice-helps-you-feel-more-in-control-study-finds

- I can participate in God's Divine Nature through His very great and precious promises (2 Peter 1:4).
- I am a Child of God (John 1:12).
- I will live in increase, prosperity, and blessing as I love and obey God (Deuteronomy 30:15-16).
- I have everything I need according to God's riches in glory through Christ Jesus (Philippians 4:19; Proverbs 3:9-10; Matthew 6:33).
- I am a member of Christ's Body (1 Corinthians 12:27).
- I am assured that all things work together for my good (Romans 8:28).
- I have been established, anointed, and sealed by God (2 Corinthians 1:21-22).
- I have everything I need for life and godliness (2 Peter 1:3).
- I have the ability to get wealth and glorify God through it (Deuteronomy 8:18; Proverbs 8:17-21; 2 Corinthians 8:9).
- l am surrounded by the favor of God (Psalm 5:12; Proverbs 11:27, 12:3).
- I am confident that God will perfect the work He has begun in me (Philippians 1:6).
- I am a citizen of heaven (Philippians 3:20).
- I am adopted as His child (Ephesians 1:5).
- I am given God's glorious grace lavishly and without restriction (Ephesians 1:5,8).
- I have been justified (Romans 5:1).
- I am Jesus' friend (John 15:15).
- I belong to God (1 Corinthians 6:20).
- I am in Him (Ephesians 1:7; 1 Corinthians 1:30).
- I have redemption (Ephesians 1:8).
- I am forgiven (Ephesians 1:8; Colossians 1:14).
- I have purpose (Ephesians 1:9, 3:11).
- I have hope (Ephesians 1:12).
- I have been given the keys of the Kingdom of Heaven to bind and loose on earth (Matthew 16:19).
- I am healed by the stripes of Jesus (1 Peter 2:24).
- I have authority over the enemy, and nothing shall hurt me (Luke 10:19).
- I am included (Ephesians 1:13).
- I am sealed with the promised Holy Spirit (Ephesians 1:13).

- I am a saint (Ephesians 1:18).
- I am salt and light of the earth (Matthew 5:13-14).
- I have been chosen and God desires me to bear fruit (John 15:1,5).
- I am a witness of Jesus Christ (Acts 1:8).
- I am a minister of reconciliation (2 Corinthians 5:17-20).
- I am alive with Christ (Ephesians 2:5).
- I am raised up and seated with Christ (Ephesians 2:6; Colossians 2:12).
- I am a member of God's household (Ephesians 2:19).
- I am secure (Ephesians 2:20).
- My body is a holy temple (Ephesians 2:21; 1 Corinthians 6:19).
- I am a dwelling for the Holy Spirit (Ephesians 2:22).
- I share in the promises of Christ Jesus (Ephesians 3:6).
- God's power works through me (Ephesians 3:7).
- I can approach God with freedom and confidence (Ephesians 3:12).
- I can grasp how wide, long, high, and deep Christ's love is (Ephesians 3:18).
- I am completed by God (Ephesians 3:19).
- I can bring glory to God (Ephesians 3:21).
- I am a light to others and can exhibit goodness, righteousness, and truth (Ephesians 5:8-9).
- I am hidden with Christ in God (Colossians 3:3).
- I have not been given a spirit of fear, but of power, love, and self-discipline (2 Timothy 1:7).
- I am born of God and the evil one cannot touch me (1 John 5:18).
- I am blessed in the heavenly realms with every spiritual blessing (Ephesians 1:3).
- I was chosen before the creation of the world (Ephesians 1:4,11).
- I am holy and blameless (Ephesians 1:4).
- I have been shown the incomparable riches of God's grace (Ephesians 2:7).
- God has expressed His kindness to me (Ephesians 2:7).
- I am God's workmanship (Ephesians 2:10).
- I have been brought near to God through Christ's blood (Ephesians 2:13).
- I have peace (Ephesians 2:14).
- I have access to the Father (Ephesians 2:18).
- I can understand what God's will is (Ephesians 5:17).

- I can give thanks for everything (Ephesians 5:20).
- I don't have to always have my own agenda (Ephesians 5:21).
- I can be strong (Ephesians 6:10).
- I have God's power (Ephesians 6:10).
- I can stand firm in the day of evil (Ephesians 6:13).
- I am dead to sin (Romans 1:12).
- I have been called and chosen (Ephesians 4:1; 2 Timothy 1:9).
- I am humble, gentle, patient, and loving toward others (Ephesians 4:2).
- I choose to mature spiritually (Ephesians 4:15).
- I can be certain of God's truths and the lifestyle which He has called me to (Ephesians 4:17).
- I can have a new attitude and a new lifestyle (Ephesians 4:21-32).
- I can be kind and compassionate to others (Ephesians 4:32).
- I can forgive others (Ephesians 4:32).
- I am not alone (Hebrews 13:5).
- I am growing in Christ (Colossians 2:7).
- I am His disciple (John 13:15).
- I have the mind of Christ (1 Corinthians 2:16).
- I am prayed for by Jesus Christ (John 17:20-23).
- I am united with other believers (John 17:20-23).
- I am not in want (Philippians 4:19).
- My heart and mind are protected with God's peace (Philippians 4:7).
- I am chosen and dearly loved (Colossians 3:12).
- I am blameless (1 Corinthians 1:8).
- I am set free (Romans 8:2; John 8:32).
- I am crucified with Christ (Galatians 2:20).
- I am a light in the world (Matthew 5:14).
- I am more than a conqueror (Romans 8:37).
- I am the righteousness of God (2 Corinthians 5:21).
- I am safe (1 John 5:18).
- I possess the mind of Christ (1 Corinthians 2:16).
- I am promised eternal life (John 6:47).
- I am promised a full life (John 10:10)
- I am victorious (1 John 5:4; 1 Corinthians 15:57).
- I am part of God's Kingdom (Revelation 1:6).
- I am healed from sin (1 Peter 2:24).
- I am no longer condemned (Romans 8:1,2).

- I am not helpless (Philippians 4:13).
- I am an overcomer (1 John 4:4).
- I am persevering (Philippians 3:14).
- I am protected (John 10:28).
- I am born again (1 Peter 1:23).
- I am a new creation (2 Corinthians 5:17).
- I am delivered (Colossians 1:13).
- I am redeemed from the curse of the Law (Galatians 3:13).
- I am qualified to share in His inheritance (Colossians 1:12).

Truth 4.2

Imagine with me a king and queen who had a beautiful little princess daughter. After an illness, the queen passed away when the princess was quite young. Not long after her passing, the king decided to remarry. His new wife had other children of her own, and she and her daughters were cruel to the princess out of envy and jealousy. The princess was beautiful and reminded the stepmother of the king's first wife whom he loved more than anything. The stepmother and her daughters hated the princess because of her beauty and because she was the apple of her father's eye. The princess was the true heir to her father's throne and all things in his kingdom. Because she was yet too young to understand her authority, she remained subject to her stepmother.

Not long after the king remarried, he went away on a long trip that lasted many years, and the princess had to remain home with her stepmother and stepsisters.

The stepmother and her daughters spoke hurtful lies to the princess, making her believe that her father didn't love her, that she was illegitimate, ugly, stupid, and would never amount to anything. They made fun of her and made her do all the housework and every menial task they didn't want to do, even though her father had left every kind of provision needed for his family's happiness. There was plenty of money to afford maids and servants, but the stepmother stole that extra money and hid it away for her own use.

The princess was forced to eat whatever was leftover that no one else wanted. While the stepmother and stepsisters ate at the table, the princess had to sit on the floor. All the beautiful clothing that she had was given to her stepsisters. She was never allowed to leave the castle, never allowed to have friends, never allowed to do any of the fun things the stepsisters did.

The king would often send letters of love to his daughter, but the stepmother always intercepted them and intentionally changed the messages so that the letters made the princess fearful of ever seeing her father again. She was told that the father hated her and that she must dutifully obey all that the stepmother demanded of her or she would be thrown into the dungeon forever.

Because of all the hateful, evil treatment that the princess received from her stepmother and stepsisters, she didn't realize that she was a princess. She forgot that she had a loving father who adored her. She never even knew that she was the heir to the throne and that all that the king owned was also hers. She had heard and listened to the lies of her stepfamily for so long she had come to accept those lies as her truth. She hated herself. She hated her life. She had given up all hope of anything positive or beautiful ever happening to her.

While this may sound almost identical to the story of Cinderella, it is an allegory of many Christians today. They've been lied to through false doctrines of the church and have been told that they are subject to the whims of satan whom the evil stepmother represents. Most Christians today don't know or understand who they are in Christ. Let's look at a few more Bible promises that tell us about our true identities. Romans 8:17 tells us that we are heirs of God and co-heirs with Christ.

In Ephesians 1:6-13 we see that:

➢ We are loved and accepted by our Father God.

➢ We were predestined for adoption as sons (and daughters) through Christ for the purpose of His will.

➢ He has blessed us *as His own Beloved.*

➢ We are redeemed (a ransom was paid for us—bought back from the penalty of sin, we were rescued, recovered from destruction, saved eternally) through His blood.

➢ We are completely forgiven.

➢ We are covered by the riches of God's grace (unmerited favor, kindness, blessings).

➢ We are blessed with wisdom and understanding.

➢ The mystery of His will and His purpose is being made known to us.

➢ We have obtained an inheritance in Him.

➢ We have heard the Word of truth—the Gospel of our salvation.

➢ We have been sealed with the Holy Spirit—our guarantee to all of this inheritance!

➢ Philippians 4:19 tells us we have provision for everything we need from the Father!

➢ 1 Corinthians 2:16 gives us the incredible news that we have the mind of Christ!

➤ Hebrews 13:21 encourages us that we are equipped for every good work.

➤ Ephesians 3:19 states that we are loved beyond measure (more than we could ever attempt to understand in this life).

➤ 2 Corinthians 5:21 says that we are righteous because of Jesus.

While there are many more incredible promises about our identity in the Word, I want to focus on the topic of righteousness a bit longer. The fact we are counted as righteous before God changes *everything* about us once we grasp this truth. When we received Jesus as our Savior, our lives and eternal destinies were changed forever. Coming to the point where we understand our righteous standing with God, we will no longer believe that we are lacking or inadequate. We stop thinking we are deserving of punishment. We don't associate ourselves with a victim mentality. We begin recognizing that we have the right to exercise the authority Jesus has given us. Guilt, fear, and self-condemnation will keep us from using that authority based on a mental state of feeling unworthy, but knowing we are seated with God in the heavenlies with Christ completely changes our perspective.

Righteousness allows us to stand before God without any guilt, shame, or condemnation. Because Christ has made us righteous, our Father God sees us in the same way that He sees Jesus—absolutely spotless! Because of this, as Barry Bennett says, "We are to reign in life. We are to activate God's promises and enforce His will. Only those who see themselves as God sees them will dare to step into this realm of authority."[22]

God doesn't want us to remain sin-conscious. Sin-consciousness keeps us under the enemy's thumb. We think we deserve whatever he might throw at us—sickness and disease, guilt, condemnation, fear, poverty, and anything else to make us miserable and keep us from overcoming him and all of his lies. Sin-consciousness is not our true identity. Instead, it's a tactic the enemy has used to defeat us, even though as new creations in Christ, there is absolutely no truth to it. It's one of his biggest bold-faced lies, and the church has seemed to adopt it as its own! Ephesians 4:23-25 reveals that our inner self, the new man, is being renewed day by day, not according to our works but the Holy Spirit working in and through us. Hebrews 10:22 states that our hearts have been sprinkled from an evil conscience. Always feeling guilty reveals that we may not be recognizing our forgiven state - or we may need to forgive ourselves. When we are constantly worried that we are sinners, we will try to keep the law on our own, (and trying to do anything on our own to please God, rather than trusting Him

---

[22] Bennett, Barry. *He Healed Them All©*. Harrison House, 2020.) p. 164

and His leading, leads to death, as Adam and Eve learned). The law brings death, pronouncing us guilty (2 Corinthians 3:7-11) because we cannot keep the law without the Holy Spirit working in and through us. The more we worry about our own actions and we focus on trying to be good and to keep the law, the more we sin. (Romans 7:9) Instead of sin-consciousness and trying to be good, when we *submit to the Holy Spirit's leading,* we are led into life and peace. Again, it is our trust in Jesus that is counted toward us as righteousness.

Romans 8:1(NKJV) reveals: "There is therefore now no condemnation to those who are in Christ Jesus, who do not walk according to the flesh, but according to the Spirit." We are accepted before God and seen in the same way He sees Jesus when we trust Him. He sees us as perfect. Because we are seen as righteous and perfect before God through faith, the righteousness of Christ restores to us everything that was lost to humanity in the garden of Eden when Adam and Eve handed over all of their rights to the enemy. We are fully restored to God in every way. We no longer have any reason to fear. Righteousness imputed to us makes all things right between us and the Father, and because of all that Jesus purchased for us we are now considered by God to be just like Him. (1 John 4:17) This is the best possible news about our true identity. It's the biggest game changer we could possibly imagine. The very lie that satan tempted Adam and Eve within the garden of Eden was, "For God knows that in the day you eat of it your eyes will be opened, and you will be like God, knowing good and evil." (Genesis 3:5 NKJV). When they stopped trusting God, they lost their righteous standing, but Jesus came to reveal that He is trustworthy so we can choose to trust Him and regain all that we lost. We can be counted just like Jesus.

It has never been about our righteousness. Since the very beginning, it's always been about us believing God for righteousness. What was Adam and Eve's greatest sin in the Garden of Eden? They stopped trusting God. Righteousness is about trusting God. They lost their righteous standing with God when they stopped trusting Him. This is why Jesus came—to reveal that He is trustworthy. And because He is trustworthy, we can be counted righteous through Him.

Truth 4.2 Application:

1. Who does the evil stepmother represent in the allegory?

_____

_____

---

2. List 5 Bible promises in this section that define your true identity in Christ:

_____

_____

_____

_____

_____

_____

3. Why does righteousness matter? "It allows us to stand before God without

any _____, _____,

or_____ "

4. In order to be counted righteous, we must _____ .
(Genesis 15:6)

Truth 4.3

His Victory is Our Victory

One of the most important pieces of a believer's identity is being an overcomer or *victor*. We fight the enemy *from* victory rather than *for* victory. Let's consider why that matters. If we are fighting *for* victory, we don't yet know the outcome, but when we fight *from* victory, we're already certain of the outcome being in our favor. Attitudes regarding our position in Christ will reveal where our beliefs are in this matter. If you find yourself feeling like a victim, take heart and know that we can change how we perceive our positions and learn to step into the victory Jesus has for us as we renew our minds (by reading the Word, meditating on it and getting it into our hearts) to this truth. Jesus tells us in John 16:33 (NKJV), "These things I have spoken to you, that in Me you may have peace. In the world you will have tribulation; but be of good cheer, I have overcome the world."

This victory that Jesus experienced over the world is our victory as well. We see this in verses such as 1 Corinthians 15:57 (NKJV): "But thanks be to God, who gives us the victory through our Lord Jesus Christ." and Romans 8:37 (NKJV) "Yet in all these things we are more than conquerors through Him who loved us." Be encouraged and take this to heart. You are an overcomer in Christ because your identity is *in Him*. You are not your own and you are not alone. You are in Christ. Because of this, Paul tells us that we can do *everything through* Christ. Philippians 4:13 (NLT) "For I can do everything through Christ, who gives me strength."

But what if we don't see this as a possibility in our current situation or circumstance? The Apostle Paul himself experienced some bumpy situations, yet the Lord revealed to him that victory would still occur. 2 Corinthians 12:9 (NLT) "Each time he said, 'My grace is all you need. My power works best in weakness.' So now I am glad to boast about my weaknesses, so that the power of Christ can work through me." Let's take a deep dive into this verse of Paul's and find out why the grace of God was enough to carry him through even the worst experiences.

The word grace here is the Greek word *charis*. While charis is well-known for its definitions of favor, kindness, and blessing, several of its less known, yet just as important meanings, are *regeneration,* which transforms man so that his "nature is brought under the dominion of righteousness," and *divine empowerment,* which enables and ensures our victory as we lean into and trust in God's power for us. God, through His *benefaction*, makes up for any lack we might have. Paul is saying in 2 Corinthians 12:9 that God told him He had everything Paul needed to succeed. God will supply His unmerited favor, His divine (supernatural) empowerment, and He would cover any lack Paul might experience.[23]

When we understand the grace and empowerment of our Papa God, we truly can overcome in every area of our lives. A few additional power verses stating the victories that are already ours as we believe and enforce them: When we struggle to understand, we find in 1 Corinthians 2:16 and 1 John 2:20 that we not only have the mind of Christ, but we've been anointed by Him and have His knowledge. His ability to overcome in *all things*: Romans 8:37 (NKJV): "Yet in all these things we are more than conquerors through Him who loved us." 1 John 5:5 ESV: "Who is it that overcomes the world except the one who believes that Jesus is the Son of God?" 1 Corinthians 15:57 NKJV: "But thanks be to God, who gives us the victory through our Lord Jesus Christ."

No weapons can harm us. Isaiah 54:17 NKJV tells us, "No weapon formed against you shall prosper, And every tongue which rises against you in judgment You shall condemn. This is the heritage of the servants of the LORD, And their righteousness is from Me," Says the LORD.

---

[23] Zodhiates, Spiros, *The Complete Word Study Dictionary for a Deeper Understanding of the Word©.* (AMG International Publishers, 1992)

You are an overcomer through Christ. Because you received Jesus as your Savior, the very power that raised Jesus from the dead lives inside of you Romans 8:11 ESV: "If the Spirit of him who raised Jesus from the dead dwells in you, he who raised Christ Jesus from the dead will also give life to your mortal bodies through his Spirit who dwells in you." Because of Jesus and His righteousness that has been counted to us, we also can overcome the enemy and every lie he throws at us. Not only that, but in Papa God's eyes, we look just like Jesus, and that is the most perfect, beautiful identity that we could ever hope to have.

Truth 4.3 Application

Is there an area, like Paul, where you need God's grace in your life today?

Zechariah 4:7 tells us, "Who are you, O great mountain? Before Zerubbabel you shall become a plain! And he shall bring forth the capstone with shouts of 'Grace, grace to it!'" Jesus told us to speak to our mountain in Mark 11:23. What kind of mountain is before you that you need to see become a plain? By the grace of God, He can ensure your victory as you believe Him for it: grace: *His unmerited favor, His divine empowerment, His benefits that have the ability to cover all lack.* Talk to Him in a message below and thank Him for giving you the victory you need in this area.

Chapter 5

WHO YOU ARE IN HIM:

The Truth About

Your Authority in Christ

Truth 5.1

Let's talk about authority. If you have the *authority* to do something, you have the right or power to do it. Here are a few definitions of authority:[24]

- The power or right to give orders or make decisions.
- Persons who exercise (administrative) control over others.
- An administrative unit of government.
- The power to enforce laws, exact obedience, command, determine, or judge.

---

[24] https://www.dictionary.com/browse/authority

- One that is invested with this power, especially a government or body of government officials.
- Power assigned to another; authorization. Such as deputies that are given authority to make arrests.

Authority in Christ isn't something that most of us were taught in the church. It's another one of those Bible truths that has been twisted and hidden by religion. We've basically been told we are subject to the enemy. I wonder where that doctrine of devils came from? What does the enemy have to lose if we were to learn that we actually have authority over him? Pretty much everything. No wonder he's worked so hard to keep this truth from the church. When we come to understand and step into our role, being seated with Christ in the heavenly realms, satan knows he has lost all of his power over us. Ephesians 2:6: "and raised us up with him and seated us with him in the heavenly places in Christ Jesus." So what does the Bible say about our authority?

In Genesis 1:26-28, God created Adam and Eve and gave them dominion over all the earth. "Dominion" in Strong's concordance (#7287 *radah*) means—make to have dominion, prevail against, reign, bear, to tread down, subjugate, make to rule over, take. God gave Adam and Eve unconditional rule, power, dominion, and authority over all of the earth. However, Lucifer, an angel that God created and who held the position as a covering cherub that ministered to God directly, became envious of God and most likely envious of Adam and Eve and the dominion and power God had given them on their new planet. God created angels to be ministering spirits. The word "angel" means messenger or ambassador. Angels were not created for the same purpose that we were. While we and the angels were all created with free will, God created man specifically for fellowship.

Psalm 103:20 (NIV): "Praise the LORD, you his angels, you mighty ones who do his bidding, who obey his word."

Hebrews 1:13-14 (NIV): "To which of the angels did God ever say, 'Sit at my right hand until I make your enemies a footstool for your feet'? Are not all angels ministering spirits sent to serve those who will inherit salvation?"

Hebrews 2:6-8 ESV: "It has been testified somewhere, 'What is man, that you are mindful of him, or the son of man, that you care for him? You made him for a little while lower than the angels; you have crowned him with glory and honor, putting everything in subjection under his feet.'"

As mentioned previously, Ephesians 2:6 says we have been seated with Christ. The angels have not. Everything has been put under man's subjection and authority. This is not true for the angels. 1 John 4:17 also tells us that as Jesus is, "... so are we in this world." (NKJV)

Jesus told the Parable of the Prodigal Son, which beautifully illustrates the authority He has restored to us:

> And the son said to him, 'Father, I have sinned against heaven and in your sight, and am no longer worthy to be called your son.'
> "But the father said to his servants, 'Bring out the best robe and put it on him, and put a ring on his hand and sandals on his feet. And bring the fatted calf here and kill it, and let us eat and be merry; for this my son was dead and is alive again; he was lost and is found.' And they began to be merry." (Luke 15:21-24 NKJV).

After the prodigal returned home, his father ran out to meet him and did several things to demonstrate to his son that he was not only received but was also being elevated to his status as a rightful heir.

Robe:

"I delight greatly in the LORD; my soul rejoices in my God. For he has clothed me with garments of salvation and arrayed me in a robe of his righteousness, as a bridegroom adorns his head like a priest, and as a bride adorns herself with her jewels" (Isaiah 61:10 NIV). As the prodigal's father did for him, so our Father God also covers us with His own robe of righteousness. Similarly to the way Jacob (given the name Israel), gave a beautiful robe to his son, Joseph, and later, Pharaoh also adorned Joseph in fine robes and linens signifying his exalted status in the kingdom, so our Father covers us with His robe. (Genesis 41:41-43)

Ring:

"'In that day,' says the LORD of hosts, 'I will take you, Zerubbabel My servant, the son of Shealtiel,' says the LORD, 'and will make you like a signet ring; for I have chosen you,' says the LORD of hosts." (Haggai 2:23 NKJV). This verse speaks specifically of God calling Zerubbabel His own signet ring, the mark of authority as a king. Similarly, in the account of Joseph, the Pharaoh put his own signet ring on Joseph's finger. A signet ring symbolized a person's authority. A signet ring had an engraving that revealed such things as name, job title, or rank. When the father placed the ring on the hand of his son, he was not only welcoming his son back into his home, but he was also welcoming the son back into his authority.

Sandals:

"Every place that the sole of your foot will tread upon I have given to you, just as I promised to Moses" (Joshua 1:3 ESV). God here has given the children of Israel authority to take any place they step. Ruth 4:7-8 explains that legal contracts were often made with sandals. (Ruth was redeemed by Boaz through a legal exchange using sandals. The close relative of Ruth handed Boaz his sandal, signifying that he was giving the right of redemption of Ruth to Boaz.) In the New Testament, Paul says, "... as shoes for your feet, having put on the readiness given by the gospel of peace" (Ephesians 6:15 ESV). These verses explain how shoes in the Bible represent legal rights and authority, and Ephesians 6:15 speaks to the authority we've been given by God to be heralds of the good news of His Kingdom, specifically giving us the responsibility as His representatives to teach the world of the gifts God has given of salvation and peace.

Truth 5.1 Application:

Begin standing in your authority over all the power of the enemy. What are you standing for today?

_____

_____

_____

_____

_____

_____

How are you choosing to reframe your thoughts based on your authority in Christ? Do you have any reason to be in fear now that you understand your authority over all the power of the enemy?

_____

_____

_____

_____

_____

_____

_____

_____

_____

_____

_____

_____

Truth 5.2

Praying With Authority:

"Prayer is not trying to twist God's arm to make Him do something. Prayer is receiving by faith what He has already done!"[25]

As shared previously, salvation includes healing, prosperity, deliverance, and basically having all of our needs met. The word "save" (*sozo* in Greek) means: To save, heal, preserve, rescue. From a primary *sos*: to save, i.e., deliver or protect. So we know that these things have already been given to us by God. We only need to receive the things He's provided.

Begging and pleading for any of those things is unnecessary because they already belong to us. As Wommack said, we can't twist God's arm to give us something we already have. Hebrews 4:16 ESV says, "Let us then with confidence draw near to the throne of grace, that we may receive mercy and find grace to help in time of need." So we know that we can always approach God in utmost confidence with any of our needs. We don't have to be timid or afraid when asking.

Philippians 4:6-7 NKJV tells us, "Be anxious for nothing, but in everything by prayer and supplication, with thanksgiving, let your requests be made known to God; and the peace of God, which surpasses all understanding, will guard your hearts and minds through Christ Jesus."

How would we have peace guarding our heart if we made a request assuming God *might* answer… Or might not. Jesus gave us some truly astounding promises of our authority in prayer in the Gospels. Let's take a look at several:

John 14:13-14 NKJV: "And whatever you ask in My name, that I will do, that the Father may be glorified in the Son. If you ask anything in My name, I will do it."

John 16:23 NKJV: "And in that day you will ask Me nothing. Most assuredly, I say to you, whatever you ask the Father in My name He will give you."

Matthew 7:7-8 ESV: "Ask, and it will be given to you; seek, and you will find; knock, and the door will be opened to you. For everyone who asks receives, and the one who seeks finds, and to the one who knocks it will be opened."

---

[25] Wommack, Andrew. *A Better Way to Pray©*. (Harrison House, 2007) p. 10

God yearns for His children to believe that all the provision they need has already been made.

When we pray "if it be Thy will" when God's will has already been stated in His Word (such as His desire to heal or provide for us) or pray begging and pleading prayers, which are not in faith but in fear, we hinder the effectiveness of our prayers. We magnify the problems, giving them energy and strength rather than magnifying God as our Source and Provision. He doesn't need a detailed list of our problems. We don't want to rehash all of the negatives in prayer. Just as we don't want to *speak* negativity over ourselves, we also don't want to *pray* negativity over ourselves.

We need to pray the answer/solution rather than the problem. If we don't know the answer or solution to ask for, then we pray in gratitude that God knows and will give us the wisdom and discernment that we need. We must ask this in faith, without doubting as James 1:6-7 admonishes us to do. Where your so-called "love language" might be tacos, God's "love language" is faith. When Adam and Eve were tempted, their trust in God was questioned. When they gave in to the temptation, their faith in Him was severed.

As discussed earlier, the entire purpose of the cross was to bring us back into a trusting relationship with God. This is why praying in faith is so important. Because of our new and right standing with God through Christ's sacrifice for us, there is no longer a barrier between us and God—except for any limitations we put upon Him. Praying God's solution from the Word releases life into the circumstance or situation.

Proverbs 18:21 (NKJV) says, "Death and life are in the power of the tongue." This includes when we pray.

Philippians 4:6 NKJV: "... with thanksgiving let your requests be made known to God." Pray and thank Him that He's already got it covered.

1 John 5:15 NKJV: "And if we know that He hears us, whatever we ask, we know that we have the petitions that we have asked of Him." We can know that we have the requests that we have asked of Him when we pray in faith. Before going any further, let's address something important. Many of us learned there are rules to prayer, and we have to pray in a specific way or through some methodology or ritual before God will hear us.

God wants us to pray to Him like we're talking to a friend. John 15:14-15 (NKJV)says, "You are My friends if you do whatever I command you. No longer do I call you servants, for a servant does not know what his master is doing; but I have called you friends, for all things that I heard from My Father I have made known to you."

Caprice Scott

When children need something from their parents, all they have to do is ask and they know their parents will take care of their needs. God is the same way—but better—because He has endless resources for us. "Ask, and it will be given to you; seek, and you will find; knock, and it will be opened to you. For everyone who asks receives, and he who seeks finds, and to him who knocks it will be opened. Or what man is there among you who, if his son asks for bread, will give him a stone? Or if he asks for a fish, will he give him a serpent? If you then, being evil, know how to give good gifts to your children, how much more will your Father who is in heaven give good things to those who ask Him!" (Matthew 7:7-11 NKJV)

"He who did not spare His own Son, but delivered Him up for us all, how shall He not with Him also freely give us all things?" (Romans 8:32, NKJV) I have found, and I believe, that man has created a lot of religions and traditions that really aren't necessary and just make seeking to have a close relationship with God more complicated than it needs to be. Much of that can become empty distractions. Religion is often a stumbling block that obscures the simplicity and beauty that connecting with God should look like. God wants relationship with us. He doesn't want prayer and communication with Him to be complicated.

When Jesus died upon the cross, the curtain in the Temple separating the Holy of Holies from the main part of the structure ripped apart, from top to bottom. (Matthew 27:51) This amazing event symbolizes that Christ's crucifixion created direct access between us and Our Father.

When we speak to a close family member, we don't have a bunch of steps to take in order for them to receive or listen to us. We just lovingly approach them in confidence. Our relationship to God should be the same. He doesn't want us to have any barriers that hinder us from coming to Him in prayer. Jesus came to make a way for us to connect with God directly. No strings, beads, or middlemen attached. Nothing separates us from the Father's Presence, at least not on His end.

As mentioned previously, God wants us to approach Him in faith. Because Adam and Eve chose to doubt God in the Garden, the relationship and bond of trust between them was severed. This severed relationship changed everything between God and man and how things on this planet have worked since, as man's authority was surrendered to the adversary at that point. Jesus purchased that authority back for us, but we've been deceived and have bought into the lie that the enemy has power over us, which simply isn't true. The only authority the devil has is our own authority that he uses against us because we don't know better.

Why does this matter when it comes to prayer? If we don't understand our authority in this world, we won't pray in faith. Instead, we'll beg God to take care of things for us, but God isn't going to step in and do things against man's free will. We have to pray in our authority and faith, knowing who we are and Whose we are. When we pray from the place of our identity as children of God and our authority in Christ, we command those things to happen that He's already promised.

Luke 10:19 NKJV: "Behold, I give you the authority to trample on serpents and scorpions, and over all the power of the enemy, and nothing shall by any means hurt you."

Matthew 16:19 NKJV: "I will give you the keys of the kingdom of heaven, and whatever you bind on earth shall be bound in heaven, and whatever you loose on earth shall be loosed in heaven."

Truth 5.2 Application:

How are you changing your words to line up according to your authority?

_____

_____

_____

_____

_____

How will you change the way that you pray as compared to the past? Write how you will pray about your health and the health of others, now that you understand your authority:

_____

_____

_____

_____

_____

_____

_____

_____

_____

Truth 5.3

The devil wants us to believe he has authority over us and our free will. The Word makes clear that the devil doesn't have authority over us. We need to stop letting him act as though he does and speak and pray from our God-given authority. Mark 11:12-14 (NKJV) says: "Now the next day, when they had come out from Bethany, He was hungry. And seeing from afar a fig tree having leaves, He went to see if perhaps He would find something on it. When He came to it, He found nothing but leaves, for it was not the season for figs. In response Jesus said to it, 'Let no one eat fruit from you ever again.' And His disciples heard it."

Mark 11:20-24 NKJV: "Now in the morning, as they passed by, they saw the fig tree dried up from the roots. And Peter, remembering, said to Him, 'Rabbi, look! The fig tree which You cursed has withered away.' So Jesus answered and said to them, 'Have faith in God. For assuredly, I say to you, whoever says to this mountain, "Be removed and be cast into the sea," and does not doubt in his heart, but believes that those things he says will be done, he will have whatever he says. Therefore I say to you, whatever things you ask when you pray, believe that you receive them, and you will have them.'"

Jesus spoke to the fig tree and commanded it to wither away. We need to speak to our "mountain." If the mountain is sickness or disease, we take our authority—believing—and we speak to the problem. This is the kind of prayer Jesus used in addressing sickness and disease. First Peter 2:24 says that by His stripes we were healed. It's up to us to address the issue and command what the Lord has already done for us in faith.

First John 4:17 says, "... as He is, so are we in this world." (NKJV) We have His authority to speak and expect results when we believe. We are to speak to the cancer and command it to dry up by its roots, to speak to the sickness and command healing . . . to speak to that depression or anxiety and command peace and joy to fill the heart and mind instead. "Now faith is the substance of things hoped for, the evidence of things not seen." (Hebrews 11:1 NKJV)

"And the Lord said, 'If you had faith like a grain of mustard seed, you could say to this mulberry tree, "Be uprooted and planted in the sea," and it would obey you'" (Luke 17:6 ESV).

In her booklet, *Quantum Faith*, Annette Capps says this about faith:

> When Jesus said in Luke 17:6, "If you have faith as a grain of mustard seed, you would say ..." He was speaking of the smallest seed that

could be seen in His time. If He were here today, He might say, "If you had faith as an atom…" Or even smaller, "If you had faith as a quark (which is a subatomic particle) …" The point He was making was that small things that cannot be easily seen manifest themselves and affect things in this larger world where we live.[26]

Capps is proposing an analogy with quantum physics, which is the study of things that are so small we can't see them. Yet everything we see in this world is made of these subatomic particles, and everything we think, believe, and speak affects them. Continuing from Capps:

> Whereas gravity works whether anyone is present or not (a tree falls down, not up, even if no one observes it), subatomic particles are not there unless someone (an observer) looks for them. We can't really know what they're doing, or even if they exist when we are not looking. It is possible that they "are not". 1 Corinthians 1:28 says that God has chosen the "things that are not to bring to naught things that are".[27]

How can a thing not be? This scripture makes no sense at all until you bring it down to the atomic level. All things are made up of atoms, which are made of subatomic particles. These particles are not really particles because they exist only in a state of possibilities until someone observes and measures them at which point they appear as a thing (particle).[28]

Again, let's read Hebrews 11:1 "Now faith is the substance of things hoped for, the evidence of things not seen." (NKJV) So in essence, Capps is saying that when we pray in faith, looking for something to happen in confident expectation and trust in the faithfulness of God, we can see it manifest. The problem is, we've reached the point at which our words don't mean much to us or others anymore. Very often, we use them flippantly and don't really mean what we say. ("These shoes are killing my feet" or "I'm so hungry I could eat a horse" are examples of the hyperbole we use in day-to-day speech that we don't mean.) We have to reach a point where we believe our words and choose them wisely, especially in prayer. Even more importantly, we must believe God's Word as our truth and that He will do what we ask when we truly expect it.

In summary, we need to believe that God is a God of His Word. When He gives His Word, He never violates it. He is trustworthy. Jesus tells us in Mark 11:22 NKJV: "… Have faith in God." We can't ask for something and then not

---

[26] Capps, Annette, *Quantum Faith*© (Capps Publishing, 2020) p. 6

[27] Capps, op cit., p. 6

[28] https://profmattstrassler.com/2025/02/10/elementary-particles-do-not-exist-part-1/

believe He will do it. That's like begging for something you already have in your hands. What we believe we will receive. It's really that simple.

Truth 5.3 Application:

1. When someone asks you to pray for them, how will this new knowledge change the way you pray, not only for health but other areas as well?

_____

_____

_____

_____

_____

_____

2. Using Biblehub.com, do a deep study on the following verses, and write them out as a message from God to you.

You can find a tutorial for the Biblehub.com site here:

https://youtu.be/PaqWWA_N56s?si=-BlCXKbLitOzOjyu

Luke 10:19 (NKJV) says, "Behold, I give you the authority to trample on serpents and scorpions, and over all the power of the enemy, and nothing shall by any means hurt you."

Matthew 16:19 (NKJV) says, "And I will give you the keys of the kingdom of heaven, and whatever you bind on earth will be bound in heaven, and whatever you loose on earth will be loosed in heaven."

Chapter 6

WHO YOU ARE IN HIM:

The Truth About Spirit, Soul, and Body

Truth 6.1

Did you know that you are a three-part being? Genesis 1:26 tells us that we were created in the image of God. God is a Spirit. First Thessalonians 5:23 (NKJV) says, "Now may the God of peace Himself sanctify you completely; and may your whole spirit, soul, and body be preserved blameless at the coming of our Lord Jesus Christ." Our spirit is our inmost part. It is *who* we are. We *are* spirits. (Consider that if our spirit was only a "breath" or simply the ability to breathe, it would not need to be sanctified.) Luke 1:46-47 says Mary glorified the Lord in her soul and rejoiced in the Lord in her spirit. A breath doesn't have the ability to "rejoice." We connect with God through our spirit. The soul is merely the channel or conduit in which we do this through our humanity.

The soul, which is our mental and emotional part, includes the will, emotions, conscience, and mind. We *have* a soul. Our body is the physical part of us. We *live* in a body. 1 Corinthians 6:19 even says that our body is a temple of the Holy Spirit. It is the dwelling place for our spirit and the Holy Spirit. We can feel our body and our soul, but our spirit cannot be accessed by any natural means.

John 3:6 (NKJV) says, "That which is born of the flesh is flesh, and that which is born of the Spirit is spirit." Though our spirits have been recreated, we can't connect to our spirit through our body. We can't connect to our spirit through our emotions. However, it is essential that we as believers know and understand who we are in the spirit so that we may know who we are in Christ— and what benefits we receive through being one with Him.

When you gave your life to Jesus and received His gift of salvation, the old you died and you became an entirely new creation. Becoming a new creation, which was a complete transformation, took place in your spirit; it was altogether changed at the decision you made to receive salvation. In 2 Corinthians 5:17 (KJV) we read, "If any man be in Christ, he is a new creature: old things are passed away; behold, all things are become new."

Your body and soul didn't change at that time, but your spirit became one with the Holy Spirit. Your soul, which is your mental and emotional part, also did not change at that time. While we can change our soul (and we are told to do so by the renewing of our mind), it wasn't changed automatically when we became believers and followers of Christ. The total transformation of our body and soul won't happen fully until we are with Jesus.

1 Corinthians 15:53 (ESV): "For this perishable body must put on the imperishable, and this mortal body must put on immortality."

However, Romans 12:1-2 (ESV) tells us that we still have a responsibility to begin changing our souls here on earth: "I appeal to you therefore, brothers, by the mercies of God, to present your bodies as a living sacrifice, holy and acceptable to God, which is your spiritual worship. Do not be conformed to this world, but be transformed by the renewal of your mind, that by testing you may discern what is the will of God, what is good and acceptable and perfect."

Notice Paul doesn't say anything about the spirit here, because our spirit is already perfect upon receiving Jesus as our Savior. It's our body and mind (or soul) that must be brought into submission to the Lord. We must renew our mind in order to experience the changes in our mind, emotions, and body. Not only does mind renewal affect our soul, but it also helps us bring the body into perfect submission. However, it's our spirit that has been changed into a new creation. Because of this new creation of our spirit, there is no longer an old sin nature left in us.

The word "conformed" is the Greek word *suschématizó* (soos-khay-mat-id'-zo) which implies being poured into and shaped by a mold. When we are not choosing to renew our minds to/with/inside/from the Word, we are being squeezed into the mold of the world, whether we are making that decision deliberately or not. Simply stated, if we are not deliberately choosing to renew our minds, we will by default be choosing the world.

The word "transformed" is the Greek word *metamorphoó* (met-am-or-fo'-o) where we get our English word metamorphosis. It's a picture of a caterpillar transforming into a butterfly. When we renew our mind to the truth of God's Word, we are transforming our soul/mind into His likeness. We learn to step into our true identity in Christ when we look at who He says we are instead of listening to who the world says we are. God's Word is a mirror for us to see ourselves through His eyes. We must behold Him and His truth in order to be changed into His image.

James 1:23-25 NKJV: "For if anyone is a hearer of the word and not a doer, he is like a man observing his natural face in a mirror; for he observes himself, goes away, and immediately forgets what kind of man he was. But he who looks into the perfect law of liberty and continues in it, and is not a forgetful hearer but a doer of the work, this one will be blessed in what he does."

As we begin looking at the Word to understand our new identity—which is who God says we are—we start to see an entirely new picture, or reflection, that appears much different than our old identity without Christ. Romans 6:2-4 (NKJV): "How shall we who died to sin live any longer in it? Or do you not know that as many of us as were baptized into Christ Jesus were baptized into His death? Therefore we were buried with Him through baptism into death, that just as Christ was raised from the dead by the glory of the Father, even so we also should walk in newness of life."[29]

Truth 6.1 Application

1. How many "parts" does a person have according to this lesson?

_____

_____

---

[29] For more information about this subject, see Andrew Wommack's Spirit, Soul, and Body: https://www.youtube.com/playlist?list=PLOER0yhdOW6CDk_OONScwq3VH1ASQ6_tD

2. Is there a part of a believer that is perfect once they have received Jesus as their Savior? Explain your answer (see 2 Corinthians 5:17; 1 Corinthians 2:10):

_____

_____

_____

_____

Truth 6.2

Our new spirit has died to sin and has been recreated into a brand-new species! God's Word reflects what our new spirit looks like. This is our TRUE identity. "That which is born of the flesh is flesh, and that which is born of the Spirit is spirit"(John 3:6 NKJV).

Our born-again spirit looks just like Jesus. 1 John 4:17 tells us that as He is, so are we in this world. It includes the mind of Christ (1 Corinthians 2:16) and knows all things because the Holy Spirit reveals all things to our spirit (1 Corinthians 2:10). Our newly created spirit is perfect and is as complete as it will be, even throughout eternity, lacking nothing. Our soul/mind however, must be renewed. The mind of Christ is part of our born-again spirit because it includes our union with the Holy Spirit. However, our souls/minds must be renewed by bringing them under submission to the Word of God. Our humanity doesn't know how to be "good" on its own. As mentioned previously, it will default to the flesh. Mind renewal isn't just about changing the way we think. It's about bringing every part of us under the authority and Lordship of Christ (and we need the Word of God *in us* in order to recognize Truth). It's about changing our brains, yes, but it's also about changing our heart beliefs and our will. Natural man is about self-preservation. The natural (or carnal) mind allows feelings and circumstances to dictate how it functions. The born again spirit, however, does not sin (1 John 3:9).

We are new creations in Christ when we become believers, but we won't know how to recognize the mind of Christ and the Spirit's voice speaking to our spirit until we begin renewing our minds. Mind renewal is a daily choice to learn from and submit to the Holy Spirit. This renewed mind acts according to the Word of God because it has been trained to do so. (Romans 8:5-7; Ephesians 4:22-27; Colossians 3:5-10)

This transformation of our spirits that God did miraculously at the time of our salvation is truly wonderful, but because of our fallen physical and soul natures, our souls/minds still must be renewed and transformed as well; otherwise, they will remain bent toward functioning like the world, that is to say carnally.

Romans 8:6 (NKJV) tells us why that's a problem: "For to be carnally minded is death, but to be spiritually minded is life and peace." As new creations in Christ, we need to begin functioning as Christ did in this world. He was not dominated by His flesh—what He could see, taste, hear, smell, and feel. He overcame the enemy by being spiritually minded. In Luke chapter 4, vs 1-12, we see that Jesus overcame the enemy and temptations by *not* focusing on fulfilling the lusts of the flesh but on submitting Himself to the will and Word of God. That doesn't mean that it's sinful to eat or do other things in the natural. What it means is that we should not be dominated by carnal thoughts that are focused on the physical realm. Remember how the enemy got Adam and Eve to sin? Being focused solely on the physical realm produces death. We must be spiritually minded—not focused on and trusting our senses, but focused on and trusting the Lord and His Word.

Ephesians 4:17 ESV: "Now this I say and testify in the Lord, that you must no longer walk as the Gentiles do, in the futility of their minds." The word "futility" here is the Greek word *mataiotés* (mat-ah-yot'-ace) which means vanity, emptiness, unreality, purposelessness, ineffectiveness, instability, frailty, false religion. God's purposes for us are high above worldly pursuits. When we focus on the Word and the Lord, no matter what our physical circumstances may be, we will remain in peace.

Isaiah 26:3 (NKJV) says, "You keep him in perfect peace whose mind is stayed on you, because he trusts in you." There is simply no other way in this world through which we can remain in true peace, because real peace only comes from God, and we must be *in* Him to experience Him. (John 15:5) He is True Peace. Ephesians 4:20-24 (NKJV) says, "But you have not so learned Christ, if indeed you have heard Him and have been taught by Him, as the truth is in Jesus: that you put off, concerning your former conduct, the old man which grows corrupt according to the deceitful lusts, and be renewed in the spirit of your mind, and that you put on the new man which was created according to God, in true righteousness and holiness." The NLT says it this way in verse 23: "Instead, let the Spirit renew your thoughts and attitudes."

2 Peter 1:3-4 (ESV) says, "His divine power has granted to us all things that pertain to life and godliness, through the knowledge of him who called us to his own glory and excellence, by which he has granted to us his precious and very

great promises, so that through them you may become partakers of the divine nature, having escaped from the corruption that is in the world because of sinful desire." As these verses state, we become partakers of God's divine nature. We must know about these great and precious promises and what His divine nature looks like in order to experience them. The more we behold Him, the more we become like Him.

Jesus Himself became our righteousness. Because of this truly extravagant gift, we are now 1/3 completely righteous! Our souls and bodies, however, must still come into alignment with this truth. God accepts our born-again spirits as righteous based on what Jesus has done for us.

1 Corinthians 1:30 (NLT): "God has united you with Christ Jesus. For our benefit God made him to be wisdom itself. Christ made us right with God; he made us pure and holy, and he freed us from sin." After we receive Jesus as our Savior, the rest of our lives as Christians should be about the renewing of our mind and learning how to release what is in our spirit into the soul and body. The more we renew our minds, the more our minds/souls will line up in agreement with that new creation of our spirit. When our souls and spirits are in agreement, we release the *life* of God that is in our spirit. If we choose not to renew our minds, our soul and body will not experience the supernatural life of God that is in our spirit. We need to get all of the benefits we received in our born-again spirits into our soul and body.

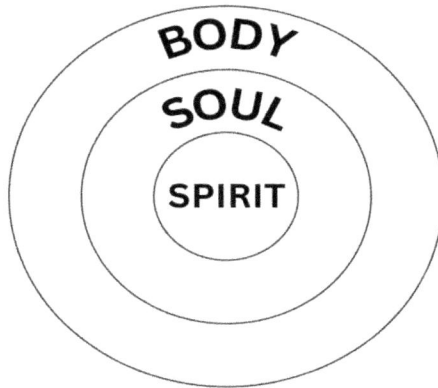

- The outer circle is your physical body, which you can see and feel.
- The second circle is your soul/mind. While you can't see it, you can feel it. It is in contact with both your body and your spirit.
- The innermost circle is your spirit. Even though this is the "true you," it can't be seen or felt. It's the life-giving part of you:

James 2:26 (NKJV) says, "For as the body without the spirit is dead, so faith without works is dead also." Genesis 2:7 (NKJV) says "And the LORD God formed man of the dust of the ground, and breathed into his nostrils the breath of life; and man became a living being." Because your spirit has no direct access to your body, everything that you need to get from your spirit to your body (such as healing) must go through your soul/mind. Your soul is like the valve between your spirit and your body. In order to release the supernatural life of the Holy Spirit that is dwelling in your spirit, you have to open that valve on the spigot to get those truths from your spirit into your body.

As I mentioned previously, most of us are dominated by our carnal/fleshly senses such as what we taste, see, hear, smell, or feel. Because of this, we have a very difficult time understanding the things happening in our spirit and the spirit realm.[30] When we are entirely tuned in to the carnal, we don't receive what God has already placed in our spirit.

So, as discussed, we now understand that God's provision for living the supernatural life has already been provided in our spirits, however, our relationship with God should not only be about trying to get things from Him. (Remember everything that salvation includes?) He can't give us something He's already given us. If we have access to His Kingdom in our spirit, the problem isn't that we don't have it (Luke 17:21, NKJV), but that we must learn to receive it. If we have $5 million sitting in the bank, we need to know that we have it and then we must go through the necessary channels to access and use it. We have to *know* that we have it before we try to spend it. The same is true about what is in our spirit. We already have healing, peace, prosperity, and safety from the Lord in our spirit, but we must know it is there before we can attempt

---

[30] The spirit realm (Romans 8:9) is where angels, demons, and God dwell. It is a realm outside of human senses.

to receive it into our soul and body. We do this by mind renewal that we may *believe* through faith that these things are already ours.

Philemon 1:6 (NKJV) tells us, "... that the sharing of your faith may become effective by the acknowledgement of every good thing which is in you in Christ Jesus." When you became born again, God placed in your spirit physical healing, peace, joy, all of His fruit, and every single thing that you need for a life of abundance and victory. You cannot access them, however, if you don't renew your mind. This, friends, is why the renewing of our mind is imperative in our Christian walk. It is the key that unlocks all of the blessings God has given us. We must believe in order to receive.

Truth 6.2 Application

1. What does your born-again spirit look like? (1 John 4:17):

_____
_____
_____

2. What kinds of things did God place in your spirit when you became born again?

_____
_____
_____
_____
_____

3. Write a prayer of gratitude to your Papa God thanking Him for all that He has done in your spirit when you gave your life to Christ and became a new creation. Thank Him for helping you as you choose to commit to renew your mind in order to get those things that are in your spirit into your mind and body.

Chapter 7

YOUR RELATIONSHIP TOGETHER:

The Truth About Prayer,

Hearing God, and Bible Study

Truth 7.1

Did you know that God desires you to hear Him speaking to you even more than you desire to hear Him? He is always speaking, always trying to reveal Himself and His love to all humans. If we aren't hearing God, it's not because He's not speaking; we may just need to adjust our hearts so we can hear Him, or we may need to get ourselves into His Word. He desires to have a close relationship with us where we can openly communicate with one another. His Word is one of the most powerful ways He communicates. For example, Psalm 85:8 (NKJV) states. "I will hear what God the LORD will speak …"

As you read earlier, I shared how to pray with authority, and while it is very important for us to know our authority in Christ and to know how to pray correctly, we also need to know how to commune with God, not just speak our dominion and authority over His creation. Knowing our authority and identity are certainly important aspects to the believer's walk, but being rooted deeply in a relationship with God goes beyond knowing who we are and how to act. Relationships involve communion. The word "communion" is made up of the words *commune*: to have a relationship; and *union*: which means oneness.

Prayer and hearing from God are about relationship, just as speaking and sharing our thoughts is a part of any relationship. Relationships are about being connected. We have to communicate, and that communication shouldn't just be one-sided. Many base their relationship and prayer life with God on begging and pleading prayers and only when they need something without realizing that God has already promised our provision, healing, and peace. When it comes to a need that God has already provided for, we can pray based on Philippians 4:6-7 (NKJV), which states: "... Be anxious for nothing, but in everything by prayer and supplication, with thanksgiving, let your requests be made known to God; and the peace of God, which surpasses all understanding, will guard your hearts and minds through Christ Jesus."

State your request with thanksgiving, expecting that He has answered. As soon as we ask, the answer is already in the spirit realm. We just need to believe in order to see it manifested in the natural (physical world). God desires to provide for our needs. He is Jehovah Jireh—He IS Provision.

Luke 11:9-13 (NKJV) states:

> So I say to you, ask, and it will be given to you; seek, and you will find; knock, and it will be opened to you. For everyone who asks receives, and he who seeks finds, and to him who knocks it will be opened. If a son asks for bread from any father among you, will he give him a stone? Or if he asks for a fish, will he give him a serpent instead of a fish? Or if he asks for an egg, will he offer him a scorpion? If you then, being evil, know how to give good gifts to your children, how much more will your heavenly Father give the Holy Spirit to those who ask Him!"

If you are in need, ask—believing—and you will receive: Matthew 21:22 (NKJV): "And whatever things you ask in prayer, believing, you will receive." James 4:3 (NKJV): "You ask and do not receive, because you ask amiss, that you may spend it on your pleasures." When our hearts are aligned correctly with the Lord's heart, we will have His desires and ask for what He wants for us, rather than asking for the wrong things.

As we learned earlier, we should also "speak to the mountain" in expectation of receiving promises such as healing, financial provision, and all of the things Jesus paid for. Our prayer life shouldn't be based on begging for things He's already said belong to us.

On that note, our prayer life also shouldn't be based on just *getting* from God. So often, Christians, especially those who need healing, seek God's hands rather than His face. That means they're narrowly focused only on what they can get from Him, instead of truly desiring Him. When we seek that love relationship that He desires to have with us, His meeting all our needs will be a fruit of that fellowship we experience with Him. (Matthew 6:33)

Because God wants to have a loving relationship with us, He is always speaking to us, desiring that we would know His love for us, His character, purposes, and ways. He not only has every answer that we need, but also, He *is* every answer. As I mentioned, He's not just "The Lord Who Heals"—He is "I Am Healing." He's not just "The Lord Who Provides"—He is "I Am Provision."

Galatians 4:6 (ESV) says, "And because you are sons, God has sent the Spirit of his Son into our hearts, crying, 'Abba! Father!'" The word "Abba" in this verse means "Daddy." I asked Him several years ago if it would be ok for me to call Him "Papa." He confirmed that this would most certainly be acceptable. He desires that we would feel so close and safe with Him. He is a very personal Papa God. A friend of mine who has visited Israel many times told me how much it blesses her to walk down the streets in Jerusalem and to hear little children who were walking with their daddies say, "Abba, Abba, Abba!" when they were addressing their fathers. The Apostle Paul is saying in this verse that through Christ we can approach our Father God as "Daddy."

Truth 7.1 Application

Listen to the example meditation on God's Word. After listening to this meditation, write down anything the Holy Spirit revealed to your heart: https://drive.google.com/file/d/1Lv6TPimGT3BNGxAfHTelPrBg8-jO3_Xy/view?usp=drive_link

_____

_____

_____

_____

_____

_____

Truth 7.2

We should pray because we desire to know God and for others to know and experience Him. Paul says in Ephesians 3:14-19 (PHILLIPS):

> When I think of the greatness of this great plan I fall on my knees before God the Father (from whom all fatherhood, earthly or heavenly, derives its name), and I pray that out of the glorious richness of his resources he will enable you to know the strength of the spirit's inner reinforcement—that Christ may actually live in your hearts by your faith. And I pray that you, firmly fixed in love yourselves, may be able to grasp (with all Christians) how wide and deep and long and high is the love of Christ—and to know for yourselves that love so far beyond our comprehension. May you be filled though all your being with God himself!

He wants us to experience the richness of His resources. He desires to enable you to know the strength of His Spirit working in you. He longs for you to grasp His great love for you. Simply stated, we should pray because we need God. First Chronicles 16:11 says, "Seek the LORD and his strength; seek his presence continually!" Jeremiah 29:11-14 adds, "For I know the thoughts that I think toward you, says the LORD, thoughts of peace and not of evil, to give you a future and a hope. Then you will call upon Me and go and pray to Me, and I will listen to you. And you will seek Me and find Me, when you search for Me with all your heart. I will be found by you, says the LORD ..." We should pray because we desire to be His hands and feet in this world.

1 Corinthians 3:9 says, "For we are God's fellow workers. You are God's field, God's building."

We should pray because we want to see, think, and feel the way that God does. Ephesians 4:22 ESV: "to put off your old self, which belongs to your former manner of life and is corrupt through deceitful desires, and to be renewed in the spirit of your minds, and to put on the new self, created after the likeness of God in true righteousness and holiness ..." We should pray for understanding and revelation from God.

James 1:5-6 (ESV) tells us, "If any of you lacks wisdom, let him ask God, who gives generously to all without reproach, and it will be given him. But let him ask in faith, with no doubting, for the one who doubts is like a wave of the sea that is driven and tossed by the wind." Remember when you are speaking to your Daddy God that He is the good, good Father. He truly desires the very best for you. Romans 8:31-32 (NKJV) states, "What then shall we say to these things? If God is for us, who can be against us? He who did not spare His own Son, but delivered Him up for us all, how shall He not with Him also freely give us all things?"

First Peter 5:7 (NKJV) says, "... casting all your care upon Him, for He cares for you." It's also important to remember that even though we may ask in faith and we have our answer in the spirit realm (where Papa God says "YES" to our request), sometimes our answer doesn't manifest immediately, due to spiritual warfare. As you can imagine, the enemy of our souls does not want our prayers answered.

Ephesians 6:12 (ESV) says, "For we do not wrestle against flesh and blood, but against the rulers, against the authorities, against the cosmic powers over this present darkness, against the spiritual forces of evil in the heavenly places." Also in the book of Daniel chapter 9, we find Daniel had been praying in faith and his prayer was answered when the angel Gabriel appeared immediately. However, in Daniel chapter 10, he was praying again and didn't see that answer manifested until 21 days after he had prayed. The following verses give us some insight into what was happening behind the scenes. Daniel 10:12-13 (NKJV) states,

> Then he said to me, "Do not fear, Daniel, for from the first day that you set your heart to understand, and to humble yourself before your God, your words were heard; and I have come because of your words. But the prince of the kingdom of Persia withstood me twenty-one days; and behold, Michael, one of the chief princes, came to help me, for I had been left alone there with the kings of Persia...'"

Just because we don't see or experience the answer to our prayers immediately doesn't mean the answers aren't already on the way. God is faithful to answer our prayers. We must remain steadfast in faith and expectation. Don't stop praying or believing; don't give up if you don't see your answer immediately. As Galatians 6:9 (ESV) reassures: "And let us not grow weary of doing good, for in due season we will reap, if we do not give up."

Jesus' disciples asked Him how to pray. He gave the example in Matthew 6:9-13 which is referred to as *The Lord's Prayer*, but it wasn't meant for us to just repeat by rote. He didn't share this example so we would recite it word by word without meaning. Let's take a look at what each line is really saying:

"Our Father in heaven, hallowed be your name."

Jesus is reminding us here that God the Father is holy. While God desires a love relationship with us, we need to remember that we are talking to the Creator of the universe. We are to respect, revere, and honor Him.

"Your kingdom come, your will be done, on earth as it is in heaven."

We are to pray that things happen on earth as they do in heaven. Is there sickness or disease in heaven? War? Poverty? Hatred? Depression? We're to pray that God's will be done on earth, and we are to keep in mind that His will is that everyone will come to the knowledge of Him and be saved. He desires that people know what Jesus has done for them—everything in the salvation package: healing, peace, prosperity, safety, and everlasting life.

"Give us this day our daily bread …"

This sounds like a demand, doesn't it? God desires to supply all of our needs. Also, remember that His Word is the Bread of Life. As I mentioned before, we can come to Him just as a child would approach their parents, asking for food or whatever they need. He is ready to provide.

"… and forgive us our debts, as we also have forgiven our debtors."

We don't need to beg and grovel for God to forgive us, but when we've done wrong, we do need to confess and repent. Remember that repentance means to make a U-turn and go the other direction. Confession is an empty, meaningless work without repentance. God is more interested in our repentance and change of heart than He is in us telling Him how wrong we were. He wants us to do an about face and change our direction. That matters more than just telling Him we're sorry. Also, notice that forgiveness is a requirement, not an option in God's Kingdom of Love, as well as here on earth. He has forgiven us for our sins; we are to forgive others for their sins against us.

"And lead us not into temptation, but deliver us from evil."

Jesus is telling us that we should request God's guidance in order to be delivered from evil. James 1:13 tells us that God doesn't lead us into temptation; He cannot do so, because He would be acting contrary to His nature. James 4:2 tells us that we have not because we ask not. We should ask God for our needs to be met and for deliverance from evil. He desires that we depend on Him, but we must come to Him in trust and faith that He will do it.

Truth 7.2 Application

1. What are five reasons we should pray?

_____

_____

_____

_____

_____

_____

2. What is a possible reason our prayers might not be answered immediately? (See Daniel 10)

_____

_____

_____

_____

_____

3. Was *The Lord's Prayer* given so that we would repeat it by rote? Explain your answer:

_____

_____

_____

_____

_____

_____

_____

_____

_____

_____

_____

_____

_____

_____

Truth 7.3

To experience that loving relationship, we need to know how to hear God. He speaks to us in many different ways, and we must learn to discern whether what we are hearing is His voice, the devil's, or our own. I shared earlier about discerning those three voices, but I want to expound here on how to hear God's voice clearly.

1. Hearing God—The Word and Meditating on the Word

The first and surest way to hear from God is through His Word. God will never contradict His Word. While we may hear something from the Holy Spirit that is applicable to our personal situation, His leading will never be contrary to the Bible. We need His Word in our hearts so that when we need His wisdom or guidance, His Spirit can bring the Word to our remembrance and enlighten us. The Word of God is the best way for us to discern whether or not we are actually hearing His voice.

Hebrews 4:12 (AMP): "For the word of God is living and active and full of power [making it operative, energizing, and effective]. It is sharper than any two-edged sword, penetrating as far as the division of the soul and spirit [the completeness of a person], and of both joints and marrow [the deepest parts of our nature], exposing and judging the very thoughts and intentions of the heart." When we prioritize putting the Word of God into our hearts, the Word of God will show us when what we are hearing is from our own flesh or from the Holy Spirit. That's why it's necessary to study and know His Word so that He can reveal His will to us.

Second Timothy 3:16-17 (ESV) tells us, "All Scripture is breathed out by God and profitable for teaching, for reproof, for correction, and for training in righteousness, that the man of God may be complete, equipped for every good work."

Romans 12:2 (NIV) says, "Do not conform to the pattern of this world, but be transformed by the renewing of your mind. Then you will be able to test and approve what God's will is—his good, pleasing and perfect will." We renew our minds by putting His Word into our minds and hearts. Just as you can't draw money from an empty bank account, you can't draw upon the knowledge and guidance of the Word if you don't have it in your mind and heart. When you put the Word into you, the Holy Spirit will bring to your remembrance specific verses that will apply to your personal circumstances.

Our relationship with God must include a commitment to spending time in His Word daily. God's Word reveals who He is, and it is the most important way we can hear His voice. When we read His Word, He is present. His Spirit is with us, revealing things to our understanding. His Word has the answers to everything we need. We not only need to read the Word, but also to meditate on it. Meditating on the Word means that we take time to ponder and think about what we've read, and seek any deeper meaning there might be for us. We need it in our hearts as well as our brains. We get it into our hearts through meditation and mixing it with our faith and even our emotions.

Recently, as I was meditating on Psalm 24, I experienced a vision about the Divine Exchange, (the meditation I suggested that you listen to in Chapter 2). This exchange refers to Jesus taking our sin upon Himself and giving us His righteousness. I chose to sit and meditate, prayerfully asking for understanding, and the Holy Spirit opened my understanding and gave me a vivid revelation of this truth. I wouldn't have received this greater understanding if I had not chosen to sit quietly in His Presence for an extended period of time to really think about what His Word was saying.

Isaiah 40:31 (AMP) says, "But those who wait for the LORD [who expect, look for, and hope in Him] Will gain new strength and renew their power; They will lift up their wings [and rise up close to God] like eagles [rising toward the sun]; They will run and not become weary, They will walk and not grow tired." Notice this verse says we need to *wait* upon the Lord. We expect, look for, and hope in Him. It's only after doing this that we gain strength and renewed power and we're able to move forward with the ease of an eagle. Eagles don't flap their wings all over the place—they glide with ease because they wait for an opportune wind to ride upon.

In *The Truth About Mind Renewal*, coming up in a couple of lessons from now, I discuss Joshua 1:8 (ESV), which states, "This Book of the Law shall not depart from your mouth, but you shall meditate on it day and night, so that you may be careful to do according to all that is written in it. For then you will make your way prosperous, and then you will have good success." This verse has a beautiful promise for us: When we meditate upon the Word of God and apply it to our lives, our ways will be prosperous, and we will have good success. We've got to put God's Word into our hearts and allow it to transform us and change us. As I mentioned, my meditation on Psalm 24 gave me a much deeper revelation and understanding of Jesus receiving my sin in His own body so that I would be completely forgiven and cleansed. While we often know Biblical truths, receiving a deeper revelation from the Holy Spirit fixes those truths into our hearts. It becomes a transformative heart belief rather than just intellectual knowledge.

This is not something we can do without the Holy Spirit's help. At the same time, when we read, pray, ponder and meditate, we are using our brains and minds to instill new information, which makes connections with existing information…and, of course, allows our brains/minds to seek, categorize, add to, expand upon what we've read/prayed/pondered…

Some may feel that the Word doesn't line up with their personal worldviews, but we don't get to pick and choose what parts of the Word we like and want to apply if we want to experience a true relationship with God. Mind renewal means that we agree with the Word of God rather than the world.

Romans 12:1 says, "I appeal to you therefore, brothers, by the mercies of God, to present your bodies as a living sacrifice, holy and acceptable to God, which is your spiritual worship." If we want to hear from God, we must choose to be a living sacrifice. Being a living sacrifice means that we agree with God rather than the world's ways. We choose to yield ourselves to Him rather than to our flesh.

1 John 2:15-16 (NKJV) says, "Do not love the world or the things in the world. If anyone loves the world, the love of the Father is not in him. For all that is in the world—the lust of the flesh, the lust of the eyes, and the pride of life—is not of the Father but is of the world." The desires of the flesh have to do with our physical appetites – in general these appetites are usually based on instant gratification for food, drink, or sensual pleasures. The desires of the eyes involve materialism, coveting and having a restless craving for more of the world, and always wanting bigger and better. Advertisers appeal to the lust of the eyes, enticing us to believe that we *need* what they sell in order to be happy. The pride of life is anything that puts us on the throne through selfish ambition or any way that we exalt self. All of these things will hinder us from hearing the Lord and we must guard our heart with all diligence (Proverbs 4:23) by being careful what we allow into our eyes and ears.

2. We Hear the Lord by Confirmation Through Peace

1 Corinthians 6:17 (NKJV) states, "But he who is joined to the Lord is one spirit with him." If you recall the earlier lesson, you'll remember that you are a spirit, you have a soul, and you live in a body. When you gave your life to Jesus, your spirit became one with His Spirit. We can hear God speaking to us through our spirit.

However, we must know His Word so we can recognize His Spirit revealing truth to our spirit. Not knowing the Word of God can leave us in a dangerous place if we're depending on our own heart to lead us. Our born-again spirit knows all things. 1 John 2:20 (NKJV) says, "But you have an anointing from the Holy One, and you know all things."

It's important to realize that our mind and our spirit are not the same. Sometimes we may feel conflicted in our heart and mind about decisions we need to make or feelings we have. These decisions may even cause us anxiety. The Greek word *merimna* (which we find in verses such as 1 Peter 5:7), means care, worry, and anxiety. It can also mean the feeling we may experience when we feel we're being pulled in two different directions. Sometimes our flesh/mind/soul may feel one way but our spirit is pulling us to submit ourselves to the Lord and trust Him. Being led by the Spirit instead of giving into our mind/flesh/soul[31] leads us to a sense of peace. This peace is a good indication of whether we are following our spirit, which is joined with the Holy Spirit, or if we are making decisions by following our flesh. The peace of Christ won't be ruling our hearts unless we are allowing Him to lead us.

Colossians 3:15 (AMP): "Let the peace of Christ [the inner calm of one who walks daily with Him] be the controlling factor in your hearts [deciding and settling questions that arise] ..." We must be in tune with the Lord, walking with Him and obeying when, by His Spirit, our heart reveals areas that we might need to change. Matthew 13:15 (NIV) says, "For this people's heart has grown dull, and with their ears they can barely hear, and their eyes they have closed, lest they should see with their eyes and hear with their ears and understand with their heart and turn, and I would heal them."

Confirmations of peace won't be occurring in our hearts if we aren't acting on the revelations God gives us, doing what He's already shown us is right, and choosing to spend time with Him. If we're listening to our flesh, focusing on our five senses, or focusing on the world, our hearts may grow dull. Notice that Matthew 13:15 says they allowed their eyes and ears to close. This wasn't something God did; this is what the people chose to do. Through that choice, they allowed the cares of this world to become more important than cultivating their relationship with the Lord. When we are listening and obedient to the Lord, we have peace in our spirits and also our consciences. Consider the times your conscience has been pricked when you knew that you were doing something wrong. Our conscience can also bear witness to the Lord speaking to us. God uses our conscience to reveal whether or not we are walking according to His truth.

---

[31]The soul is made up of the mind, will, heart, and emotions. (Matthew 22:37; Mark 12:30; Luke 10:27)

Caprice Scott

God speaks from His Spirit to our spirit. When we delight ourselves in Him, He leads us by our desires. It's important to realize that our desires will only line up with His when we submit to Him; then He will give us the desires of our heart. We learn from Psalm 37:4 (NKJV), "Delight yourself in the LORD, and he shall give you the desires of your heart." God's heart's desires become ours when we delight ourselves in Him. Ephesians 1:17-18 (NKJV) says, "... that the God of our Lord Jesus Christ, the Father of glory, may give to you the spirit of wisdom and revelation in the knowledge of Him, the eyes of your understanding being enlightened; that you may know what is the hope of His calling, what are the riches of the glory of His inheritance in the saints."

3. Baptism of the Spirit and Gifts of the Spirit—How God Speaks Through Them

The baptism of the Holy Spirit, which comes with speaking (or more specifically praying) in tongues, is a gift that helps us hear from God. In 1 Corinthians 12, we learn about the different gifts of the Spirit which include signs and wonders such as the message of wisdom, the message of knowledge, faith, gifts of healing, miraculous powers, discerning of spirits, tongues, and interpretation of tongues.

A "word of knowledge" is what we receive when the Holy Spirit downloads His specific knowledge to us about something we ourselves would not or could not perceive or understand through our own knowledge. This can happen while we are meditating on the Word of God, or through other methods that God may choose. A few examples of what a word of knowledge could look like:

➢ Receiving a sudden solution to a problem you're experiencing.

➢ Finding something that you have misplaced and the Spirit brings its location to your mind.

➢ A greater understanding of a specific verse and how the answer may apply to your life.

➢ The Spirit may reveal an answer to your heart about something that pertains to a person to whom you are ministering. I've known people whom the Holy Spirit will impress to speak to strangers, and the Spirit tells them the stranger's name and what their problem is before they speak to these strangers.

➢ A revelation from the Lord to help set a person free from past issues.

➢ Answers to resolve disputes between others.

➢ An idea or innovation the Spirit puts upon your heart.

➢ A personal revelation on Scripture that God desires you to understand.

➢ Warnings to avoid dangerous situations.

Praying in tongues is an incredible gift. When we do this, even though we don't know with our minds what we are praying (or our understanding, as Paul says in 1 Corinthians 14:14-15), our spirits are communicating directly with the Holy Spirit. When we pray in the Spirit, we are building ourselves up. Jude 1:20 (ESV) says, "But you, beloved, building yourselves up in your most holy faith and praying in the Holy Spirit ..."

As I shared previously, some of the many benefits of praying in tongues are:

➢ Building up your spirit man—1 Corinthians 14:4

➢ Declares mysteries of God to you—1 Corinthians 14:2

➢ Increased intimacy and communion between you and God—1 Corinthians 14:14

➢ Helps in intercession—when we don't know what to pray, the Holy Spirit prays through us—Romans 8:26

➢ Glorifies God—Acts 10:46

➢ Helps in spiritual warfare—Ephesians 6:18

➢ Releases a supernatural peace and rest in your spirit—1 Corinthians 14:14-15

As I have also mentioned, the Holy Spirit can give us dreams and visions to reveal truths to our hearts that we wouldn't have known or understood otherwise. There have been multiple times in the last few years when the Holy Spirit has given me very specific visions to help me overcome struggles in some areas. Several of those visions have been included in this program. When I was struggling with deep hurt and not seeing a way to forgive those who had hurt me, Jesus revealed that He had taken in His own body every wound I experienced by the hands of others. You'll run across two of these visions in the chapter on forgiveness.

Truth 7.3 Application

If you haven't done so already, go back and watch my demonstration on the Biblehub app and Biblehub.com where I explain how to use these tools to study the original meanings of each word in Hebrew and Greek through the use of Strong's Concordance. You can also purchase a paper copy of Strong's Concordance, but it won't be quite as fast and handy to use.

See my Tutorial "Learn to Use Biblehub.com" in Appendix 1.

Caprice Scott

Truth 7.4

How to Study the Bible

If you're having a difficult time knowing how to get started in studying your Bible, you aren't alone. It can feel overwhelming when you don't know where to begin, but there's good news. There are all kinds of great Bible study options. While we can (and should) read the Bible from cover to cover, there are many other ways to get into Scripture. My personal favorite way of reading the Bible from cover to cover is using Andrew Wommack's Bible reading plan which contains his notes.[32] First and foremost, we need to ask the Author of the Word to guide our hearts and minds and interpret His Word, opening our spiritual eyes and ears, revealing His truths to us as we read. When we open the Word of God, unlike any other book, the Author is present, but we should always invite the Holy Spirit to reveal what He desires us to learn and understand before we read. Let's discuss several other ways to study the Word:

- The Inductive Method: This method includes the who, what, where, when, why, and how approach. Who is speaking? Who is the audience? What is the message? When is it taking place? What time period? Where is this event taking place? Why was this message needed, and is it relevant today? How does this change what I know about God? How can I apply it to my life? I personally use this kind of method when reading through a specific book of the Bible (see *Application 7.4*).[33]

- The SOAP Method[34]: SOAP stands for **S**cripture, **O**bservation, **A**pplication, and **P**rayer: Sometimes a specific verse will stand out to me and I'll feel so impressed that I need to do a deep dive. I will write out the scripture by hand and then use Strong's Concordance to study every word in the original Hebrew (OT) or Greek (NT). This is also referred to as "exegesis" which means, "the critical interpretation of the biblical text to discover its intended meaning."[35] Once I've studied each word's original meaning, I will consider how the verse applies to

---

[32] https://www.awmi.net/bibleplan/

[33] Information about the study methods in this list can be found at
    https://www.biblegateway.com/learn/bible-101/about-the-bible/bible-study-methods

[34] Pastor Wayne Cordeiro of New Hope Christian Fellowship in Honolulu, Hawaii, created the SOAP Method of Bible study, outlined in his book *The Divine Mentor: Growing Your Faith as You Sit on the Feet of the Savior*© (Bethany House, 2008).

[35] https://www.britannica.com/topic/exegesis

me and my situation, then I'll write it out as a personal letter from God to me, or as a prayer from me to God.

- The TEXT Method: This kind of study can be either a verse-by-verse study or topical. Begin by **T**alking to God in prayer before you read (which you should always do anyway, as you want the Holy Spirit to direct your thoughts and give you understanding). **E**ncounter God and humanity in this Scripture and ask—what does this teach me about God and what does this teach me about humanity? **EX**amine your heart and consider what needs to be changed in your life based on this Scripture. **T**alk to God, thanking Him for revealing truths to you, and talk with others about what you learned.

- The Verse-Mapping Method: Write out your chosen verse(s). Write them out in at least two other translations. (You can find other translations by using Biblehub.com or Biblehub App and look under "Parallel" or "PAR.") Circle key words to look up in Strong's Concordance and write down their definitions. Explore the meaning of the verses as you consider the context—people and time period involved—and make connections with other relevant verses, passages, and concepts throughout Scripture. Write a short summary of what you learned.

- The Topical Study Method: Choose a specific topic you want to learn more about. Some examples might be the love of God, the gifts of the Spirit, or healing in the atonement. Look up references for this topic. (Biblehub.com and Strong's Concordance are my favorite choices for this.) Choose the verses you want to study. Begin asking questions about the topic, and then read the verses to see how they address your questions. Summarize your conclusions and write down how they apply to you.

- The Character Study Method: Choose a Biblical character you wish to study, and find relevant passages about him or her. Maybe you want to study the life of the Apostle Paul, so you might begin by reading the book of Acts. If you wanted to study Moses, you might begin with reading Exodus. You'd also find that Moses is mentioned throughout the New Testament as well. Once you've read your passages, dig into some other tools such as Bible dictionaries (Biblehub.com also has a Bible dictionary). You can begin to find answers to questions such as who, what, where, when, why, and how regarding the details of your subject's life. Consider how these findings might apply to your own life.

Those are a few ways you can study the Bible on your own. We're living in the age of information. We can look up any topic or verse by using a search engine and have answers immediately at our fingertips. While this is an incredible option, sometimes it's also good for us to get into a physical Bible without the use of so much technology. You can purchase Bible dictionaries, Bible concordances, and many other wonderful study tools to help you glean the most from God's Word.

Truth 7.4 Application

1. If you have funds to do so, you might consider purchasing Andrew Wommack's Living Commentary.[36] While there are many Bible commentaries available, including on Biblehub.com, not all theologians and writers teach that the gifts of the Spirit are still flowing today. This is unfortunate, as it can hinder our faith and trust in the Lord. Andrew also offers a free sample of his commentary which includes Matthew through 2 Timothy.[37] A good study Bible and maybe a parallel Bible will be helpful for you to be able to compare versions/translations.

2. "O HEAR" Inductive Bible Study[38]
"O HEAR" Inductive Bible Study (see Appendix 2)
Helps & Hints
Open My Eyes and Ears - Invite a Search
Before you begin your study, pray for the Holy Spirit to open your eyes and ears to God's Word. Invite the Holy Spirit to shine His light into your heart and soul and to give you revelation and understanding.

Highlight and Listen - Note Key Words or Phrases
Read the passage you've chosen through twice, then go back and highlight words or phrases that stand out to you personally. Remember, being transparent before the Father is the key to being transformed into the image of His Son.

---

[36] https://www.awmi.net/lc/
[37] https://www.awmi.net/reading/online-bible-commentary/?utm_source=awmi.net&utm_medium=internal&utm_campaign=commentary&utm_content=view-sample-button
[38] https://www.lifeway.com/en/articles/bible-journaling-method-to-hear-god-speak

Examine the Passage - Who, What, Where, How, Why, When

Go back and re-read the passage. Write and answer questions that come to you as you read. (Who, what, where, how, and why questions.) Here are a few to get you started:

- Who is the intended audience?
- What is the primary purpose of this passage?
- Why do you think the Holy Spirit had this passage written & included in Scripture?

Write and answer one or two other questions that relate to your examination of this passage. Remember to keep to the facts. Select and look up some key words. Write down a parallel passage. Consider using a Bible dictionary, concordance or other study helps to deepen your understanding of the meaning in this context. (Vine's, Strong's, etc.)

Apply - Moving from Head to Heart - What Does this Mean to Me Personally?

How am 1 encouraged and strengthened through this passage? What is the Father saying to me personally? Is there an example to follow, a sin to forsake, an error to avoid, a promise to claim, a command to obey?

Respond to the Word - Write a Prayer or Action Plan

A personal response can take many forms.

Write out a prayer that expresses your heart as you respond to His Word, or write out an action plan, and/or describe any personal changes in your perspective. Ask God for help. It is a good idea to build in a point of accountability to yourself or someone else. This passage means to me _____ so 1 can or will _____.

Chapter 8

YOUR RELATIONSHIP TOGETHER:

The Truth About Faith

and Belief—Uprooting Doubt

Truth 8.1

Hebrews 11:6 (NIV) says, "And without faith it is impossible to please God, because anyone who comes to him must believe that he exists and that he rewards those who earnestly seek him."

Earlier, I shared that everything from Genesis to Revelation was written to reveal to us that God is love, and He is trustworthy. The entire point of all He has done has been to win us back to Himself. It only makes sense, then, that we must believe Him in order to please Him. Choosing not to believe Him was the reason for the fall of humanity in the first place.

So how do we grow our faith? Romans 10:17 (ESV) tells us, "So faith comes from hearing, and hearing through the word of Christ." We have got to get into the Word of God. As I mentioned above, it's impossible to renew our minds to be able to believe and receive all that God has placed in our spirits if we aren't reading His Word.

Hebrews 4:12 (BSB) tells us, "... For the word of God is living and active. Sharper than any double-edged sword, it pierces even to dividing soul and spirit, joints and marrow. It judges the thoughts and intentions of the heart." Jesus said that the words He spoke were "spirit and life" (John 6:63). John 1:1 (NKJV) reveals, "In the beginning was the Word, and the Word was with God, and the Word was God." If we are avoiding getting into the Word, we are avoiding Jesus. So, the first step in growing your faith is getting into the Word of God daily. This is a daily habit of mind renewal.

So let's discuss some other practical ways we might grow our faith. Recently, a friend related to me something one of her professors in Bible college said in class. He said you can begin by trusting God and growing your faith for things that you know are very likely to happen. You might choose to begin thanking Him for each meal before you even sit down to eat. Before driving anywhere, thank Him for a safe trip to your destination. You can also be grateful for every paycheck before it arrives. Once each of these things occurs, express your gratitude. By doing so, you are training your brain, mind, and heart to expect His provision and goodness to come to pass. As you continue receiving these things each day, begin asking for abundant health and blessings of increase in the areas you have need.

Faith and gratitude work together. Philippians 4:6-7 (NKJV) says, "... Be anxious for nothing, but in everything by prayer and supplication, with thanksgiving, let your requests be made known to God; and the peace of God, which surpasses all understanding, will guard your hearts and minds through Christ Jesus." In this verse, we see we have no need to be anxious or afraid. Instead, when we bring a prayer before the Lord, asking with thanksgiving, letting our requests be made known to Him, not only are we more likely to receive the answers to those requests, but we also are more likely to have peace because we pray in expectation rather than begging out of fear.

My friend, Leigh-Ann, had a little crepe myrtle tree in a pot. The tree had been over-watered, and as she says, became "a lifeless stick" that she transplanted into soil. She declared Psalm 118:17 (NKJV) which states, "I shall not die, but live, and declare the works of the LORD" over it often, asking God to revive the tree to give her a new hope for her own healing. After a while, the first bud appeared in the spring, and the tree began bearing its fruit of beautiful flowers. Overnight, the little tree developed five blooms, the number that symbolizes grace.[39] Through this little tree, her hope was reborn and restored, and she knew she would also experience the same healing in her body that her tree experienced. Leigh-Ann likens this to her own journey as she herself is being "planted in the fertile soil of God's Word, rooted and grounded in the love and grace of Christ Jesus." She knows that her own life is bearing witness and producing fruit to serve His Kingdom. After sharing this testimony with my group, Leigh-Ann said later, when she and her husband viewed some Christmas lights in an area where they'd never been and that was about an hour from their home, they passed New Hope Street—a beautiful confirmation of the new hope she had found. I love how Leigh-Ann chose to use a little tree to help grow her own faith.

In my own healing journey God used doves to grow my faith that I would experience healing. On Valentine's Day in 2019, I was very sick and bedridden and not expecting to survive. I asked the Lord to give me a sign—specifically a dove—if He was going to (as I said that day) "pull me out of it" and heal me. Within ten minutes, I saw a white clay dove in a potter's hand online. This happened without me searching for any doves. This was especially meaningful for me because I was a professional potter, and years prior, Papa God had given me Isaiah 64:8 (ESV) which says, "But now, O LORD, you are our Father; we are the clay, and you are our potter; we are all the work of your hand." Several days later, I told Him I would need to see at least one dove every day until I healed. At first, I only saw doves online while scrolling through social media sites, but after I began regaining my strength, my husband and I would take walks. We'd see doves just about every morning. If I didn't see a dove on our walk, God had other methods of making sure I saw one. Sometimes a dove would be on a flier in the mail. As my story began circulating to friends and family, people would send me doves through email. Occasionally I'd receive a card with a dove. Several people sent me ceramic doves. One friend even bought me a dove necklace on an evening when I was having an especially rough time and I hadn't seen a dove that day. I think the biggest shock came when my husband and I were on one of our walks and we passed a house that had at least 20 pure white doves that lived there. I had lived in that town for 11 years and never once had seen these beautiful birds until I asked God to allow me to see some in order to increase my faith and belief that I would heal. God taught me so much about faith through those sweet doves.

---

[39] https://christianfaithguide.com/what-does-the-number-5-mean-in-the-bible/

Start considering how you might ask God to increase your faith. Maybe ask Him for something as simple as a free cup of coffee sometime. You can start small and go from there. Another way that God taught me to grow my faith was to begin keeping a faith journal. Every time God answered a prayer or revealed Himself to me in some way, I wrote it down. We are told not to forget the things God has done for us, but to meditate on them. Psalm 77:11-12 (NKJV) states, "I will remember the works of the LORD; Surely I will remember Your wonders of old. I will also meditate on all Your work, And talk of Your deeds." Doing so reminds us that He is indeed faithful and we can trust Him.

There's a story in the book of Joshua where God told the Israelites to do something similar. After they had wandered in the desert for 40 years, God told Joshua to take them through the Jordan River. First, the priests had to step into the water of the Jordan while carrying the Ark of the Covenant. Once they did this, the waters of the Jordan River stopped flowing and they all walked across on dry ground. They were to take the stones from the river, one for each tribe, and build a memorial to remind them of the way that God had fulfilled His promise in bringing them into the promised land. This was an incredible feat and was a reminder to all who passed by this memorial.

Joshua 4:1-3,6-7 (NKJV):

> And it came to pass, when all the people had completely crossed over the Jordan, that the LORD spoke to Joshua, saying: 'Take for yourselves twelve men from the people, one man from every tribe, and command them, saying, 'Take for yourselves twelve stones from here, out of the midst of the Jordan, from the place where the priests' feet stood firm. You shall carry them over with you and leave them in the lodging place where you lodge tonight.'" ... that this may be a sign among you when your children ask in time to come, saying, 'What do these stones *mean* to you?' Then you shall answer them that the waters of the Jordan were cut off before the ark of the covenant of the LORD; when it crossed over the Jordan, the waters of the Jordan were cut off. And these stones shall be for a memorial to the children of Israel forever.

When we recall the ways God has revealed Himself trustworthy in the past, our faith is increased. When we write things down, we tend to remember them better.

Truth 8.1 Application

1. We must _____ God in order to please Him.
2. How do we grow our faith?

_____
_____
_____
_____
_____

3. What are some practical ways that my friend's Bible College instructor suggests we can grow our faith?

_____
_____
_____
_____

4. Leigh-Ann declared Psalm 118:17 over her little tree. What does this verse say?

_____
_____
_____
_____

5. What was the name of the street that Leigh-Ann passed that confirmed the new hope she had found?

_____
_____
_____
_____

Truth 8.2

What to Do With Doubt

Have you ever experienced doubt that:

> ➢ God wants you well
>
> ➢ you can heal
>
> ➢ you can change
>
> ➢ you can overcome childhood trauma
>
> ➢ God loves you

➢ you are righteous

➢ you are forgiven

➢ you can prosper in life

➢ you will ever find peace

When it comes to healing or having faith for anything, doubt can be a major hindrance. If fear is the antithesis of faith, then doubt is fear's evil twin. Doubt tends to speak in direct opposition to every promise of God:

➢ *God says He's our Healer.* → Doubt and fear say we can't heal.

➢ *God says He's provided for all of our needs.* → Doubt and fear say we will never have what we need and we will always be poor or in some constant state of lack.

➢ *God says Jesus was the propitiation (the sacrifice necessary for us to gain right standing with Him) for our peace.* → Doubt and fear say true inner peace is unattainable in this world.

So how do we overcome doubt and fear? The simple answer is found in 1 John 4:18 (ESV), "Perfect love casts out all fear." The rest of this verse is revealing of our true problem: "For fear has to do with punishment, and whoever fears has not been perfected in love." If we are expecting punishment in the form of sickness, disease, or remaining poor and never having enough, that's living in a state of fear and doubt, and it's contrary to God revealing Himself and manifesting Himself in our lives.

Understanding, knowing, and receiving the love God has for us changes everything, but we know that this *simple* understanding isn't always easy. This is why we need to know where doubt and fear come from and how to begin dismantling them in order to tear down those strongholds and replace them with the knowledge and truth of God.

2 Corinthians 10:5 (ESV) says, "We destroy arguments and every lofty opinion raised against the knowledge of God, and take every thought captive to obey Christ." So, let's begin by answering the question: Does God want you well? God's very name, Jehovah Rapha means "the God who heals." God isn't going to behave in a way contrary to Himself and His character.

1 Peter 2:24 (KJV) says, "Who his own self bore our sins in his own body on the tree, that we, being dead to sins, should live unto righteousness: by whose stripes ye were healed." This verse echoes Isaiah 53:4-5 which states that Jesus would come to take not only our punishment for sin—which meant that we were no longer destined to be eternally separated from God—but also our physical and emotional healing and well-being.

In Matthew 8:16-17 (NKJV), we find that Jesus healed *all who were sick* and in 8:2-3, the leper tells Jesus, "if You are willing, You can make me clean." Jesus' answer says it all: "I am willing." Hebrews 13:8 (NKJV) says, "Jesus Christ is the same yesterday, today, and forever." He hasn't changed. His will to heal hasn't changed. So if God hasn't changed, why do we doubt His Word?

Doubt That You Can Heal:
We live in a world that teaches the motto, "If it sounds too good to be true, it probably is." When it comes to humans, that's true. Luke 18:27 (BSB) says, "… What is impossible with man is possible with God." While the medical community and doctors may "practice medicine" to treat the symptoms, the kind of healing God wants for us is thorough and complete. God understands that healing is not only done physically, but also is a spiritual matter. The kind of healing God has for us gets at the root of the problem. Where sin was the initial cause for sickness and death, Jesus dealt with the root, taking our sins upon Himself, thus changing the fruit.

Some research is now revealing that almost all disease begins in our brains and with our thoughts.[40][41] When we learn to agree with God's Word and step out of that fear cycle of lies, applying and trusting God's Word to every circumstance and situation, we begin changing our thoughts, which then changes our brain chemistry and structure. Changing our brain chemistry from "CAN" chemicals (cortisol, adrenaline, norepinephrine), which are created by fear and doubt, to "DOSE" chemicals (dopamine, oxytocin, serotonin, endorphins), which are created by trust and love, and allow for emotional healing that leads to the manifestation of physical healing. In her book, *Switch on Your Brain; the Key to Peak Happiness, Thinking, and Health©*, Dr. Caroline Leaf states, "We are constantly reacting to circumstances and events, and as this cycle goes on, our brains become shaped by the process in either a positive, good-quality-of-life direction or a negative, toxic, poor-quality-of-life direction. So it is the quality of our thinking and choices… and our reactions that determine our 'brain architecture' –the shape or design of the brain and *resultant* quality of the health of our minds and bodies."[42] In another article, Dr. Leaf shares that "What we say, think, and do changes the structure of the brain, including the flow of neurochemicals. Toxic stress…changes the brain, flooding it with an

---

[40] https://www.fearlessmotivation.com/2019/08/26/bruce-lipton-explains-how-thoughts-cause-disease-in-the-body/

[41] Leaf, Caroline, *Switch on Your Brain; the Key to Peak Happiness, Thinking, and Health©* (Baker Books, 2013) p. 33

[42] Leaf, Caroline, op cit., p. 34

unhealthy imbalance of neurochemicals like cortisol, which, in turn, impacts both our mental and physical health."[43] On the flip side, Dr. Leaf shares that *love* in a healthy "community involvement has been associated with mental health and cognitive resilience, reduction of chronic pain, lower blood pressure, and improved cardiovascular health!"[44]

Doubt That You Can Change:

It's a common belief that change isn't possible – changing our lives, our thoughts, our behaviors, or even our health seems out of the question.

- "I am the way I am."
- "I can't overcome or change the way I think."
- "I have no control over my thoughts or feelings."
- "My parents and family members are this way, so it's in my genes."

These beliefs and others like them are untrue. While it may not *seem* easy to change our beliefs or thoughts, it is entirely possible. This is the beauty of neuroplasticity, the brain's ability to change, and the gift of mind renewal which helps us write God's truths upon our hearts.

Mind renewal is about changing our focus and choosing to meditate on new truths. What we focus on expands, and as we choose to focus and meditate on the Word of God, we begin shifting and wiring new thoughts, beliefs, and values into our brains and hearts.

As Romans 12:2 (NIV) states, we can be "…transformed by the renewing of our mind." Philippians 1:6 (NIV) tells us that "…he who began a good work in you will carry it on to completion." This transformation isn't something we do on our own but with the help of the indwelling Holy Spirit and God promises to complete it. Ephesians 3:20 (NLT) even states that God "…is able, through His mighty power at work within us, to accomplish infinitely more than we might ask or think." That's a pretty powerful promise, and we should take great comfort in the fact that God promises to help us change in truly miraculous ways.

Truth 8.2 Application

See it: We need to see with our mind what those promises of God look like by vividly imagining His truths.

---

[43] https://drleaf.com/blogs/news/the-chemical-imbalance-myth

[44] op cit

Speak it: Instead of speaking doubts and complaining, we must learn to speak the Word in agreement over ourselves, our circumstances, and our lives.

Catch it: Catch every thought and bring it into obedience to the knowledge of God.

Pray it: When tempted to fear or doubt, turn that thought into a prayer of praise and gratitude, thanking God for what you want rather than what you may be feeling or experiencing.

Think it: Once you catch those negative thoughts, repeat the truth from the Word of God that counters those negative thoughts.

Study it: Study the Word in depth. The original Hebrew and Greek are rich in application, cutting to the joints and marrow. Make sure you are in the Word daily. Man does not live by bread alone, but by every Word that proceeds from the mouth of the Lord.

Watch it: Steep yourself in the Word and also healing testimonies and teachings that encourage your heart and mind to keep going. If these things can happen they absolutely can happen for you!

Truth 8.3

Doubt That You Will Overcome Childhood or Other Trauma

How do we heal from trauma? While it is true that trauma and abuse can be an entry point for the enemy to take advantage of, especially when this happens to us in early childhood, it *is* possible to heal. Core beliefs related to trauma may be written upon your heart and need to be changed or uprooted. Several of the things the Lord revealed to me that were necessary for overcoming the trauma that I had experienced were things such as understanding my new identity in Christ; forgiving others and myself; letting go of bitterness and resentment toward others and myself; learning who God says I am, and replacing the things I experienced in childhood with *His* truths about me. I had to learn how to allow myself to receive God's love for me. Jesus didn't only come to fix things for us to go to heaven, He came that we might also experience abundant life here - today. That includes physical and emotional healing.

Isaiah 61:1 tells us, "The Spirit of the Lord GOD is upon me, because the LORD has anointed me to bring good news to the poor; he has sent me to bind up the brokenhearted, to proclaim liberty to the captives, and the opening of the prison to those who are bound." One of the reasons Jesus came was to bind up our broken hearts and heal them. We experience this kind of healing through His love. Focusing on the "old me" isn't helpful. The "old me" relates to what others did to me and said about me. The "old me" saw myself as a wounded victim. The "old me" internalized the opinions and behaviors of other *broken people* above the opinion of God and the freedom through the new identity Christ purchased for me. 2 Corinthians 5:17 says, "Therefore, if anyone is in Christ, he is a new creation. The old has passed away; behold, the new has come."

Once I realized the deep significance of this verse, I came to understand that the trauma I had experienced actually happened to someone in the past— it released me to embrace being a completely new creation. As a new creation, do I need to hold on to what happened to me previously? No, I do not. As a new creation, I am in union with the Holy Spirit. Does the Holy Spirit have a need to relive those traumatic situations and see the "old me?" Or does He see me as someone entirely new? This perspective helped me shift my understanding and allowed me to begin seeing myself in a very different light. It brought all kinds of freedom.

But What if You Doubt That God Loves You?

Most of us are more than a little familiar with John 3:16-17. We have probably heard these two verses enough times that they may have lost their true meaning for us. It can also be difficult to remember to put our names in these verses, but we need to because *we* are *"whosoever."* Let's try it and do so from our hearts. Repeat after me: *God so loved me that He gave His only Son that I would not perish but have eternal life. God didn't send His Son to condemn me, but in order that I might be saved through Him.* As mentioned, John 10:10 tells us that Jesus came that we may have life and have it abundantly. The Good Shepherd laid down His life for us, His sheep. He laid down His life for you. Say that out loud right now: *Jesus laid down His life for me.*

In her book, *Unveiling Jesus: Beholding Him in His Amazing Grace©*, Tricia Gunn says this about John 10:

> In John 10 Jesus called Himself the Good Shepherd who gives up His life for the sheep so that we could have life abundantly. The abundant "life" He gave TO us is the Greek word "zoe" and it means the supernatural life of God. The "life" He gave FOR us is the Greek word "psyche" which means the emotions, affections, desires, His heart. Jesus literally gave up His *soul* for you! He left His position, His title, His royalty to give you supernatural life. The point of Jesus living a perfect, sinless life on earth was not for us to imitate Him, it was for

Him to qualify to take our place. Now He lives His resurrection life through us![45]

There are a couple of things for us to consider from this. First, He calls us sheep. Sheep are kind of dumb, and they need guidance. The great news is, after we accept Him, He not only gives us His life but also His characteristics (the fruit of the Spirit), and 1 Corinthians 2:16 also tells us He's given us His mind. There's that amazing transformation again. Jesus, our Shepherd, loves us so much that He not only gave up His life for us to be saved eternally, but He also gave up His soul. Romans 5:6-8 says, "For while we were still weak, at the right time Christ died for the ungodly. For one will scarcely die for a righteous person—though perhaps for a good person one would dare even to die—but God shows his love for us in that while we were still sinners, Christ died for us."

Doubting That You Are Forgiven:

In chapter 10 of the book of Hebrews (ESV), we find that the sacrifice of Jesus was for everyone. Verse 10 says, "...we have been sanctified through the offering of the body of Jesus Christ once for all." And verse 14, "For by a single offering he has perfected for all time those who are being sanctified." Verse 17 goes even further to say, "... I will remember their sins and their lawless deeds no more." When we receive the gift of salvation through Christ, every sin we have ever committed or will ever commit has been covered, paid for, forgiven, and taken off our records. Jesus died once—for all—for all people who receive Him and for all sin ever committed. As verse 14 states, He has already perfected us for all time, and verse 17 says God doesn't remember our sins. They are not part of us any longer as they have been separated from us "...as far as the east is from the west" (Psalm 103:12).

So where do all of the guilt and shame come from that may be keeping us in fear that somehow we're worse than anyone else? Though Jesus died to save everyone, for some reason we struggle to believe that truth is for us. I shared with you earlier how the accuser of the brethren attempts to sow lies into our hearts. The enemy of our souls *works to steal, kill, and destroy*, as John 10:10 tells us. Just as Jesus shared in the parable of the sower and the seed (Matthew 13), the enemy works to choke out the truth through worldly cares, by tribulation and persecution, and through keeping us so occupied that we don't sink our roots deep into the truth of the Word. If we're not in the Word, we're not in

---

[45] Gunn, Tricia, *Unveiling Jesus: Beholding Him in His Amazing Grace*© (Patricia Gunn, 2014) p. 175

the promises. If we aren't in the promises, we can't really apply what we don't know. I want to encourage you that if you received Jesus as your Savior, you are forgiven, and not only are you forgiven, but you are also counted righteous. And this leads us to our next question.

Do you Doubt you are Righteous?

Of course, we know and have heard often that our righteousness is as filthy rags (Isaiah 64:6). But once we receive Jesus, His very righteousness becomes our righteousness. Romans 3:22-24 (NKJV) tells us, "... even the righteousness of God, through faith in Jesus Christ, to all and on all who believe. For there is no difference; for all have sinned and fall short of the glory of God, being justified freely by His grace through the redemption that is in Christ Jesus." Philippians 3:9 (NIV) says, "... and be found in Him, not having a righteousness of my own that comes from the law, but that which comes through faith in Christ ..."

Are you Doubting that God Wants you Prosperous?

The very word "salvation" in the New Testament Greek is the word *sótéria*. Strong's Concordance #4991 tells us that this word means: welfare, prosperity, deliverance, preservation, salvation, safety. Bob Yandian, in *A New Testament Commentary: Galatians*. (Harrison House Publishers, 2016) says, "These are the three categories of the curse of the law: poverty, sickness, and spiritual death. In each of these cases, Jesus Christ became the curse that we might be set free from the curse."[46]

Yandian bases this on the curses listed in Deuteronomy 28:15-68. Jesus became these curses in order to set us free. Poverty was among them. Jesus *paid* for every one of your needs to be met, friends—spiritual, emotional, physical, and even financial. Now while that financial aspect doesn't mean that He's raining money down from heaven for you (though He does love to provide for us in miraculous ways), it does mean that He will make a way for you to be prosperous.

Deuteronomy 8:18 (NKJV) tells us, "But remember the LORD your God, for it is he who gives you the ability to produce wealth, and so confirms his covenant, which he swore to your ancestors, as it is today."

Now there is a catch: God gives us the ability to produce wealth so that we use our wealth, not to store up riches for ourselves here on earth, but that we may bless others. While God wants us to be prosperous so that the world may

---

[46] Yandian, Bob, *A New Testament Commentary: Galatians*. (Harrison House Publishers, 2016) p. 97

see that He takes care of His kids, we are blessed by Him in order to be a blessing. Genesis 12:2 (NIV) says, "I will make you into a great nation, and I will bless you; I will make your name great, and you will be a blessing." Proverbs 3:16 (NLT) says, "She [wisdom] offers you long life in her right hand, and riches and honor in her left." God grants us the ability to prosper so that we will use His provision to bless others as well as experience peace from fear of want and lack ourselves.

Do you Doubt you Will Ever Find True Peace?

Peace comes from trusting God. Paul tells us here not to be anxious about anything. Look at Philippians 4:7 (NKJV) which states, "And the peace of God, which surpasses all understanding, will guard your hearts and your minds in Christ Jesus." This is a wonderful promise, but we need to look at the previous verse to find the answer to how this peace works. Philippians 4:6 (ESV) tells us, "… do not be anxious about anything, but in everything by prayer and supplication with thanksgiving let your requests be made known to God." Later, in Philippians 4:19 (NKJV), Paul says, "And my God will supply every need of yours according to his riches in glory in Christ Jesus." Every need? God will supply every single need? Matthew 6:25-33 (NKJV) states:

> Therefore I say to you, do not worry about your life, what you will eat or what you will drink; nor about your body, what you will put on. Is not life more than food and the body more than clothing? Look at the birds of the air, for they neither sow nor reap nor gather into barns; yet your heavenly Father feeds them. Are you not of more value than they? Which of you by worrying can add one cubit to his stature? So why do you worry about clothing? Consider the lilies of the field, how they grow: they neither toil nor spin; and yet I say to you that even Solomon in all his glory was not arrayed like one of these. Now if God so clothes the grass of the field, which today is, and tomorrow is thrown into the oven, *will He* not much more *clothe* you, O you of little faith? Therefore do not worry, saying, 'What shall we eat?' or 'What shall we drink?' or 'What shall we wear?' For after all these things the Gentiles seek. For your heavenly Father knows that you need all these things. But seek first the kingdom of God and His righteousness, and all these things shall be added to you.

Friends, if we know Jesus and trust Him fully, we have absolutely no reason to be worried, fearful, or doubtful. He has got us fully covered in every single area of our lives. That's the most wonderful news. So now that we have a greater understanding of who we *are*, according to what the Word of God says about us and helping us apply the faith that God has given us, and who we *are not*, according to the lies of the enemy that are crafted and designed to keep us in fear and doubt, how do we overcome doubt?

Truth 8.3 Application

How to overcome doubt, insecurity, anxiety:

1. Using your imagination
2. Saying what you want to be your truth
3. Speaking the Word over yourself and your situation
4. Catching your negative thoughts
5. Expressing trust in God through praise and gratitude
6. Watching/reading healing testimonies
7. Filling your mind with God's Word
8. Studying Scripture
9. Don't agree with everything you think. If it doesn't agree with the Word, it's not your truth.
10. Don't assume that what you feel is always your truth (physical or emotional) especially when those feelings are negative.

Chapter 9

YOUR RELATIONSHIP TOGETHER:

The Truth About Mind Renewal

"Do not be conformed to this world, but be transformed by the renewal of your mind, that by testing you may discern what is the will of God, what is good and acceptable and perfect" (Romans 12:2 ESV). So you've given your heart to the Lord and you know that your spirit is perfect and identical to the Spirit of Jesus, but you've noticed that your thoughts aren't always lining up with the Word of God, and maybe you aren't yet experiencing all of the promises of God. Why is that? What's missing? As we learned earlier, merely because our spirits were changed when we gave our lives to the Lord doesn't mean our minds/souls and bodies were changed. We have a part to play in mind renewal.

Our born again, newly created spirits are perfect and one with the Holy Spirit. Our body is the physical "suit" in which we live. It's the vehicle for the soul and spirit. Our souls constitute our minds, wills, personalities, and everything that isn't part of the physical body or spirit. Our soul, which includes our mind, must be renewed through the washing of the water of Word of God. (Ephesians 5:26)

Maybe you've wondered how to experience the peace of God of Philippians 4:7, or you've questioned how to truly believe the provision that Philippians 4:19 states. You might even be asking, "How do I get all of that healing to manifest that 1 Peter 2:24 says has already happened?"

Truth 9.1

We must renew our minds so they will line up with our spirits. Thankfully, the Word of God gives us instruction on how to do this. God created our incredible brains, and even our bodies, with the facility to change as we choose to change our thoughts, emotions, attitudes, and imaginations.

As mentioned above, Ephesians 5:25-26 (NKJV) tells us, "... Husbands, love your wives, just as Christ also loved the church and gave Himself for her, that He might sanctify and cleanse her with the washing of water by the Word..." What does that mean? It means that we are washed, cleansed, and sanctified through the Word of God. That's how the change takes place. However, we must get into the Word and get the Word into us for this transformation to happen. In Mark chapter 4 we find the parable of the seed that's growing. Verses 26-29 liken the seed to the Word of God. 1 Peter 1:23 explains: "... being born again, not of corruptible seed, but of incorruptible, by the word of God, which liveth and abideth forever" (KJV).

Truth 9.1 Application:

2 Timothy 1:7 (NKJV): "For God has not given us a spirit of fear, but of power and of love and of a sound mind."

Go to Biblehub.com (or use your physical copy) of Strong's Concordance to write down the definitions of: *fear*, *power*, and *sound mind*.

_____

_____

_____

_____

_____

_____

Philippians 4:6-7 (NKJV) states, "Be anxious for nothing, but in everything by prayer and supplication, with thanksgiving, let your requests be made known to God; and the peace of God, which surpasses all understanding, will guard your hearts and minds through Christ Jesus."

Using Biblehub.com or another Bible Concordance, what are the full meanings of *anxiety, peace, guard, hearts,* and *minds* in this verse?

_____

_____

_____

_____

_____

_____

_____

_____

_____

_____

_____

_____

_____

_____

_____

Truth 9.2

The Word of God is the seed that is incorruptible; it will not decay and cannot be destroyed. It remains faithful to doing what it was created to do. So back to the question of why we may not be experiencing all of those promises of God. First, we need to ask ourselves if we have planted God's Word in our hearts, or if we've got something else planted in its place. Then, for example, if you want God's peace, do you have His Word and promises of peace planted firmly in your heart, or do you have the worries and cares of the world there, which the parable refers to as "weeds"? Second, we need to look at the soil in which the seed/Word is planted. Mark 4:28 (ESV) says, "The earth produces by itself, first the blade, then the ear, then the full grain in the ear." Notice the words, "by itself." This implies that this production is not something *we* do, but something the seed does on its own in connection with fertile earth. If you're a gardener, you know that you can't force anything to grow. You plant the seed, and then you find that it springs up on its own under the right conditions. The Word of God works in the same way in our hearts and lives. We don't have to understand how it works—it does the work by itself. Our hearts are the ground, and they will produce, based on the seed that is planted and the condition of the "soil" of our hearts.

This verse gives us an idea of what must be planted in order to get the crop that we desire. If we're putting negative things in our hearts, we're going to reap negative, unhealthy fruits. If we are putting positive things in our hearts—specifically the Word of God— we are going to produce and reap good fruits. When the conditions are right, plants produce fruits effortlessly. We must sow the Word of God into our hearts and leave it there so that it will produce fruit. Again, if you've ever had a garden or fruit tree, you might sow a seed, but you know better than to expect all of the fruit to be produced at once. It takes time, and when it comes to gardens, it takes cultivation. *Cultivation is our part in mind renewal.* We have to take care of the soil of our heart. Matthew 13:3-8 (NKJV) states:

> Then He spoke many things to them in parables, saying: "Behold, a sower went out to sow. And as he sowed, some seed fell by the wayside; and the birds came and devoured them. Some fell on stony places, where they did not have much earth; and they immediately sprang up because they had no depth of earth. But when the sun was up they were scorched, and because they had no root they withered away. And some fell among thorns, and the thorns sprang up and choked them. But others fell on good ground and yielded a crop: some a hundredfold, some sixty, some thirty.

Jesus then explained this parable in Matthew 13 verses 19-23 (ESV):

Verse 19) "When anyone hears the word of the kingdom and does not understand it, the evil one comes and snatches away what has been sown in his heart. This is what was sown along the path." Now this verse isn't saying that if we don't understand the Word of God, we should just give up. It's saying that it's easier for satan to steal the Word of God from our hearts when we first hear the Word.

Verses 20-21: "As for what was sown on rocky ground, this is the one who hears the word and immediately receives it with joy, yet he has no root in himself, but endures for a while, and when tribulation or persecution arises on account of the word, immediately he falls away." We can look at each of these heart/soil conditions as progressive steps. When you first hear the Word it may not make much sense to you, but as you grow in your understanding, the seed/Word will begin to take root in your heart. The rocky ground may be a place where the seed actually begins taking root, but the roots don't get deep enough; things begin to get difficult. Maybe family members or friends don't agree with your decision to follow the Lord. Allowing their opinions to sway you would be an example of rocky soil.

Verse 22 says, "As for what was sown among thorns, this is the one who hears the word, but the cares of the world and the deceitfulness of riches choke the word, and it proves unfruitful." This verse reveals that many people fall away because of things happening in the world. This is based on focusing on what's happening in the carnal/natural realm rather than focusing on and trusting the Lord.

The word "cares" here is the Greek word *merimna*, which means "worries," "anxiety," "fractured," and "distraction." It's possible that they received the Word at first, but then felt torn between their own worldview and personal beliefs, or even the opinions of others, which didn't line up with the Word of God. People may also become distracted by focusing on worldly gain and materialism, or on financial issues. While having money in itself is not evil, when it becomes an idol and our focus, there's a problem. God blesses us so that we can bless others. Satan loves to distract us with things that aren't important. We must remove distractions (weeds) so they don't choke out the Word in our hearts. God must be our first priority. Verse 23 says, "But the seed sown on good soil is the one who hears the word and understands it. He indeed bears fruit and produces a crop—a hundredfold, sixtyfold, or thirtyfold" (BSB). Of course, this is what we want to have happen. We want the Word of God to grow in our hearts. We want to have understanding and to bear healthy fruit in our lives.

Truth 9.2 Application:

Choose one or several of the verses below to meditate on for at least 10 minutes each day over the next several weeks. Meditation means to mull it over in your mind. Think about each word's meaning. Think about each verse and how you might rephrase it in your own words. Ask the Holy Spirit to help you renew your mind by receiving and planting these truths into your heart. You might choose to write the verses you chose on a sticky note or note card to tape up around your house or keep with you.

Ephesians 4:23 (NKJV) says, "... and be renewed in the spirit of your mind..."

Philippians 2:5 (BSB) says, "Let this mind be in you which was also in Christ Jesus..."

Philippians 4:8 (BSB) says, "Finally, brothers, whatever is true, whatever is honorable, whatever is right, whatever is pure, whatever is lovely, whatever is admirable—if anything is excellent or praiseworthy—think on these things."

Joshua 1:8 (NKJV) states, "This Book of the Law shall not depart from your mouth, but you shall meditate in it day and night, that you may observe to do according to all that is written in it. For then you will make your way prosperous, and then you will have good success."

2 Corinthians 10:4-5 (NKJV) says, "For the weapons of our warfare are not carnal but mighty in God for pulling down strongholds, casting down arguments and every high thing that exalts itself against the knowledge of God, bringing every thought into captivity to the obedience of Christ…"

Ephesians 4:23-24 (NIV) says, "…to be made new in the attitude of your minds; and to put on the new self, created to be like God in true righteousness and holiness."

Colossians 3:9-10 (NIV) states, "…since you have taken off your old self with its practices and have put on the new self, which is being renewed in knowledge in the image of its Creator."

Ephesians 4:22-24 (NKJV) tells us, "… that you put off, concerning your former conduct, the old man which grows corrupt according to the deceitful lusts, and be renewed in the spirit of your mind, and that you put on the new man which was created according to God, in true righteousness and holiness."

1 John 2:15-16 (NKJV) states, "Do not love the world or the things in the world. If anyone loves the world, the love of the Father is not in him. For all that is in the world—the lust of the flesh, the lust of the eyes, and the pride of life—is not of the Father but is of the world."

Truth 9.3

The same seed was sown in every condition, but only the seed sown in good soil remained and produced healthy fruit. The seed is never the problem; it is the soil. As I said, this is where mind renewal comes in to play. It is our responsibility to make certain the soil of our heart is good.[47] How do we do that? Proverbs 4:20-27 (NKJV) gives us some great guidance:

---

[47]Remember, mind/soul/heart are often used interchangeably in the Bible: Matthew 22:37; Mark 12:30; Luke 10:27

My son, give attention to my words; Incline your ear to my sayings. Do not let them depart from your eyes; Keep them in the midst of your heart; For they are life to those who find them, And health to all their flesh. Keep your heart with all diligence, For out of it spring the issues of life. Put away from you a deceitful mouth, And put perverse lips far from you. Let your eyes look straight ahead, And your eyelids look right before you. Ponder the path of your feet, And let all your ways be established. Do not turn to the right or the left; Remove your foot from evil.

These verses reveal so much about mind renewal and how we cultivate the soil of our hearts. Renewing our minds is the part we are responsible for. It's our job to get the Word into our hearts, meditating on its truth, choosing to agree with what It says. It's the Holy Spirit's job to transform our hearts as we yield to Him.

Let's break each of these verses down and dig a bit deeper into Scripture:

→ Verse 20: *Be attentive to God's Word.* We've got to read it in order to be attentive. Pay careful, close attention to what it says:

2 Timothy 3:16 (BSB) says, "All Scripture is God-breathed and is useful for instruction, for conviction, for correction, and for training in righteousness," John 8:32 (NLT) says, "... and you will know the truth, and the truth will set you free." We begin by getting into the Word of God and getting that seed/Word into us. When we do that, we will know the truth.

→ Verse 20 (continued): *Incline your ear to His sayings. Listen intently:*

Isaiah 55:3 (NKJV) states, "Incline your ear, and come to Me. Hear, and your soul shall live; And I will make an everlasting covenant with you …" We need to listen carefully to what God's Word instructs us to do. This means we must remove distractions that would keep us from being in His Word and intently focusing on what it's saying. When we follow these instructions, our souls will *live* and *thrive* in His abundance.

→ Verse 21: *Don't let them escape your sight.* This means, do not forget the Word that you read. Set your mind on it. Focus.

Colossians 3:2 says, "Set your minds on things that are above, not on things that are on earth." The Word of God reveals to us what things are "above," or in heaven. Romans 8:6 (NKJV) states, "For to be carnally minded is death, but to be spiritually minded is life and peace." It's easy to forget what we've read in the Word if we don't remain in it consistently. This needs to be a daily habit. We've got to remain focused on spiritual things and not allow our minds and hearts to get caught up in the things of this world.

→ Verse 21 (continued): *Keep them in your heart. Make them your truth by meditating on them:*

Joshua 1:8 (NKJV): "This Book of the Law shall not depart from your mouth, but you shall meditate in it day and night, that you may observe to do according to all that is written in it. For then you will make your way prosperous, and then you will have good success." Meditating on the Word of God is one of the most important ways to cultivate the soil of our hearts in order to renew our minds. To meditate on the Word means that we actively engage our minds in order to better understand. This is a mental exercise which includes what 17th century minister Thomas Watson called, "a serious and solemn thinking upon God."[48]

Biblical meditation requires a deep reflection on our part, and then consideration of how we will apply these truths of the Word to our lives. Not only should we meditate on the Word of God, but also we need to be using the power of our imaginations in a positive way; that means seeing in our minds the promises of God coming to fruition.

Verse 22: *They are LIFE and healing to your flesh.* (Here's a huge promise in the middle of these instructions.)

Proverbs 3:8 (NLT) says, "Then you will have healing for your body and strength for your bones."

Did you know that your immune system is in your bone marrow? When we receive and apply the truths of Word of God to our lives, we are strengthening our immune systems and causing our bodies to heal. Because what and how we think affect how our bodies function, as the Word of God tells us, when we choose to meditate on His truths and write them upon our hearts, we not only have an impact on how our brains function, but we also help our bodies heal.

Verse 23: *Keep your heart with all vigilance.* This means we must choose godly thoughts and defend our hearts and minds against anything ungodly. Guard your heart and mind.

Psalm 101:3 (NLT): "I will refuse to look at anything vile and vulgar. I hate all who deal crookedly; I will have nothing to do with them." Are there things that you may need to remove from your sight? The world produces a lot of unhealthy information: TV, movies, secular music, news, and many things on social media. The things of the world can contaminate our heart soil and render the Word of God of no effect, because they may sow weeds of doubt and unbelief, among other things. Consider that many things we see on the news or

---

[48] Watson, Thomas, *The Divine Cordial.* (Public domain, 1663) p. 33

in the world are things that God hates so much that He sent Jesus to pay the price for them. Why would we consider those things "entertainment"?

Philippians 4:8 (ESV) tells us what kinds of things we should be putting into our hearts and minds instead: "Finally, brothers, whatever is true, whatever is honorable, whatever is just, whatever is pure, whatever is lovely, whatever is commendable, if there is any excellence, if there is anything worthy of praise, think about these things."

Your heart contains the springs of LIFE when you take care of what is allowed into it. Consider how the healthy soil of your heart allows the seed to grow and mature. Luke 6:45 (BLB) says, "The good man out of the good treasure of his heart brings forth that which *is* good; and the evil out of the evil brings forth that which *is* evil. For out of the abundance of his heart, his mouth speaks."

Matthew 7:16-17 (ESV) tells us, "You will recognize them by their fruits. Are grapes gathered from thornbushes, or figs from thistles? So, every healthy tree bears good fruit, but the diseased tree bears bad fruit." If you ever want to know what's in a person's heart, just look at the fruits in their life.

Verse 24: *Put away crooked speech.* Our words matter! I often tell those I minister to - think of it this way: WORDS = MATTER. We create our reality with our thoughts and words.

Proverbs 23:7 (NKJV) states, "For as he thinks in his heart, so is he." Isaiah 57:19 (NKJV) says, "'I create the fruit of the lips: Peace, peace to him who is far off and to him who is near,' Says the LORD, 'And I will heal him.'" Did you catch the fact that the fruit of the lips and a reference to healing are in the same verse? Maybe there's a connection. Our thoughts and words shape our lives. Most people don't consider how powerful their words are. When God spoke the world into existence, it was by His words that all things were created. Because we are created in His image, we also have power to create with our words. We have the power to build up and tear down. In Mark 11:23 Jesus tells us to "speak to the mountain" (any issue that needs to be removed or changed), and it will be done for us, as long as we *believe*, as James 1:6-8 also tells us. That's powerful.

Recall that Matthew 6:31 (KJV) says, "Therefore take no thought, saying, 'What shall we eat?' or, 'What shall we drink?' or 'Wherewithal shall we be clothed?'" Notice the word "thought" in the first part of this verse; in other versions, this word is translated as "do not worry" or "do not be anxious." When we have worries or anxieties, we should *not* take those thoughts and say them. Instead of verbalizing them, we should cast them away. We don't want to come into agreement with worry and anxiety; worry and anxiety are unnecessary when we realize that God has promised to provide for all of our needs. God takes how we use our words so seriously that Jesus gave this warning. Matthew 12:36-37 (ESV) tells us, "I tell you, on the day of judgment people will give account for every careless word they speak, for by your words you will be justified, and by your words you will be condemned." No devious talk; no deceptive talk, profanity, dishonesty, slander, or troublemaking. Instead, speak life, grace, and truth.

Proverbs 18:21 (NKJV) says, "Death and life are in the power of the tongue, and those who love it will eat its fruits." Ephesians 4:29 (NIV) states, "Do not let any unwholesome talk come out of your mouths, but only what is helpful for building others up according to their needs, that it may benefit those who listen." Our words need to be life-giving, not only toward others, but also toward ourselves.

Verse 25: *Keep your focus—remain steadfast in the direction that you are going with the Lord.* In other words, don't get sidetracked.

Philippians 3:12-14 (NLT) tells us, "I don't mean to say that I have already achieved these things or that I have already reached perfection. But I press on to possess that perfection for which Christ Jesus first possessed me. No, dear brothers and sisters, I have not achieved it, but I focus on this one thing: Forgetting the past and looking forward to what lies ahead, I press on to reach the end of the race and receive the heavenly prize for which God, through Christ Jesus, is calling us." Don't get bogged down and frustrated in the process. Even Paul admitted he had not achieved perfection in this area, but continued striving for the goal. That should be very encouraging for us. We also shouldn't focus on what happened in the past. We can't change that. Paul says to "look forward to what lies ahead." That's where our focus needs to be. Besides, we are new creations. What happened in the past, happened to the *old* us. We are brand new creations.

Verse 26: *We need to be single-minded, walking with the Lord and by the guidance of His Holy Spirit:*

Galatians 5:16-17 (NKJV) says, "I say then: Walk in the Spirit, and you shall not fulfill the lust of the flesh. For the flesh lusts against the Spirit, and the Spirit against the flesh; and these are contrary to one another, so that you do not do the things that you wish."

Our flesh will want to have its own way. The great news is, the less we surrender to the flesh and the more we renew our minds, the less this will occur.

Verse 27: *Don't swerve to the right or to the left. Don't let your feet turn toward anything evil.* We cannot flirt with sin.

Hebrews 12:1-2 (NKJV): "Therefore we also, since we are surrounded by so great a cloud of witnesses, let us lay aside every weight, and the sin which so easily ensnares us, and let us run with endurance the race that is set before us, looking unto Jesus, the author and finisher of our faith, who for the joy that was set before Him endured the cross, despising the shame, and has sat down at the right hand of the throne of God."

Truth 9.3 Application:

List the 11 directives from Proverbs 4 that reveal how to cultivate the soil of our hearts in your own words:

1. _____
2. _____
3. _____
4. _____
5. _____
6. _____
7. _____
8. _____
9. _____
10. _____
11. _____

And, on the subject of sin, we need to talk about repentance…

Truth 9.4

Repentance

"Do not be conformed to this world, but be transformed by the renewal of your mind, that by testing you may discern what is the will of God, what is good and acceptable and perfect" (Romans 12:2 ESV). Do I hear an echo? We've covered being transformed by the renewing of the mind, we need to address the rest of this verse—not being conformed to this world, and discerning the will of God, which is good, acceptable, and perfect. You may be wondering what could possibly be left to cover under the subject of repentance that wasn't under mind renewal. The truth is, these two subjects go hand in hand, but are not the same.

So what is repentance? Let's start with what repentance is *not*. Repentance is not crying, pleading, and begging for forgiveness. Repentance, instead, is choosing to agree with God and then having a heart change. Repentance is like going south and doing a complete U-turn and going north. It's no longer going your own direction, but instead, going God's direction.

Amos 3:3 (BSB) asks, "Can two walk together without agreeing where to go?" It's a common (mis)belief that just saying the sinner's prayer is enough, but God doesn't want lip service. He wants our hearts. As Pastor Mark Cowart said in a live interview with Joseph Z, we can't just be "mouth professors," we must be "heart possessors."[49] If we only confess that we love God, but our fruit says otherwise, we are only "mouth professors." Jesus said in Matthew 7:16 we would know a person by their fruit, and James 1:22 states that we must be doers of the word. True conversion is being faithful to Christ in our hearts, not just our actions. When we are faithful to Him in our hearts, our actions will naturally reveal this.

Mark 12:29-31 (ESV): "Jesus answered, 'The most important is, "Hear, O Israel: The Lord our God, the Lord is one. And you shall love the Lord your God with all your heart and with all your soul and with all your mind and with all your strength." The second is this: "You shall love your neighbor as yourself." There is no other commandment greater than these.'"

Jesus calls us His bride. He wants us to belong completely to Him—every part of us. We can't have one foot in bed with the devil and the other in the Kingdom of God. We have to be "all in", otherwise we're committing adultery against Him. He is calling us to belong fully and completely to Him and to not commit "spiritual adultery." What is spiritual adultery, you might ask?

James 4:4 (ESV) tells us, "You adulterous people! Do you not know that friendship with the world is enmity with God? Therefore whoever wishes to be a friend of the world makes himself an enemy of God." Jesus doesn't want us, His bride, flirting with the world. Repentance puts us back on the right track - rather than being sidetracked by the world. It takes repentance to be converted (changed). We have to choose to turn away from our own way of doing things and the way that the world does things (because the world is under the influence of the devil), and then a conversion will take place—a state of sinfulness changing into a state of holiness. This is what it means to be a true child of God.

First Thessalonians 4:7 (BSB) says, "For God has not called us to impurity, but to holiness." Holiness isn't simply about our behavior—holiness is a heart matter. Holiness means to be set apart to God, consecrated, sacred. God desires that we turn away from the world, and fully and completely surrender to Him. Why would this matter? Because satan is God's enemy and that means he is our enemy, too. Satan hates God, and he hates God's kids. His only purpose is to

---

[49] https://video.josephz.com/channel/ZMinistries/video/1833

destroy us. Doing what satan wants us to do is destructive. It hurts us. John 12:31 (NKJV) says, "Now is the judgment of this world; now the ruler of this world will be cast out."

God isn't trying to be mean when He tells us we can't be lovers of this world and lovers of God. Luke 16:13 tells us that we can't serve two masters. If we are lovers of this world, God won't have our hearts. If we are lovers of this world, then we are still under the grip of the enemy and his influence. This would lead to our own destruction. God is calling us out of this world because He loves us. We must repent, convert, and walk in holiness.

Acts 3:19-20 (NKJV) states, "Repent therefore and be converted, that your sins may be blotted out, so that times of refreshing may come from the presence of the Lord, and that He may send Jesus Christ, who was preached to you before." Think of it this way: I love my husband. He has my heart. I don't commit adultery with someone else because I love my husband, not because I'm afraid he's going to punish me. I don't want to hurt him, and I don't want to destroy our relationship.

Ephesians 4:27 (NASB) states, "...and do not give the devil an opportunity." John 1:12-13 (NKJV) tells us, "But as many as received Him, to them He gave the right to become children of God, to those who believe in His name: who were born, not of blood, nor of the will of the flesh, nor of the will of man, but of God." True repentance and conversion mean that we agree with God and allow Him to change our hearts. Again, this isn't something we can do without Him; this isn't about us doing everything right in the flesh on our own. Our own works are "dead works" for which we need to repent.

Hebrews 6:1 (ESV) says, "Therefore let us leave the elementary doctrine of Christ and go on to maturity, not laying again a foundation of repentance from dead works and of faith toward God ..." We've got to embrace the power of Christ and His Spirit in us that can transform us. This takes us back to the seed/Word of God. When that seed not only gets into our heads, but also into our hearts, it begins growing and taking root. This is what changes us and transforms us. When we give the seed healthy soil to grow in and the right conditions, God begins changing us from the inside out. This is what true mind renewal is all about.

Truth 9.4 Application

1. Spend some time journaling, specifically writing a letter from you to God about Romans 8:4-8:

> ... that the righteous requirement of the law might be fulfilled in us who do not walk according to the flesh but according to the Spirit. For those

who live according to the flesh set their minds on the things of the flesh, but those who live according to the Spirit, the things of the Spirit. For to be carnally minded is death, but to be spiritually minded is life and peace. Because the carnal mind is enmity against God; for it is not subject to the law of God, nor indeed can be. So then, those who are in the flesh cannot please God.

_____

_____

_____

_____

_____

_____

_____

_____

_____

_____

_____

_____

_____

_____

_____

2. Consider these verses below about the tongue and the power it holds. Ask the Holy Spirit if you need to repent in any area that concerns the words you've spoken against others or yourself. There is no condemnation against you, but your Papa God wants you to have a pure heart and words that bring edification and healing to yourself and others. Write out anything that God speaks to you about this subject as you read the verses and pray.

_____

_____

_____

_____

_____

_____

_____

_____

_____

James 3:5-10 NKJV:

Even so the tongue is a little member and boasts great things. See how great a forest a little fire kindles! And the tongue is a fire, a world of iniquity. The tongue is so set among our members that it defiles the whole body, and sets on fire the course of nature; and it is set on fire by hell. For every kind of beast and bird, of reptile and creature of the sea, is tamed and has been tamed by mankind. But no man can tame the tongue. It is an unruly evil, full of deadly poison. With it we bless our God and Father, and with it we curse men, who have been made in the similitude of God. Out of the same mouth proceed blessing and cursing. My brethren, these things ought not to be so.

Chapter 10

YOUR RELATIONSHIP TOGETHER:

The Truth About "Thinking

on These Things"—Dream Big!

Truth 10.1

God wants us to use our imaginations and to dream big. If we have small thinking, we will experience small outcomes. When I first began using the power of imagination in 2019 in the way I'm about to share with you, I began to see myself coaching and speaking in public. If you had known me then you would have thought there would be no way for me to be able to do these things, and I would have agreed with you. By imagining and "seeing" myself doing these things, I trained my brain to believe they were possible. Now I use my imagination to see even bigger things in my future. I use creative imagery in my mind to see God blessing my ministry and making it possible for me to make an incredible impact on millions of lives. While that may seem far-fetched, I know that nothing is impossible for one who is submitted to God and dreaming big dreams with Him, especially dreams that will be a blessing for others and bring Him glory. We limit God with small dreams. When we are walking in close communion with Him, He puts His own desires in our hearts, and when we trust Him, He brings those desires to fruition. It may not happen all at once, but He begins opening doors and setting things in motion. Getting to where I am today didn't happen overnight, but step by step He has brought me here. I know that the things I am imagining and dreaming with Him about the future are also being set in motion today. Let's take a deeper look at what this entails.

Our Mind's Eye

Our brains see in pictures rather than words. You may think that isn't true, but if you decided you didn't want to eat a cookie and you repeated to yourself over and over, "I'm not going to eat that cookie. I'm not going to eat that cookie", what is the thing you are thinking about? The cookie, right? You're probably thinking about what that cookie looks like, the crumbly texture, the light brown color with dark chocolate chips. You "see" the cookie before you imagine tasting it. When we read a book, we "see" what we are reading. Our imagination goes to work and we can see according to our brain's visual interpretation of what the author had in mind. An ocean scene? A dark alley? A beautiful sunset?

One study suggests that planning for a vacation can be just as emotionally rewarding as being on that vacation.[50] Why? Because we imagine the good things and feelings attached to being on vacation. Maybe we're planning to go to the beach? We imagine how beautiful the water will be, sparkling in the sunshine. We "see" ourselves standing in the sand as the waves come, even before we can imagine feeling those waves. And we attach emotions to these mental pictures.

Because the mind sees and thinks in pictures, we can imagine either good things or bad things, and "see" them before they happen. Now, I'm not talking about some strange kind of clairvoyance, but we can often imagine things that may become reality in our future. Our emotions come into play when we imagine. If we imagine negative or harmful actions, outcomes, or consequences, our emotions can include fear and write those beliefs upon our hearts. This can create unhealthy neural pathways of fear which can lead to poor health.

---

[50] https://pmc.ncbi.nlm.nih.gov/articles/PMC2837207/

If we imagine the best, we may see ourselves working on or realizing and living goals we have set. When we imagine positive things, we create healthy brain connections; we can produce healthy brain chemistry. Changing the substances which the brain releases can change how it/we function and may allow our bodies to heal, return to, and remain in homeostasis, keeping us in peace. For example, author Steven Ray Ozanich explains "Visualizing a healthy body reverses, or interrupts, prior false experiences by breaking the long-term neural relationships. It…is an invaluable tool in healing. You can't heal until you can imagine yourself as "okay" and as being healthy and happy and pain-free."[51]

We can also consider how quantum physics may be applied here. If you think back to what I mentioned in the section, *The Truth About Your Authority in Christ,* specifically *Praying With Authority,* you may remember that subatomic particles are not there unless an observer looks for them. We can't really know what they're doing, or even if they exist when we are not looking. It is possible that they "are not." When we take time to imagine or "visualize" our future the way we want it to be, looking for something to happen in expectation, we can see it in our minds before it is made manifest in our lives.

If that sounds strange, think about this: When you decide you want tacos for dinner, the first thing your mind does is think of tacos, what they look like, and how happy you are when you eat them. Then, you consider the process, thinking about and "seeing" the ingredients, and you may "see" in your mind's eye what you have on hand in your fridge and pantry. You have to see all of these things before they happen. Seeing the process in your mind allows you to begin fixing dinner. Hopefully, the end result looks a whole lot like what you envisioned when you first decided to fix tacos for dinner.

Scripture has a lot to say about the use and power of imagination. Isaiah 26:3 tells us that the word "mind" includes *imagination*: "You keep him in perfect peace whose mind (or imagination) is stayed on you, because he trusts in you." (ESV) Consider that the Bible is full of imagery. We can't read a verse about being under the shadow of God's wings without imagining something like a mother hen with her chicks and seeing God's wings over us in a similar manner. (Psalm 17:8) God created all that we see through His imagination.

Hebrews 11:3 (BLB) tells us, "By faith we understand the universe to have been formed by the word of God, so that the things being seen have not been made from the things being visible." Genesis 11:5-6 (KJV) might be the most

---

[51] Ozanich, Steven Ray, *The Great Pain Deception: Faulty Medical Advice is Making Us Worse*© (Silver Cord Records, 2011) pp. 299-300

revealing verses of all when it comes to the use of imagination: "And the LORD came down to see the city and the tower, which the children of men builded. And the LORD said, 'Behold, the people is one, and they have all one language; and this they begin to do: and now nothing will be restrained from them, which they have imagined to do.'"

Did you catch that? *Nothing* will be restrained from them which they have imagined to do. Imagination is *powerful.* As Jesus tells us in Mark 9:23, "…If you can believe, all things are possible to him who believes." (NKJV).

Psalm 37:4-5 (NKJV) says, "Delight yourself also in the LORD, And He shall give you the desires of your heart. Commit your way to the LORD, Trust also in Him, And He shall bring it to pass."

We have to learn to see ourselves the way God sees us. If we continue seeing ourselves from the world's perspective, nothing will change for the better, and many things will seem impossible. When God says we are healed, accepted, in His peace, and even prosperous, we have to use our imaginations to see in our mind what that actually looks like in order to receive those things by faith.

Since "… faith is the substance of things hoped for, the evidence of things not seen" (Hebrews 11:1 KJV), we've got to see through our spiritual eyes the promises of God being ours …see our bank accounts full, see ourselves doing all of the things that we hadn't been able to do when we were sick, see ourselves standing in the peace of God in the midst of a storm. The way we see ourselves on the inside will dictate how we respond to God's promises.

It's easy to use our imaginations to see the worst. Allowing vain imagination to run through our minds will keep us from receiving God's promises due to doubt and unbelief. Seeing with natural eyes rather than spiritual ones causes us to remain stagnant in our lives. In his book, *The Power of Imagination*© Andrew Wommack likens the imagination to a spiritual womb. We must plant the seed of the Word in our hearts and minds. Peter 1:23 (NIV) illustrates this, saying "For you have been born again, not of perishable seed, but of imperishable, through the living and enduring word of God." We also must continue to guard over that Word, not allowing doubt or unbelief to affect it. We do this by using our imaginations to continue growing that seed until it comes to maturity and manifests.

Truth 10.1 Application:

Create a "Think on These Things" Binder:

- Brainstorm some specific ways you will use your imagination and add them to your notebook for quick referencing when it's time to do them. Some ideas to get your creative juices flowing:

- Think about *who* you want to be—physically and emotionally, and *why*. This is especially important. We need to see ourselves healed emotionally as well as physically. We need to see ourselves living out our purpose, experiencing the peace and abundant life God desires for us. Consider the qualities you see in others, especially Jesus. How did He handle things? Journal about how you will handle things in the future, and use those notes to create these imaginative experiences.

- Go back to *Your Identity in Christ* and read over who you are. Think about how that new identity in Christ functions. How do you feel now that you have the mind of Christ? How do you respond to situations and people? Imagine it.

- When you need to have a difficult discussion with someone, journal about how you'd like the discussion to go and how you want to feel and respond, rather than react. Speak this out as you picture and imagine how you would like this conversation to look:

  ➤ "I am calm."

  ➤ "_____ hears my concerns and remains calm as well." Thank God while you are imagining the way you remain calm and are able to articulate in a peaceful manner:

  ➤ "Thank You God that _____ hears me."

  ➤ "Thank You God that this meeting is going smoothly."

  ➤ "Thank You God that we are able to work things out well through this discussion," etc.

  ➤ Use your imagination for everything that you want to change about your life.

- Your physical health—see yourself whole and well. What kind of activities are you doing? Who are you with? How do you feel about it? Be descriptive.

- Your emotional health—you remain joyful, calm, and peaceful.

- Your spiritual health—see yourself in a close relationship with Jesus.

- Finances—see and trust that God is providing for all of your needs. You do not lack anything. Maybe you are in need of some kind of provision? Begin imagining and seeing that need being fulfilled.

- Your career or ministry—if you are not currently doing what you feel is your calling, begin asking the Holy Spirit to help you imagine what living out that job or ministry might look like.

- Your relationships—mentally create conversations and imagine the way you want to respond, rather than reacting.

- Bring God into your imaginative times: Do a short devotion in Scripture. Read a chapter in the Bible and journal about it. Create a story in your mind based on stepping into the past with Jesus (as yourself) and imagining that you are part of His group of followers. Pray before these visuals and ask the Holy Spirit to reveal God's character to you so that you may see Him as He is. In this Bible chapter, is He joyful and loving? Can you see joy on His face and hear it in His voice? How does He look at those He is healing? Imagine going for hikes with Jesus. What do you talk about? Take Jesus to the grocery store with you. What foods would He choose? Think about doing art with Jesus. What would He paint? Sculpt? Would those things come to life?

- Imagine sitting out under the stars and singing praises to Papa God with Jesus. Or singing praise songs to Jesus. You can sing praises during all kinds of mental imagination processes.

- Are you hiking in your imagination? Sing a song to the Lord about how beautiful His creation is.

- Are you shopping? Sing to Him about His goodness and provision. (Maybe the other shoppers in this creative mental story will join in?)

- Are you watching Him heal someone? Is that someone you? Sing praises to Him for being your healer.

- In your creative imagination sessions, take time to thank God for what He is doing in your life. If you're visualizing being healed and living your best life, thank Him for that healing.

Thank Him for the answer before you see it. It's His will for you to be well. Thank Him for making that a reality while you imagine this in your mind. 1 John 5:14-15 (NIV) says, "This is the confidence we have in approaching God: that if we ask anything according to his will he hears us. And if we know that he hears us—whatever we ask—we know that we have what we asked of him."

In Mark 11:24 (NIV) we see, "Therefore, I tell you, whatever you ask for in prayer, believe that you have received it, and it will be yours." Thanking God while you are seeing these things happen in your mind invites Him to work, and allows your faith—through the renewing of your mind—to change your circumstances.

Be descriptive in these creative imagination sessions:

➢ Use words to explain what things look like in detail.

➢ How do you want to feel?

➢ Are there smells? Sounds?

➢ Really work up your emotions in a positive way to the point that you feel like this is a very real experience. This is how you write new messages upon your heart and change your beliefs. (Remember, the brain doesn't know the difference between what is real and imaginary. You're training your brain to believe what you are seeing in your imagination to be your truth.)

➢ Imagining positive things and *feeling* them helps your brain create happy neurotransmitters, which are part of your brain chemistry. **D**opamine, **O**xytocin, **S**erotonin, and **E**ndorphins. You're giving yourself a "DOSE" of wellness.

Truth 10.2

The Hebrew word *yetser* (#3336 Strong's Concordance), translated "imagination" or "imaginations", means "to form or conceive in order to give birth." It also means "framework," or something similar to what a potter does with clay when molding and shaping it. We must conceive/form an image of God's truth in our minds in order to see it born as a reality in the natural realm, as well as use our imaginations to build the framework and shape our minds and realities. We must keep our imaginations fixed upon God and His truth rather than allowing our thoughts to be contrary to the Word. We can take thoughts captive to obey Christ when we keep a tight rein on our imaginations. Your imagination is a creative force and a gift from God. Proverbs 29:18 (KJV) says, "Where there is no vision, the people perish …"

Consider the fact that you can't set goals without seeing in your mind what you want the outcome to be. If you want to get an education to become a teacher, you first set that goal by imagining yourself standing in front of a classroom. That's where you first conceptualize the goal which allows you to move forward. Words paint pictures and plant seeds. We can be influenced by the words of the world that plant seeds of fear and discontent which may lead to anxiety or sickness in the body, or we can be influenced by the Word of God that tells us who we are and what our inheritance is which leads to peace and health. 2 Corinthians 10:5 (NIV) tells us that we must "...demolish arguments and every pretension that sets itself up against the knowledge of God, and we take captive every thought to make it obedient to Christ." God not only wants us to use our imaginations to conceive walking in His truth for the future, but also to recall the things He has done for us in the past.

1 Chronicles 29:14-18 (KJV) states, "But who am I, and what is my people, that we should be able to offer so willingly after this sort? for all things come of thee, and of thine own have we given thee … O LORD God of Abraham, Isaac, and of Israel, our fathers, keep this forever in the imagination of the thoughts of the heart of thy people, and prepare their heart unto thee."

In these verses, David was saying, "Lord, don't let the people forget all that You have done for them! Keep it in their imaginations." It's when we forget the things that God has done for us in the past that our imaginations take off and go into doubt and fear. By using our memories to remember what God has done for us, we grow in our faith and trust that He is always for us and continues to have good plans for our lives. (Jeremiah 29:11)

> ➤ Rehearse what He's done for you in your mind.
> ➤ Recount His faithfulness and kindness to you.
> ➤ Ruminate and reflect on verses that reveal how much he loves you.
> ➤ Reiterate what you know to be His truth for you and your life.
> ➤ Remind yourself of the goodness of God.

Reminding ourselves of the goodness of God and the character of God helps us to receive the truths He speaks about us in His Word. When we know that He wants us well, prosperous, at peace, and in a deep and abiding love relationship with Him, we can begin imagining these things. God's character and His will toward us are only good and loving. He only desires good things for us. He loves and adores us and has purchased for us through Christ *all* things that pertain to *life* and *godliness*. (2 Peter 1:3) This includes healing, health, peace, abundance, and prosperity, in that we have every single provision met. We can be in absolute faith, and trust that God has these things for us. When we *believe* this, we receive it. Using our minds to "see" these promises fulfilled helps us to believe.

We can also use our imaginations to change the pictures that were written upon our hearts in the past. We have all experienced negative things at some point. How those things affected us is dependent upon how we experienced them by mixing them with specific emotions. The more negative the emotions, the deeper the wounds were written. The good news is, we can choose to rewrite those memories by imagining they had a different outcome, or by reframing what we experienced and seeing the best in the situation, wherever possible.

When I was a child in grade school, gangs of girls often bullied me. In one instance, I remember being surrounded by a group of girls who took turns hitting me and being verbally abusive toward me. It was a very traumatic event in my life, and it made me fearful and distrusting. As I learned the things I'm sharing with you, I realized it was possible for me to change how I *saw* what had happened and how I remember it. I've created a new memory. I chose to imagine Jesus with me (though at the time I did not realize He had been there, I now realize He was), guarding over me so the girls couldn't touch me. I felt safe and at peace while choosing to see this new picture. That doesn't mean that I don't remember what happened, but I am now able to picture it in a different way in my mind that removes the hurt and helps me to feel safe and loved, rather than wounded and fearful.

One of the most powerful ways the Holy Spirit revealed using my imagination was to begin seeing myself in Bible accounts. I prayed first and asked the Lord to give me a revelation and understanding of His character and love for me and asked if I would be able to see and experience Him in a personal way. I didn't see myself as a character in a Bible story, but I imagined that Jesus took my hand and led me back in time to see firsthand what occurred. I saw myself as part of His group of followers, and He would single me out and share inside information with me based on what was happening. To begin, I would read a paragraph or a short story (the Gospels are the best place to start) and then write things in my own words. Once I did this, I began imagining and verbalizing what I was seeing. I realized that by doing this, I could imagine seeing the expressions on Jesus' face. I could imagine hearing the inflection and love in His voice. I could truly imagine *experiencing* Jesus in a way that simply reading His Word didn't allow me to do.

I've discussed how the brain works in pictures, what the Bible says about using our imaginations for the future and the past, and the fact that God wants us to see and believe Him for the good things He's promised us. Now I want to give you some ideas for using your imagination in order to change your present circumstances—in order to *see* yourself well and living the abundant life

God has for you. In the application part of this section I will give you the how-to instructions on using your imagination in the ways I've discussed.

Truth 10.2 Application:

1. Other ways to use Scripture in conjunction with your imagination: For example, look closely at Psalm 23 (NASB). I love picturing this entire psalm and considering how I can apply each verse to my life. I've given a few suggestions of how you might envision these things, but don't limit yourself to what I've shared:

1. The LORD is my shepherd.

What does it mean to you that Jesus is your Shepherd? How might you imagine this?
I shall not be in need.
God provides everything that you need. Is there an area that you need for Him to supply? Begin imagining His provision.

2 He lets me lie down in green pastures.

Imagine lying under a tree in the warm grass in the middle of summer with Jesus guarding over you. His peace is yours.

2b He leads me beside quiet waters.

You might imagine sitting on a beach next to a lake with Jesus—calm, joyful, and relaxed.

3 He restores my soul.

Jesus gives you His peace and removes all of the emotional trauma and pain you've ever experienced. You feel peaceful and light.

3b He guides me in the paths of righteousness for the sake of His name.

Maybe you see yourself walking a road or hiking a beautiful trail with Jesus as you enjoy His company. He is changing and transforming every area of your life.

4 Even though I walk through the valley of the shadow of death, I fear no evil, for You are with me; Your rod and Your staff, they comfort me.

Consider whatever trial you might be going through right now. How might you see Jesus changing circumstances and working them out for your good? He is giving you the wisdom and guidance you need.

5 You prepare a table before me in the presence of my enemies.

What might be on a table that Jesus prepares for you? What kinds of blessings would be included that your enemies would see? Jesus is showing off how He is providing for you.

5b You have anointed my head with oil; My cup overflows.

You are the Lord's special guest. He anoints your head and gives you a place of honor. Your cup of blessings never runs dry. Similar to "I shall not want," this verse echoes that in God's blessings and supply for us, there is never any lack. Again, what is an area in your life in which you need His abundance to overtake you? What might that look like?

6 Certainly goodness and faithfulness will follow me all the days of my life;
All of the goodness God has for you chases after you. You don't even need to go looking for it. God's provision and goodness comes upon you and overtakes you. What does this look like when you see it in your mind?

6b and my dwelling will be in the house of the LORD forever.
What does your mind see when you try to imagine the splendor and beauty of heaven? You get to live with God.

OK, friends, let's start imagining our amazing futures with Jesus!

Chapter 11

YOUR RELATIONSHIP TOGETHER:

The Truth About Worship, Praise,

and Gratitude: By Beholding We Become

———— ⊱ ⟨⟨⟨⟩⟩⟩ ⊰ ————

H ave you ever noticed that the longer a couple is together the more similar they become? This is also true of many close friends. They pick up some of each other's mannerisms and behaviors. They might even begin using the same phrases. This happens because we become like those we spend time with. Consider children who admire role models. The closer they watch their role model, the more they begin to emulate and mimic them. How many of us have said we'd never become like our parents, yet due to the environment in which we were raised and the behaviors we saw modeled, (even when we didn't want to emulate those behaviors), we've done so. Something as simple as growing up in a certain region where everyone has a similar accent can cause us to speak with that accent even when we aren't aware of it happening. It's part of our design—by beholding, we become.

Truth 11.1

Worship is a form of beholding and being transformed. When we choose to worship God, we are changed and become like Him. 2 Corinthians 3:18 (AMP) says, "And we all, with unveiled face, continually seeing as in a mirror the glory of the Lord, are progressively being transformed into His image from [one degree of] glory to [even more] glory, which comes from the Lord, [who is] the Spirit." As we behold Him, we are transformed into His likeness. Worship can change us into His likeness, though we must also be in the Word so we can renew our minds to who He says we are. It's also a way that we experience intimacy with the Father. I would compare prayer and praise as part of our relationship with the Lord to a date between a husband and wife. They sit at a candle-lit dinner and share their hearts with each other, expressing their love and gratitude for one another. But worship is where we go into an even deeper form of intimacy in which we enjoy God and He enjoys us. Author Kristi Winkler explains that "Praise is opening up, worship is entering in. Praise is boldly declaring, worship is humbly bowing in the presence of a Holy God. Praise applauds what God has done, worship is honoring God for who He is."[52] We can praise anyone for anything, but our worship belongs solely to God. Our English word "worship" comes from two old English words: *weorth*, which means "worth," and *scipe* (ship), which means "quality" or "condition." So, "worth-ship" is the quality of having worth. By worshiping God, Winkler continues, "we are ascribing worth to Him and proclaiming that He alone is worthy."[53]

There really is no one else who is worthy of our worship. Paraphrasing Winker, intimacy through our worship is not head knowledge, but an expression and experience of the heart. We experience Him through understanding, sharing, and belonging. Worship is immersing ourselves in Him. We immerse ourselves in His Presence, but we do so in deep reverence. He is holy, pure, perfect, immaculate, and complete. He is unlike any being that He has created. Worship is a way that we honor and glorify the Lord because of these traits.

We express our gratitude, love Him, and bless Him, similarly to the way we bless others with words of appreciation or the way we express love and adoration to a spouse, but when we worship, we hold God in highest esteem

---

[52] https://www.sharefaith.com/blog/2013/11/worship-praise-difference/
[53] op cit

above all else. In worshiping God, we magnify Him. To magnify means that we make Him greater than anyone or anything else in our hearts.

Worship doesn't have to be limited to singing songs in church, though corporate worship with the family of God is something we should not neglect, as Hebrews 10:25 tells us.

In the Old Testament, the word, "worship" in the Hebrew is *shachah* (Strong's #7812). It means to bow ourselves down, to do or give homage (having reverence and paying respect), to prostrate oneself, and obeisance (submitting to authority in obedience.) Using the definition of worship that we find in the American Dictionary of the English Language, when we worship God we are ascribing:

> Excellence of character; dignity; worth; worthiness…Chiefly and eminently, the act of paying divine honors to the Supreme Being; or the reverence and homage paid to him in religious exercises, consisting in adoration, confession, prayer, thanksgiving and the like…To adore; to reverence with supreme respect and veneration. To honor with extravagant love and extreme submission; as a lover. To perform acts of adoration…[54]

In the New Testament, Paul enlarges our understanding of worship by showing us our relationship with the Lord is not simply about going to the temple to worship Him. Our relationship with Him has changed, because now *we* are the temple of the Holy Spirit. That changes everything. In Romans 12:1 (ESV), Paul tells us, "I appeal to you therefore, brothers, by the mercies of God, to present your bodies as a living sacrifice, holy and acceptable to God, which is your spiritual worship." Paul says in 1 Corinthians 10:31 (NIV) "So, whether you eat or drink, or whatever you do, do all for the glory of God." And in Colossians 3, verses 17 and 23 (ESV) he adds, "And whatever you do, in word or deed, do everything in the name of the Lord Jesus, giving thanks to God the Father through him … Whatever you do, work heartily, as for the Lord and not for men …"

Paul is telling us that worship is not limited to church services, praise songs, or prayer. Because we are now the temple of the Holy Spirit, everything we do should be a form of worship. Everything we do should be done to honor and glorify the Lord.

I want to speak a bit about another act of worship that many may not have considered as worship. Our worship should include every part of our lifestyles. It should include giving Him our time, energy, abilities, and resources. Worship

---

[54] https://webstersdictionary1828.com/Dictionary/worship

may also include tithing or giving Him monetary gifts. For example, we read in 2 Corinthians 9:6-15 (ESV):

> ….whoever sows sparingly will also reap sparingly, and whoever sows bountifully will also reap bountifully. Each one must give as he has decided in his heart, not reluctantly or under compulsion, for God loves a cheerful giver. And God is able to make all grace abound to you, so that having all sufficiency in all things at all times, you may abound in every good work. As it is written, 'He has distributed freely, he has given to the poor; his righteousness endures forever.' He who supplies seed to the sower and bread for food will supply and multiply your seed for sowing and increase the harvest of your righteousness. You will be enriched in every way to be generous in every way, which through us will produce thanksgiving to God. For the ministry of this service is not only supplying the needs of the saints but is also overflowing in many thanksgivings to God. By their approval of this service, they will glorify God because of your submission that comes from your confession of the gospel of Christ, and the generosity of your contribution for them and for all others, while they long for you and pray for you, because of the surpassing grace of God upon you. Thanks be to God for his inexpressible gift!

Giving to others for the sake of God's Kingdom is an act of worship on our part, and it's something that God calls us to do. He wants us to be like Him—to behave like His children. He is selflessness; He is love; He is compassion. Here's the beautiful thing about God and His Kingdom. Giving, with God, is like a never-ending cycle. It's like a river that never runs dry. The more we give, the more we receive. That's the principle of sowing and reaping. It's an important part of our relationship with Him.

Truth 11.1 Application:

Carve out some time to just sit and worship God. If you aren't sure where to begin, watch one of Pastor Chris Garcia's YouTube videos:
https://www.fathersglory.org/
https://www.youtube.com/live/rI3bONsqyOE

Truth 11.2

Praise and Gratitude

Psalm 100:4 tells us, "Enter his gates with thanksgiving, and his courts with praise! Give thanks to him; bless his name!" Webster's 1828 Dictionary says this about praise: "...commendation bestowed on a person for his personal virtues or worthy actions, on meritorious actions themselves, or on anything valuable..."[55] Praise applies to what someone has done rather than to who they are. So when we praise God, we are giving Him glory and honor for His actions. Praise is like saying, "Wow, God! I am amazed at what You have done!" While worship might be more like, "Wow, God, I am amazed at who You are!" Both are important in our relationship with Him.

Praising God can be a weapon against the enemy, but we shouldn't only think of it as a tool. Praise is an act of love on our part toward the Lord that deepens our relationship with Him and blesses Him. However, let's look at how praise and gratitude can change our circumstances for the better, because praise invites the Lord into those areas of our lives. Psalm 22:3 (KJV) tells us, "But thou art holy, O thou that inhabitest the praises of Israel." God inhabits the praises of His people. Let's think about that. God inhabiting our praises means that He occupies and is present in, or dwells in, our praises. What a powerful promise. It's no wonder that things change when we praise Him.

There are several incredible accounts of God stepping in because of the praises of His people.

The Old Testament shares the occurrence of a city coming to its ruin after the children of Israel marched around it six times, and on the seventh time, shouting! We find this story in Joshua chapters 5 and 6 (NIV) . While I don't know the exact words they shouted, I do know they did so out of obedience, and in this they glorified God and gave Him credit. This is what ultimately caused the walls of Jericho to fall. **(10)** But Joshua had commanded the army, "Do not give a war cry, do not raise your voices, do not say a word until the day I tell you to shout. Then shout!" ... **(20)** When the trumpets sounded, the army shouted, and at the sound of the trumpet, when the men gave a loud shout, the wall collapsed; so everyone charged straight in, and they took the city." Isn't it easy to imagine they shouted words of praise to God? Another example is found in Acts chapter 16. After being stripped and beaten with wooden rods, Paul and

---

[55] https://webstersdictionary1828.com/Dictionary/praise

Silas are sitting in their prison cell praising God and singing hymns. While they are doing this, a truly miraculous event happens—an earthquake—the prison doors begin to open, and the prisoners' shackles are undone.

Praise works that way—it tears down the walls of opposition. It opens doors for us and releases us from the shackles and chains of the enemy. Praise sets us free. I began learning in my healing journey that praise could truly change my circumstances. I learned to praise God when I needed help overcoming symptoms, fear, financial issues, and even relationship difficulties. Instead of saying negative things over these issues and complaining, I began to learn that praising God for what I wanted to have happen (like overcoming a headache) could change what I was experiencing. I also learned to see trials as opportunities for God to come through for me, instead of always expecting the worst.

James 1:2-4 (ESV) tells us, "Count it all joy, my brothers, when you meet trials of various kinds, for you know that the testing of your faith produces steadfastness. And let steadfastness have its full effect, that you may be perfect and complete, lacking in nothing." I remember the first time I decided to test this verse. My husband and I were camping in the Utah desert and I had just gone to use an outhouse. When I went to open the door, I realized this big metal latch was stuck. I tried to open it for about ten minutes and started to panic. The Holy Spirit then reminded me to "count it all joy." So... I said out loud, "Oh, joy!" and started laughing. Immediately, I checked the latch and the door opened. Now that may sound like a silly example, but it worked. Looking back, I imagine that my guardian angel (Psalm 91:11-12) heard me speaking God's language of praise and moved the latch for me.

Let's Talk About Gratitude

Gratitude and thankfulness fill us with hope and joy, while focusing on lack, what is distasteful and complaining about what we don't have or how awful things are can attract more of the same. Gratitude and thankfulness have the opposite effect. Gratitude reminds us that God is always faithful, and has never and will never let us down. An attitude of gratitude and thankfulness on our part brings us peace. Colossians 3:15 and 17 instructs us, "And let the peace of Christ rule in your hearts, to which indeed you were called in one body. And be thankful ... And whatever you do, in word or deed, do everything in the name of the Lord Jesus, giving thanks to God the Father through him." (ESV)

Worship, praise, gratitude, and thankfulness shouldn't be things that we do in order to get God to move on our behalf. They should naturally spring from a relationship with Him. A heart that is in love with Him will desire to communicate these things to Him. Just as we shower affection on our family members we love, even more should we shower our Heavenly Father with affection through worship, praise, and thankfulness. I don't tell those in my family that I love them in order to get things from them; I tell them in order to let them know I value them. We don't worship in order to endear ourselves to God, to earn His favor or to receive blessings, but because we're in a love relationship with Him. God created us for relationship. He created us to commune with Him. We exist because He desired to share His love with us. Worship, gratitude, and praise enrich that relationship. Worship, gratitude, and praise are part of how we show our love to Him; when we speak to Him lovingly—and God is Love—the floodgates of heaven open and blessings pour out in such abundance that we don't have enough room to receive them all at once. Matthew 6:33 (BSB) says, "But seek first the kingdom of God and His righteousness, and all these things shall be added unto you."

I'm not just talking about financial blessings. God owns everything. He doesn't need our money. He longs to bless us and provide for us. When we express our love, praise, gratitude, and worship Him through faith, we open ourselves to receive *all* He has to give. When we speak in faith, it allows Him to bless us in the areas of our need and the ways He desires. My challenge for you today is: How might you begin changing your life so everything you do can become acts of worship? Do you have an attitude of gratitude? Are you speaking God's language of faith?

Truth 11.2 Application:

For a deeper study on the power of praise, read: 2 Chronicles 20:1-24; Joshua 5:13-6:27; Acts 16:16-34

1. Begin by keeping a journal where you write down at least 10 of the things for which you are most grateful. I've heard the statement, "If on Tuesday you only received the things you were grateful for on Monday, what would you have?" Gratitude is important for a number of reasons—it tells your brain that there were positive things that happened during the day. It helps you sleep and also reminds your brain to look for positive things the following day.

2. Use the rest of the list for other thanksgiving. For example, if you had only two wins for the day, you would fill in eight other things you were grateful for during that day. These things could be as simple as, "I'm grateful that the sky was blue and sunny today

because I got natural vitamin D," or "I'm grateful for my dishwasher because I don't have to wash dishes by hand."

Chapter 12

YOUR RELATIONSHIP TOGETHER:

The Truth About Forgiveness

Truth 12.1

Forgiving Others

L et's start by defining what forgiveness *is* and what forgiveness is *not*:

- Forgiveness is (and does):
  - o   peace when you learn to release the offense
  - o   for you and not the offender
  - o   taking back your power
  - o   taking responsibility for how you feel
  - o   about your healing
  - o   help you get control over your feelings

- o improve your mental and physical health
- o free you from being a victim
- o a choice
- o something everyone can learn to do
- Forgiveness is not:
  - o condoning unkindness
  - o forgetting that something painful happened
  - o excusing poor behavior
  - o denying or minimizing that you were hurt
- Forgiveness does not mean
  - o you have to be reconciled to the offender
  - o you have to give up having feelings
  - o condoning lying

Most of us have probably heard some version of the quote: "Resentment is like drinking poison and waiting for the other person to die"[56] from St. Augustine. While we may have shrugged that off, there's actually scientific proof to back this up. Let's take a look at what happens in the brain and body when we choose to remain in unforgiveness, bitterness, and resentment toward others, God, or even ourselves.

When someone hurts us, it sends the brain into survival (fight /flight/freeze) mode. The limbic system, specifically the amygdala, is activated, which leads to a series of biochemical processes in the brain and body. The adrenal glands release the stress hormone cortisol into our bodies, and the brain releases neurotransmitters into the brain. This then activates the sympathetic nervous system. When this system is activated, among other things, our attention gets highly focused on survival—our digestive system stops, our pupils dilate, our saliva glands slow, our blood pressure and heart rate increase, and our muscles tense to get ready for action.

The problem with unforgiveness is that it can keep our bodies and brains in this state of high alertness. According to Pastor Charles Stone, who holds a master's degree in the area of neuroscience, this leads to the following unhealthy physical and emotional results:[57]

- *"Rumination:* we nurse and rehearse the hurt, which reinforces our negative emotions and burns the event and pain even deeper into

---

[56] https://www.socratic-method.com/quote-meanings/saint-augustine-resentment-is-like-drinking-poison-and-waiting-for-the-other-person-to-die

[57] https://charlesstone.com/what-unforgiveness-does-to-your-brain/

our neural pathways. When we're not focused on a task, our inner self-talk will often default to rehearsing the painful situation."

- *"Diminished memory:* when we remain stressed for long periods of time (i.e., refusing to forgive), cortisol actually causes our brain to atrophy, especially our memory center called the hippocampus."
- *"Amplified negative emotions:* prolonged stress also amplifies our amygdala's sensitivity, making us even more susceptible to further hurt and pain."
- *"Schadenfreude:* this concept describes the secret pleasure we feel when we see those who have hurt us experience misfortune themselves. It causes our brains to produce the pleasure neurotransmitter dopamine. It actually feels good to see bad things happen to those we don't forgive. It's the opposite of praying for your enemies, which Jesus commanded us to do."

Another effect of unforgiveness is the power of entanglement. Dr. Caroline Leaf, a communication pathologist and neuroscientist shares in her video *On FORGIVENESS and How it Affects Our Bodies*:

Whenever two particles (or people) are in a relationship together, no matter how geographically far apart they are, they still influence each other. When we're in a toxic mindset, we are generating toxic energy that damages ourselves and others, but when we choose to forgive, sever that entanglement which enables us to heal. We can't heal as long as we choose to remain in a bitter state toward another person, because the toxic connection remains. When we stay in unforgiveness, we remain connected to the source of pain. Similar to charging your phone and keeping it on the charger, you continue recharging the negative energy.[58]

Holding on to toxicity means that you hold on to toxic stress. Being unforgiving constricts the blood vessels around the heart, which makes one much more susceptible to heart attack or stroke. It also reduces the amount of oxygen to the brain. I've shared Mark 11:22-25 previously in this program, but because it sheds even more light on the necessity of forgiveness I'd like for us to look at it again:

And Jesus answered them, 'Have faith in God. Truly, I say to you, whoever says to this mountain, "Be taken up and thrown into the sea," and does not doubt in his heart, but believes that what he says will come to pass, it will be done for him. Therefore I tell you, whatever

[58] https://youtu.be/EzR4H4oJbAc?si=OvzzyZW3taoXUwJR

you ask in prayer, believe that you have received it, and it will be yours. And whenever you stand praying, forgive, if you have anything against anyone, so that your Father also who is in heaven may forgive you your trespasses.' (ESV)

It's interesting that there seems to be a qualification here for having our prayers heard. Harboring unforgiveness in our hearts can block our prayers from being answered. According to Pastor Stone, unforgiveness can also hinder our healing because it keeps our brains creating unhealthy neurotransmitters that wreak havoc on our bodies. Unforgiveness is truly destructive for us physically, emotionally, and spiritually.

Truth 12.1 Application:

Listen to the visualization of "Hurts Done to Us" which was a vision Papa God gave to me in 2023:
https://drive.google.com/file/d/1yX6PmVd4uTPGTMWzRBHKCSRzEZP HM5tO/view?usp=drive_link

Pray about how this visualization is applicable to you, and write your thoughts in the form of a prayer to God, including any confessions and repentance that the Holy Spirit impresses on you:

_____

_____

_____

_____

_____

_____

_____

_____

_____

_____

_____

_____

_____

_____

Truth 12.2

God's Forgiveness Toward Us

I want to affirm that when it comes to God's forgiveness of us, we have nothing to fear. Once we have received Christ as our Savior, we have been completely reconciled to God. 2 Corinthians 5:17-21 (NKJV) states:

> Therefore, if anyone is in Christ, he is a new creation. The old has passed away; behold, the new has come. All this is from God, who through Christ reconciled us to himself and gave us the ministry of reconciliation; that is, in Christ God was reconciling the world to himself, not counting their trespasses against them, and entrusting to us the message of reconciliation. Therefore, we are ambassadors for Christ, God making his appeal through us. We implore you on behalf of Christ, be reconciled to God. For our sake he made him to be sin who knew no sin, so that in him we might become the righteousness of God.

Romans 6:6-11(NKJV) tells us:

> We know that our old self was crucified with him in order that the body of sin might be brought to nothing, so that we would no longer be enslaved to sin. For one who has died has been set free from sin. Now if we have died with Christ, we believe that we will also live with him. We know that Christ, being raised from the dead, will never die again; death no longer has dominion over him. For the death he died he died to sin, once for all, but the life he lives he lives to God. So you also must consider yourselves dead to sin and alive to God in Christ Jesus.

If you have accepted Jesus as your Savior and have received the gift of salvation, your sins are forgiven. You don't need to beg and plead with God to forgive you, because Jesus already took those sins upon Himself. Hebrews 9:25-26 (ESV) says, "Nor was it to offer himself repeatedly, as the high priest enters the holy places every year with blood not his own, for then he would have had to suffer repeatedly since the foundation of the world. But as it is, he has appeared once for all at the end of the ages to put away sin by the sacrifice of himself." Jesus' sacrifice covered every sin—from our very first parents who lived in the Garden of Eden until Jesus' return. We only need to receive what

He's done for us. When we understand the depth of the forgiveness God has toward us, it becomes easier to forgive others for the things they've done to us.

The biggest problem with what many churches teach today is that we must beg God to forgive us. When we don't believe we've been forgiven, it's difficult to forgive others.

In Matthew 18:21-35, we find the parable of the unforgiving servant. Just before Jesus gives this parable, Peter asks the question: "Lord, how often will my brother sin against me, and I forgive him? As many as seven times?" Jesus said to him, "I do not say to you seven times, but seventy- times seven times." Peter thought he was being generous. Jesus basically says: don't stop forgiving. There's no limit to how many times you may need to forgive your brother.

Heart Forgiveness—for Ourselves and Others

So the question becomes, how do we forgive from our hearts? True godly forgiveness has three parts:

1. Coming to an understanding of God's nature and love toward us;
2. Beginning to see ourselves through our new identity in Christ, in which we are able to love, value, and forgive ourselves, and
3. Allowing us to love and forgive others through the power of God.

True forgiveness of self and others is possible only when we know and believe the true character of God. Remember, God is Love. Let's consider the reality that the love of God is something each of us needs to cultivate in our hearts. We simply cannot neglect this just because we think we already know it. Knowing something in your mind doesn't mean that you know and accept it in your heart. Many of us who grew up attending church may think we know the love of God, but we still haven't come to accept His love in the depths of our souls. This comes through reading the promises in His Word, meditating on them, and saying them out loud. God has to come alive for us. For most of us, many of the verses on the love of God, such as John 3:16, have been repeated so many times that they've lost their meaning for us. We've become numb to the power of the Cross and the gifts our Father has bestowed upon us. They've simply become words.

I encourage you to spend time really meditating on the meaning of all Christ has done for you; meditate on specific verses that speak of the love God has for His children—for you. Consider that God the Father gave Jesus to die for us, for our salvation. It wasn't just Jesus' sacrifice—it was also the *Father's sacrifice*—for you. Then visualize God revealing His love for you. See yourself as the object of Jesus' attention and love in a Bible account. Ephesians 3:17-19 (NIV) says: ...so that Christ may dwell in your hearts through faith. And I pray

Caprice Scott

that you, being rooted and established in love, may have power, together with all the Lord's holy people, to grasp how wide and long and high and deep is the love of Christ, and to know this love that surpasses knowledge—that you may be filled to the measure of all the fullness of God" When we begin seeing ourselves through our new identity in Christ, we are better able to love, value, and forgive ourselves. Self-forgiveness is easier after realizing the love God has for us. If God loves and forgives us, then surely we are valuable to Him. Because we are valuable to Him we've been made into completely new creations in Christ, and all our sins are forgiven, we begin to see ourselves as different. If we're new creations, this means we aren't the same people we had been when we committed those sins. When you are in Christ, you should see yourself as a completely new person. The old self, who had done things that you may be ashamed of, is now dead and was buried with Jesus. All those sins died on the cross. You are a new creation. God doesn't remember them so why should you? As Hebrews 8:12 (NIV) states 'For I will forgive their wickedness and will remember their sins no more"

Lamentations 3:22-23 (ESV) says, "The steadfast love of the Lord never ceases; his mercies never come to an end; they are new every morning; great is your faithfulness." You get to start over with a clean slate each day. That means yesterday and the past are gone. You are not the person you were yesterday or one year ago, 10 years ago. You're a new creation. 2 Corinthians 5:17 (ESV) says, "Therefore, if anyone is in Christ, he is a new creation. The old has passed away; behold, the new has come." Because you're a new creation in Christ, you don't need to remain angry or bitter with yourself. You've changed. That doesn't mean, however, that you may not need to deal with some of the consequences of past behaviors, but you don't need to hold on to negative feelings toward yourself.

Say the truths of who you are in Christ. This includes finding Bible promises that reveal your new identity. Read them, study them, meditate on them, and see yourself as that person.

Truth 12.2 Application:

Listen to the visualization "Holding Onto Hurts":
https://drive.google.com/file/d/1_flMMZOcQjLxu5GzgbCTxlvdBCdNpkOs/view?usp=drive_link

179

Pray about how this visualization is applicable to you and write your thoughts in the form of a prayer to God, including any confessions and repentance that the Holy Spirit impresses on you:

_____

_____

_____

_____

_____

_____

_____

_____

_____

_____

_____

_____

Truth 12.3

Releasing Resentment and Bitterness

I want to share several keys regarding forgiveness that can help you release the resentment you may still have toward an offender. Let's take a look at Philemon 1:18-19 (ESV) as two powerful verses on forgiveness: "If he has wronged you at all, or owes you anything, charge that to my account. I, Paul, write this with my own hand: I will repay it—to say nothing of your owing me even your own self." Although this is Paul speaking, we can hear this as Jesus speaking to us. Jesus wants us to understand that ALL manner of sin has been forgiven through His death upon the cross, not just *our* sins. We are to charge to His account anything that anyone else has done to us. Any sins that were committed against us went to the cross. Jesus paid the price for the sins of others just as much as He paid the price for our own sins. Consider looking at the cross and seeing the sins that were committed against you nailed to the cross. Those sins—no matter how heinous—were put upon Jesus; He paid the price. Those sins committed against you hung upon that cross in Christ. Why would we choose to hold on to that? What kind of effect do you think that might have?

The next thing we need to do to forgive is humble ourselves. Humility doesn't mean we have to get on our faces and grovel. Humility before the Lord can also be synonymous with repentance. Again, we often misunderstand what true repentance is. Repentance is not begging God to forgive us. Repentance means we agree with God. In this case, we surrender our right to be right, our right to hold on to offense, etc., and agree with God that Christ has covered the sins of our offenders.

When Jesus died, all that anyone else had done to hurt us went to the cross. All those horrible sins were PAID for. We also know that God says He is our vindicator. He not only paid for those sins through the body of Christ, but He will repay us and our offender. The seeds that we sow we also reap—good or bad. We can choose to sow forgiveness and reap forgiveness from God and others, or we can choose to sow bitterness and resentment and reap those consequences, often in our bodies. As I shared previously, 2 Corinthians 5:17 says, "Therefore, if anyone is in Christ, he is a new creation. The old has passed away; behold, the new has come."

Whatever the offender did to you, s/he did to the OLD you. That person has passed away. You don't need to hold on to any of that because it wasn't even done to *you*! As Paul reminds us, we must choose to die to self and live for Christ. If Jesus lives in you, you get to choose to live for Him rather than to live to that old person you no longer need to be.

The final point comes from Ephesians 6:10-20 (NIV):

> Finally, be strong in the Lord and in his mighty power. Put on the full armor of God, so that you can take your stand against the devil's schemes. For our struggle is not against flesh and blood, but against the rulers, against the authorities, against the powers of this dark world and against the spiritual forces of evil in the heavenly realms. Therefore put on the full armor of God, so that when the day of evil comes, you may be able to stand your ground, and after you have done everything, to stand. Stand firm then, with the belt of truth buckled around your waist, with the breastplate of righteousness in place, and with your feet fitted with the readiness that comes from the gospel of peace. In addition to all this, take up the shield of faith, with which you can extinguish all the flaming arrows of the evil one. Take the helmet of salvation and the sword of the Spirit, which is the word of God. And pray in the Spirit on all occasions with all kinds of prayers and requests. With this in mind, be alert and always keep on praying for all the Lord's people. Pray also for me, that whenever I speak, words may be given me so that I will fearlessly make known the mystery of the gospel, for which I am an ambassador in chains. Pray that I may declare it fearlessly, as I should.

I'd like to draw special attention to verse 12 which says "For we do not wrestle against flesh and blood, but against the rulers, against the authorities, against the cosmic powers over this present darkness, against the spiritual forces of evil in the heavenly places."

Understanding that our battle isn't with people but with the enemy can be a major key in forgiveness. It's possible to love the one who hurt us without liking or approving of what they did—to separate the sin from the sinner.

Near the end of 2023, the Holy Spirit gave me two visions that illustrate several reasons we must forgive others. In the first vision, as I was praying about forgiveness, I was reminded of Philemon 18-19 that God had given me previously. I then saw Jesus standing before me. Jesus had His back turned to me as if He were guarding me. In one particular instance, all of the things that someone had done to hurt me were hitting *Him*; all the pain hit Him, and hit Him hard. Every blow Jesus received was either a word or action that had negatively affected me. Now I had a choice whether to allow all of it to hit me as well, or to allow Him to filter out the pain, fear, and all of the consequences of what they had done to me as those blows were hitting Him. When all of these incidents were filtered through Him—while He received them all, the filtering process changed what they had done into blessings. Yet indeed, He received all the pain. He received every blow, every offense, every word. He turned around to look at me, and I saw He had a gaping wound in His face under His right eye on His cheek. He was wearing the wound they caused me. They did this to JESUS.

The Holy Spirit said (Matthew 25:45 ESV) to my heart, "Then he will answer them, saying, 'Truly, I say to you, as you did not do it to one of the least of these, you did not do it to me.'" He told me that the opposite is also true— what others have done to me, they have also done to Him. (More about this shortly.) John 17:23 tells us that we are in union with Jesus. John 15:4-5 explains this union as a vine and branches. What affects us as well as other believers directly affects Jesus. Psalm 33:20-22 explains that God is our shield. We can allow Him to shield us, or we can step out of His safety. The choice is ours. In this vision, I had the choice either to allow Jesus to receive each blow and let it be filtered before it reached me, or I could also receive the pain after He had already received it Himself. Jesus received the wounds regardless, but I got to choose how those wounds would affect me—either Jesus and I *both* receiving the pain, or Jesus receiving the pain and filtering it so that when all of the blows reached me, they were blessings. They were filtered through Him for my good.

Immediately after this vision, I experienced a second vision in which I saw the body of Christ as the Church. The body was made up of glowing energy.

The energy was a mixture of blue and green turquoise in the form of a physical body, but with many flickering lights. I asked the Lord why it was so important for us to forgive others in the body of Christ when they had hurt us. He revealed that His church body would always have some kind of sickness if we didn't forgive. He reminded me that "a house divided cannot stand." (Matthew 12:25) Anything that is not love between us is a sickness in His body. He revealed to me a yellow/orange flicker that turned red in the body and was spreading like cancer. When we don't forgive ourselves or others, it poisons His body, and we are all part of the same body. We are entangled and connected. Once again, when we hurt one another, it affects Him directly because we are part of Him, but it also harms the entire body. I had a much clearer understanding of the body of Christ as a living organism. It is a spiritual organism, but no less an organism than our own physical bodies.

The Lord revealed to me that as Hebrews 8:12 says He remembers our sins (and the sins of others) no more. (my paraphrase.) If God doesn't remember them, why should we? He chooses to forget our sins because they were placed upon Jesus. God changed the memories that He had of our sins by seeing them all punished and forgiven through Christ's sacrifice. We are one with the Lord. If we choose to hang on to bitterness and unforgiveness, we who are united with the Lord remind Him of our own faults and the faults of others, when He has already chosen to forget. We are doing a disservice to the Lord and His body, not to mention ourselves, when we refuse to release the hurts we've experienced or even the hurts we have caused others. We must forgive ourselves as well. Jesus already knows what we've done, but we need to speak with Him about it when we've hurt another – admitting to Him what we've done. When we've sinned, we need to confess. Confessing leads to our own healing and restoration to others, ourselves and to God. (1 John 1:9; James 5:16) The enemy cannot hold us in bondage when we take responsibility for the things we've done wrong and bring them into the light. It's through the light that we are cleansed and set free and the wrongs done lose their power over us.

While we are on this subject, we need to consider that what we have done to others, we have also done to Jesus. This is sobering when we realize the negative thoughts we've had toward others, words we have spoken about those who have upset or hurt us, or actions we have taken against them. I wonder how many things would be done differently and how many words would never be spoken out loud against another, if—as believers— we considered our words were being spoken *to Jesus*. Do we truly want to harm others who are created in the image of God? Have we considered that our words against others devalue those that God adores so much that His Son died for them?

Forgiveness is so important that Christ not only modeled it for us, He died for it. One might ask, how do we know that we've truly forgiven someone? First Peter 4:8 (ESV) tells us, "Above all, keep loving one another earnestly, since love covers a multitude of sins." The love of God in our hearts doesn't want to expose how someone has hurt us. It wants to cover them, to protect them from hurt. I realize that's very difficult to accept. We would be lying if we said it's something we can do on our own. God's love through us can do this. When we choose to truly forgive our offenders, God changes our hearts, and we no longer want vengeance. Once we understand that true heart forgiveness towards those who have wronged us, God gives us a heart change that reflects His love for them. Our part is to be willing. Luke 6:28 (ESV) gives us a final tool to use in our ability to forgive: "... bless those who curse you, pray for those who abuse you."

In praying for others, we invite the Holy Spirit to work in their lives, and then He is also able to work on our hearts. It's almost impossible to hate someone you are praying for—that's because the miraculous power of God changes everything when we're willing. And finally, take back your power. As I mentioned regarding the power of entanglement, the effects of unforgiveness continue to entangle us in the negative energy of the offender. Choosing to forgive allows us to take back our power. Don't allow unforgiveness to have any root in your heart. Doing so gives your power away to the offender and allows them to continue hurting you. Nail what they did to the cross of Christ and walk away into freedom.

Truth 12.3 Application:

Steps to Forgiveness

Start by making a list of all of the people you need to forgive, including yourself. Did you blame yourself? Parents? Anyone that should have protected you? Next to each name write—emotions and circumstances—be specific.

- Write a letter to each person you need to forgive. These letters can help you work through your memories and emotions. *You will not send any letters.*
- Write a letter to yourself from God saying how much He loves you; He never abandoned you; He never wanted you to experience trauma, abuse or sickness from these circumstances.
- Do a visualization of/with each person who offended or hurt you.

- Imagine a safe place (maybe a room in a church with many windows or an open place outside), a place where you feel safe to be with the person you need to forgive.
- There are two chairs next to each other—one for you, and one for the offender.
- Tell the offender all the things you wrote about them and how that affected any areas of your life—be specific (e.g., "Because it happened in the dark, I've been afraid of the dark, and it's affected my ability to sleep well.")
- Tell the offender that you forgive them.
- Forgiveness does *not* mean you forget or excuse the wrongdoing. Forgiveness is to free the person doing the forgiving from bitterness, resentment, hatred, fear, and other negative feelings.
- Tell the offender that you recognize that someone hurt them in their past and they dealt with it by hurting you in return.
- See yourself kneeling at the offender's feet and, one foot at a time, washing the foot in a basin and then drying the foot with a towel.
- Take the dirty water that you can imagine is filled with whatever the offenses were and pour that water down the drain to symbolize forgiveness, letting go of all of the negative feelings you have and all of the awful things that were done to you.
- See the offender as a broken child, fragile, and take their hands in yours. Pray and ask God to forgive them for all that they did and express to God that you forgive them.
- Feel a huge weight being lifted both physically and emotionally as you hand the offender over to God, and you now walk in freedom.

The 4 R's of Self-Forgiveness

Responsibility: The first step toward forgiving yourself is taking personal responsibility. This is probably the hardest step, because most of us want to rationalize, make excuses, and justify our actions in order to make them acceptable. Taking responsibility for anything is a difficult step, but it's also the most freeing. Once you decide to take responsibility and ownership of whatever you have done—accepting what happened, whatever consequences might have come with your actions/decisions—then you need to show yourself compassion. When we take responsibility and accept what we've done that may have hurt others, we can avoid things such as regret, guilt, and shame. Forgiving self requires us to confront those actions and behaviors, showing remorse for them, but allows us to be honest with ourselves and others. It helps to "clean the wound."

Look at yourself as you would a friend or family member. Don't beat yourself up over and over but approach everything with a great deal of self-compassion. Show yourself kindness as you would a loved one.

Remorse: Having remorse and admitting guilt imply that you are a good person who did something wrong. Shame makes you see yourself as a person who is wrong. A wrong action does not make you a bad person. Feelings of self-hatred or worthlessness can lead to depression and other harmful behaviors. *Making a mistake does not mean you are a mistake.* Remorse for a wrong behavior means you feel sorry for that action, but you don't continue to ruminate on guilt, and especially not shame. We all make mistakes and bad choices sometimes. Express your remorse for the bad action and move to the next step. Experiencing guilt is realizing that we may have made a mistake. Shame, on the other hand, says that *we* are a mistake. Remorse is a deeper sense of sorrow for the wrongdoing.

Restoration: If your action/behavior hurt others, you need to make amends, even if the person you need to forgive is yourself. When we don't take personal responsibility for our actions and behavior, we often continue in condemnation, guilt, and shame. When we do what is necessary to make things right, it's much easier to forgive ourselves.

If you need to apologize, do so. If there is some way that you can rectify the wrong, work to do that. Doing this will take away all concern that you didn't do everything that you could have done to make things right.

Renewal: Rumination, self-hatred, and even self-pity are nasty traps that send the brain into fight/flight mode. We want to hide and isolate ourselves from others when we allow ourselves to ruminate on the negative things we've done. Consider that God has already forgiven you and He is much bigger than any wrong thing you could have done. Remember when Jesus said to forgive 70 x 7? That applies to forgiving yourself, too. The renewal step is about finding a way to learn from the experience and grow as a person. How will you change your behavior in the future? Allow this to be a learning experience that can make you a better person.

In an interview, Stanford Director Emerita of Student Wellness, Carole Pertofsky, MEd explains that when people practice self-forgiveness, they experience lower levels of anxiety and depression. Self-compassion allows for higher levels of productivity, success, and mental clarity.[59]

[59] https://scopeblog.stanford.edu/2019/08/02/the-benefits-of-self-forgiveness/

Chapter 13

YOUR RELATIONSHIP TOGETHER:

The Truth About the Fruit of

the Spirit and the Armor of God

❧⎯⎯⎯⎯∞⎯⎯⎯⎯❧

Who You Are and Whose You Are

The Fruit of the Spirit – Who you are in Christ

"But the fruit of the Spirit is love, joy, peace, patience, kindness, goodness, faithfulness, gentleness, self-control; against such things there is no law." (Galatians 5:22-23)

Truth 13.1

The fruit of the Spirit is part of our new identity in Christ. This fruit becomes our identity through the indwelling of the Holy Spirit; it is our character, and our character will remain throughout eternity. The fruit of the Spirit is singular (notice I didn't say "fruits") and indivisible, because each of the characteristics of this fruit is a characteristic of LOVE, and as 1 John 4:8 states, "God is love." So, each of the characteristics of love reveals the nature of Christ. Once we received Jesus as our Savior, we became entirely new creations *as one* with Him. Because of this incredible transformation that happened in our spirit, His characteristics became ours. That seed of God was transplanted into us and made us part of the Vine and Branch of Christ, as I will discuss shortly.

While our spirits received this transformation into the character of Christ, our minds/souls did not. This means that while our spirits are perfect, our minds/souls still need to be renewed to the truths in the Word of God. We also must choose to crucify the flesh—which is something we are able to do through our will (mind) and the Holy Spirit's fruit of self-control at work in us. Galatians 5:24-25 (ESV) says, "And those who belong to Christ Jesus have crucified the flesh with its passions and desires. If we live by the Spirit, let us also keep in step with the Spirit." The fruit of the Spirit evident in us is that it does not prioritize self above others. *Agapao* love (which I'll share about soon), reveals Christ in us, and is self-sacrificing. All nine of these characteristics are part of who God is and are manifestations of this kind of love. The Holy Spirit begins producing these characteristics of love in us when we walk in step with Him. We learn that by the fruit we exhibit others will recognize that we belong to Him. The fruit is visible in us, just as the works of the flesh can be visible in us. For example, Matthew 7:17-20 (ESV) says, "So, every healthy tree bears good fruit, but the diseased tree bears bad fruit. A healthy tree cannot bear bad fruit, nor can a diseased tree bear good fruit. Every tree that does not bear good fruit is cut down and thrown into the fire. Thus you will recognize them by their fruits."

We want people to be able to "taste and see that the Lord is good" (Psalm 34:8 NIV) by our conduct as the Spirit lives and functions through us, but the fruit of the Spirit isn't revealed by "acts" that *we* can do. Only the Holy Spirit can produce this fruit in us. This fruit ripens and manifests in our lives, transforming our personalities and characters to reflect Jesus as we grow and mature in Him. When we walk in the Spirit, we don't have to try to perform these characteristics. They occur naturally and are byproducts of our relationship with Him. When we surrender to our flesh—or our carnal nature— by focusing on the five senses that cause us to be occupied with earthly things, rather than focusing on following the Holy Spirit's leading and the Word of God, we forfeit our ability to function in the fruit of the Spirit. We forfeit our inheritance in Christ; walking in our authority and our identity in Christ are part of our inheritance.

Galatians 5:16 (NIV) tells us, "So I say, walk by the Spirit, and you will not gratify the desires of the flesh." Fruit comes by a process of gradual growth which may be cultivated deliberately. That means we have to make the choice daily to submit ourselves to the Lord, to spend time with Him, to crucify our flesh, and to walk in the Spirit.

Truth 13.1 Application

1. The fruit of the Spirit is our _____, and our _____ will remain throughout eternity.

2. While our spirits received the transformation into the character of Christ, our souls did not. Because of this, what must we do to change our minds? There are two answers:

_____

_____

_____

_____

_____

3. What causes us to forfeit our ability to function in the fruit of the Spirit and forfeit our inheritance in Christ?

_____

_____

_____

_____

_____

4. How can we avoid this?

_____

_____

_____

_____

_____

Truth 13.2

Next, we'll take a look at each of Love's characteristics. The first three characteristics of the fruit of love are *love*, *joy*, and *peace*. These represent our attitude toward God.[60]

Love

LOVE is the primary fruit and can only be born in us through God. The English language has one word for love, while the Greeks have many words for love, so for our benefit, we're going to focus solely on the love of God, which is called *agapao*. *Agapao* is the highest form of love. It is self-sacrificing, willing to give up its rights even to the extent of giving up itself for the benefit of others. We see this *agapao* love in John 3:16 (NKJV). "For God so loved the world that He gave His only begotten Son, that whoever believes in Him should not perish but have everlasting life"(NKJV).

- **Loved** – *agapao* (Strong's #25): *Agapao* literally means "BELOVED; greatly loved and dear to the heart." *Agapao* love is unconditional love with no strings attached. It's given and offered even if it's not reciprocated. It is a preferential love, which means it puts the needs of the beloved in higher regard than itself, and it is chosen and acted out by the will. *Agapao* is not based on goodness of the beloved or upon natural affinity or emotion. This means that it exists and functions regardless of the unworthiness of the beloved. This kind of love does what is right and best for someone, even if it involves negative feelings. It concerns itself only with the well-being of the object of its love. Self-devotion (devoting oneself for the good of others)—NOT self-satisfaction, is the dominant trait.

Agapao delights in making the beloved happy, and desires to provide security and self-worth, both of which are important because when we don't feel loved, we feel insecure and don't recognize our worth. *Agapao* is sacrificial, a verb that calls for action—not an emotion. It's about what it gives, not what it gets, and this causes God to behold us with great esteem and respect—we are prized by Him.

---

[60] *Fruit of the Spirit* (lesson outline), Greg Mohr. Charis Bible College

This kind of love stands in awe, amazement, and wonder, as David says in Psalm 139:14: "I praise you, for I am fearfully and wonderfully made." I imagine him saying, "*Wow*, look at how amazingly I was created!" and God saying, "*Right?* I made you, and just *wow*! Look at how amazing you are!" It's a kind of admiration—a feeling of excitement and even surprise, as well as sincere appreciation that's awakened by an estimate of one's worth or value. Possibly the most important aspect of *agapao* is that it honors free will because it is a deliberate choice of the WILL, rather than being emotionally based. Its perfect expression is in the Lord Jesus: "... not My will, but Yours, be done." (Luke 22:42 NKJV) Many other kinds of love do not do this. *Agapao* doesn't take offense, yet longs for and hungers for our companionship. The *agapao* love God has for us is the entire reason for His plan of Redemption.

Joy

Contrary to what you may have heard, happiness and joy are not the same. While most people strive to be happy, happiness is fleeting. Happiness is usually based on external circumstances, while joy is based on what God is doing in our hearts. So how do we cultivate joy in our hearts? Psalm 51:12 (NKJV) tells us, "Restore to me the joy of Your salvation, and uphold me by Your generous Spirit." Salvation and knowing we are safe in Christ create joy. Also, Isaiah 56:7 (ESV) says "... these I will bring to my holy mountain, and make them joyful in my house of prayer; their burnt offerings and their sacrifices will be accepted on my altar; for my house shall be called a house of prayer for all peoples." Prayer and communion with our Papa God cultivate joy.

Jeremiah 15:16 (ESV) says, "Your words were found, and I ate them, and your words became to me a joy and the delight of my heart, for I am called by your name, O LORD, God of hosts."

The Word of God, its truth, and knowing that we belong to the Lord create joy in our hearts. Acts 20:35 (ESV) says, "In all things I have shown you that by working hard in this way we must help the weak and remember the words of the Lord Jesus, how he himself said, 'It is more blessed to give than to receive.'" Giving to others, doing for others, blesses us and ignites joy—in us and the receiver. In Psalm 126:5-6 (ESV) we learn, "Those who sow in tears shall reap with shouts of joy! He who goes out weeping, bearing the seed for sowing, shall come home with shouts of joy, bringing his sheaves with him." We reap what we sow, in every area of our lives. If we have sown in God's Kingdom and to His purposes, we will reap an abundance of souls. I can't think of anything that could make my heart happier. Can you?

A favorite verse that I have used in my healing journey is Nehemiah 8:10 (ESV): "… do not be grieved, for the joy of the LORD is your strength." God's joy is our strength. I love this. It means I don't have to do anything on my own, but I can do all things through His joy.

Truth 13.2 Application

Meditation on Psalm 139:14 - *Amazing Creation - Love from God - Love for self*: https://drive.google.com/file/d/1Z_yqVP1lQ4tVbuVJYN0jAb3j_IGe5zmd /view?usp=drive_link

After listening to this meditation, write a letter from God to you. Then write your reply to God, discussing how you feel about being His very own work of art.

_____
_____
_____
_____
_____
_____
_____
_____
_____
_____
_____
_____
_____
_____
_____
_____
_____
_____
_____
_____
_____

Truth 13.3

Peace

The Greek word for peace is *eirene* (Strong's #1515). It means: "One, peace, quietness, rest, peace of mind, sense of health (welfare) of an individual, when all essential parts are joined together into a whole, wholeness, prosperity." When we are joined with Christ, we are one with Him. The biblical definition of peace[61] includes that oneness. Peace is not only a fruit of the Spirit, but also Jesus paid for our peace in the garden of Gethsemane. From Isaiah 53:5 (BSB) we see, "But He was pierced for our transgressions, He was crushed for our iniquities; the punishment that brought us peace was upon Him, and by His stripes we are healed."

Romans 15:13 tells us that He fills us "with all joy and peace as [we] trust in him, so that [we] may overflow with hope by the power of the Holy Spirit" (NIV). Because we have the mind of Christ (1 Corinthians 2:16) and we are filled with the Holy Spirit and His fruit, peace is already ours as our inheritance in Christ. It's not something we have to ask for, because peace is a part of the character of God, who dwells in us.

Romans 14:17 ESV: "For the kingdom of God is not a matter of eating and drinking but of righteousness and peace and joy in the Holy Spirit."

Righteousness is not something we can manufacture or create on our own (Romans 3:22). Joy is also not something we can produce on our own but instead comes through the indwelling of the Holy Spirit (Nehemiah 8:10). Peace that passes all understanding guards our hearts and minds through Christ Jesus (Philippians 4:7). These aren't things we can create. These are gifts from God. All we need to do is receive. How do we receive? - by thanking Him for this gift and trusting that it is ours. Isaiah 26:3 (NKJV) tells us, "You keep him in perfect peace, whose mind is stayed on you, because he trusts in you."

Let's take a deeper look at several of these words. The NASB states Isaiah 26:3 this way, "The steadfast of mind You will keep in perfect peace, Because he trusts in You." The term, "steadfast" is *samak* (Strong's Heb. #5564) and means: "rest, support, uphold, sustain, brace oneself, refresh, lean against, lay upon, rest upon, and to be committed and focused." The term, "of mind", or *yetser* (Strong's Heb. #3336): means "purpose, imagination, form, framing,

---

[61](based on our studies of peace: G1515. eiréné in Strong's Concordance)

framework [like framing a house or building], intent and intentions, and pottery—formed by the potter, conception." Andrew Wommack, in his book *Power of Imagination; Unlocking Your Ability to Receive from God*© calls this our spiritual "womb" where we are creating our future![62]

"You will keep": *natsar* (Strong's Heb. #5341): "watch, guard, keep, watch over, preserve, to be kept close, guard from dangers, watchman." Next, "in perfect peace" is *shalom shalom* (Strong's Heb. #7965): "completeness, soundness, welfare, peace, safety, health, prosperity, quiet, tranquility, contentment, with God especially in a covenant relationship." "Trusts" is the word, *batach* (Strong's Heb. #982) and means, "trust, to feel safe, care-less, have confidence, to be secure or make secure, to be bold, takes refuge in God with hope and confident expectation." Therefore, this verse is telling us that as we focus our imaginations on God, resting in Him, allowing Him to uphold and sustain us, bracing ourselves and our thoughts completely upon Him, molding and conforming our minds and brains, shaping them as a potter shapes clay, and we could even go as far as to say restructuring those neural pathways and building and reshaping them into the proper framework, using our intentions to do so, *then* God will keep us in completeness, causing us to remain in safety, health, tranquility, and contentment, and experiencing His prosperity.

You may have noticed that the word *shalom* (peace) is stated twice in a row. Whenever God repeats the same word twice, He is adding emphasis, and He wants us to pay attention. Because we trust in Him and have complete confidence in Him, we are without worry or care. He makes us secure, and we boldly take refuge in Him with hope and confident expectation. We must CHOOSE to stay our mind upon God. In so doing, He keeps us in *shalom shalom*—perfect peace!

Stress causes us to focus inward. The fight/flight/freeze (limbic response) makes us believe that we have to save ourselves. If, instead, we take our eyes and attention off of self and negative circumstances, and choose to trust in our God, putting our imaginations upon Him and His goodness and promises to us, He will hold our hearts and minds in peace. Remember that because you have the mind of Christ, negative thoughts are not yours. Don't receive them. Negative thoughts and any thoughts contrary to God's Word are from the enemy, and we can choose whether to receive or reject them.

Truth 13.3 Application

1. What are the 6 benefits of keeping our minds focused upon God?

---

[62] Wommack, Andrew, *A Better Way to Pray*© (Harrison House, 2007)

1) _____
2) _____
3) _____
4) _____
5) _____
6) _____

2. What does "shalom shalom" mean?

_____
_____
_____
_____

3. Stress causes us to focus inward. Why is that bad? Be specific:

_____
_____
_____
_____
_____

Truth 13.4

The second three characteristics of love are: *patience*, *kindness*, and *goodness*—represent our social relationships.[63]

Patience

Patience is resting in God, fully resigned to trust Him. Patience is remaining consistently and constantly the same in our attitudes towards whatever we're believing Him for. Our culture today is often referred to as a microwave or fast-food culture, but God doesn't work that way. In Genesis 12 God promised Abraham a son and that promise didn't seem to be fulfilled in the natural for 25 years. Patience is resting in Him and trusting that His promises will manifest in our lives, but this means we must walk with Him rather than running ahead of Him and trying to make things happen on our own, in our own timing. Patience helps us grow in faith and maturity:

---

[63] *Fruit of the Spirit* (lesson outline), Greg Mohr. Charis Bible College

James 1:4 (NKJV) states, "But let patience have its perfect work, that you may be perfect and complete, lacking nothing." Patience makes us perfect, complete, and lacking nothing.

Hebrews 6:12 (NKJV) says, "... that you do not become sluggish, but imitate those who through faith and patience inherit the promises." Not many of us enjoy waiting, but consider the waiting that many of the greatest heroes of faith did, (as we find in Hebrews 11)—men such as Abraham, Moses, Joseph, and David. These men all had to wait for many years before they experienced God's promises. Everything that happened during their waiting was used to prepare them inwardly as well as outwardly. Let's look at Moses and Joseph specifically. Moses tried to stand up for his people in his own strength by murdering an Egyptian he saw abusing an Israelite, and we know how that turned out. God had to take him to the desert for 40 years in order to get him out of the flesh and into faith—into a trusting relationship with Him. During this long period of time, God was growing and preparing Moses to bring the children of Israel out of Egypt. Imagine Moses trying to perform these great exploits without God's training and help! It would have been impossible.

Joseph was sold into slavery by his brothers, and his entire ordeal took him through all kinds of horrific experiences—from being sold to Potiphar, to Potiphar's wife falsely accusing him of violating her, to being put in prison and left there for years after interpreting the dreams of Pharaoh's cupbearer and baker who had promised Joseph they would mention him to Pharaoh . . . What would have happened had Joseph been set free long before any of these experiences? He wouldn't have been able to save Egypt or his family. Millions of lives would have been lost, and it's possible that Joseph would never have been reunited or reconciled with his family. Galatians 6:9 (NKJV) says, "And let us not grow weary while doing good, for in due season we shall reap if we do not lose heart." Patience has the potential to change us as we learn to rely upon God rather than self or others, or substances. God has been trying to teach us that He is trustworthy and true, and when we choose to submit to Him, things fall into place. He can take much better care of us than we can of ourselves.

Kindness

Jeremiah 31:3 (NKJV) tells us, "The LORD has appeared of old to me, saying: 'Yes, I have loved you with an everlasting love; Therefore with lovingkindness I have drawn you.'" God's lovingkindness is what has drawn us to Him. Because we are His children and we are *As One* with Christ, it is also our kindness that draws others to Him. In Ephesians 4:32 (ESV) we read, "Be kind to one another, tenderhearted, forgiving one another, as God in Christ forgave you." We've already reviewed a great deal about forgiveness, but it is through *kindness* that we choose to forgive one another. Consider that we also need to show kindness to ourselves. It's often true that we may express these things toward others, yet have a tendency to be much harsher toward ourselves. Because of the high value God places upon us, we need to give ourselves grace through kindness. Recognize the love God has for you and the price He paid for you.

Goodness

Whereas kindness is expressed in attitude, goodness is demonstrated through actions. These two must work together. Psalm 136:1 (NKJV) says, "Oh, give thanks to the LORD, for He is good! For His mercy endures forever." God's goodness is merciful. Exodus 34:6 lets us know that through His goodness we experience His mercy, grace, and long-suffering.

God *is* good continually. That never changes. While the devil and his devices are always bad, God and His ways are always good, as shown in Psalm 34:8 and Psalm 52:1. Romans 2:4 (NKJV) says, "Or do you despise the riches of His goodness, forbearance, and longsuffering, not knowing that the goodness of God leads you to repentance?" It is God's goodness that leads us to repent and turn from destruction, and that same goodness chases us down! He desires that we *expect* His goodness in our lives. It is *in His Presence* that we experience His goodness. Recall from Psalm 23:6 (NKJV), "Surely goodness and mercy shall follow me all the days of my life, and I shall dwell in the house of the LORD forever."

Truth 13.4 Application

1. The second three characteristics of love: _____,
_____,_____ represent our social relationships.

2. Why did Moses need to spend the first 40 years in the desert?
_____
_____
_____
_____
_____

3. What would have happened had Joseph been set free long before any of the adverse experiences he endured?

_____

_____

_____

_____

_____

Truth 13.5

The last three characteristics of love are *faithfulness*, *gentleness*, and *self-control*. These three characteristics of love guide our conduct.[64]

Faithfulness

Webster's 1828 Dictionary defines faithfulness as "fidelity; loyalty; firm adherence to allegiance and duty."[65] This means that we must be true and loyal to Jesus, to our spouse, and to employers, friends, and family, in handling finances and anything else that has been entrusted to us. We also have a duty as Christians to be faithful in our spiritual authority. Faithfulness to God goes back to trusting God. Faithfulness to the Lord means depending on Him, rather than trying to do everything on our own and trusting in ourselves. Proverbs 3:5-8 (NKJV) goes as far as to say, "Trust in the LORD with all your heart, And lean not on your own understanding; In all your ways acknowledge Him, And He shall direct your paths. Do not be wise in your own eyes; Fear the LORD and depart from evil. It will be health to your flesh, And strength to your bones."

Faithfulness is going where He leads, sticking with it, not giving up, persevering no matter what comes our way, and remaining steadfast in following the Lord. Faithfulness requires self-discipline and determination to see things through. Luke 9:62 (ESV) says, "Jesus said to him, 'No one who puts his hand to the plow and looks back is fit for the kingdom of God.'" Even the Apostle Paul stated in Philippians 3:13 (AMP), "Brothers and sisters, I do not consider that I have made it my own yet; but one thing I do: forgetting what lies behind and reaching forward to what lies ahead..." Being faithful means we

---

[64] *Fruit of the Spirit* (lesson outline), Greg Mohr. Charis Bible College
[65] https://webstersdictionary1828.com/Dictionary/faithfulness

keep trusting, keep doing good, keep submitting to the Lord, keep moving forward, and keep believing even when it's challenging. In Hebrews 11:1 (BSB) we read, "Now faith is the assurance of what we hope for and the certainty of what we do not see."

Gentleness/Meekness

What is meekness? According to Strong's Concordance, *prautés* (Greek #4420, prah-oo'-tace) means: "mildness, gentleness, 'gentle strength' which expresses *power* with *reserve and gentleness.*" The Complete WordStudy Dictionary says that meekness is "inward grace of the soul, calmness toward God in particular . . . the acceptance of God's dealings with us considering them as good in that [His dealings with us] enhance the closeness of our relationship with Him."[66] It is not *weakness*, but can also exist in one's heart from being actively angry at evil. So while meekness is a gentle strength, it's also a calm acceptance of the way God works in our lives and deals with us, which includes having a sense of righteous anger toward evil.

Colossians 3:12-13 (NKJV) says, "Therefore, as the elect of God, holy and beloved, put on tender mercies, kindness, humility, meekness, longsuffering; bearing with one another, and forgiving one another, if anyone has a complaint against another; even as Christ forgave you, so you also must do." Ephesians 4:1-3 (ESV) states, "I therefore, a prisoner for the Lord, urge you to walk in a manner worthy of the calling to which you have been called, with all humility and gentleness, with patience, bearing with one another in love, eager to maintain the unity of the Spirit in the bond of peace." You'll notice a common theme in these verses: meekness is usually connected with patience and forgiveness.

Self-Control/Temperance

Strong's Concordance defines self-control *egkrateia* (Greek #1466, eng-krat'-i-ah) as "self-mastery, self-restraint, dominion within or true mastery from within." Self-control and temperance also mean being sober and of sound mind. Self-control is a means of reining in our flesh and resisting and overcoming temptation. James 1:19-20 NKJV: "So then, my beloved brethren, let every man be swift to hear, slow to speak, slow to wrath; for the wrath of man does not produce the righteousness of God." Self-control will, at times, mean that we "hold our peace" rather than "speaking our piece." We don't function out of our emotions and *react* rather than *respond*. We control our tongues, our

---

[66] Zodhiates, Spiros, *The Complete WordStudy Dictionary* (AMG Publishers, 1993) entry #4236

emotions, and attitudes. It applies to every part of our lives—from how we manage our finances and physical and emotional relationships, to how we care for our bodies with the food we eat, the things we drink, and even physical exercise. It means we are in control of our behaviors, our thoughts, and our words. Self-control is the *power* the Holy Spirit gives us to overcome the flesh.

Truth 13.5 Application

Fruit of the Spirit Meditation:

Once you are filled with the Holy Spirit, you have the fruit of the Spirit in you. Think about and meditate on each characteristic of the fruit and what these look like in your life. Work this into your daily routine. Consider the Scripture references to help you see these characteristics. You might imagine or visualize them taking root in your life like this:

> ➤ *Love* flows down your head from the crown down to your chin— "God's perfect love flows through me and casts out all fear" (1 John 4:18). Take a moment to consider how you see and hear things differently through a filter of Love.

> ➤ *Joy* flows down your neck from the base of your head to your shoulders—"The joy of the Lord is my strength" (Nehemiah 8:10). When God's joy is your strength, what are you able to do differently? Physically? Mentally?

> ➤ *Peace* is flowing around your heart and chest—"The peace of God which passes all understanding guards my heart and mind through Christ Jesus." (Philippians 4:7). When you are focusing on the peace of Christ, how will your day be different? How will you look at challenges? Other people? Yourself?

> ➤ *Patience* flows down into your stomach and liver—"I am patient with myself and others." (1 Corinthians 13:4-5). What will your relationships look like as you experience patience in them? What will you experience in your heart and mind as you are patient with yourself?

> ➤ *Kindness* flows into your belly—"I am kind to myself and others" (1 Corinthians 13:4). How do you choose to express kindness to yourself? And others?

> ➤ *Goodness* flows down your shoulders into your arms and hands— "The goodness of God leads me to repentance; it works through my hands, and I bless others" (Romans 2:4). Are there actions that you have done that you might need to repent for as God's

goodness speaks to your heart? How might you bless someone else today?

➤ ***Faithfulness*** flows down your back—first over your shoulders, between your shoulder blades, mid-back and lower back—"I am filled with the faith of Jesus, and I am faithful to Him and myself" (Galatians 2:16). Did you know that you not only have a measure of faith, but you have the faith of Jesus? (Revelation 14:12) What kinds of things can the faith of Jesus do? How might that change your life?

➤ ***Gentleness*** flows down your buttocks, hips and thighs to your knees—"A gentle answer turns away wrath; I am gentle with myself and others" (Proverbs 15:1). Consider how you might begin answering everyone with a gentle answer. Are you gentle with yourself? How does your inner voice sound? How might you change the way you speak to yourself to reveal gentleness and grace in a way that you might speak to your best friend?

➤ ***Self-control*** flows from your knees to your toes—"I am self-controlled in every way" (1 Corinthians 10:13). Self-control helps us to make godly choices. By using self-control, how might your choices today look different? Will you exercise? Eat healthily? Spend dedicated, uninterrupted time with the Lord? Avoid things that may not be beneficial for you physically? Emotionally? Spiritually?

Truth 13.6

The Armor of God → Whose you are

Ephesians 6:11 (ESV) tells us, "Put on the whole armor of God, that you may be able to stand against the schemes of the devil." Every day, we need to choose to "put on" the armor of God, keeping in mind that we belong to Him, and we are safe and secure, ready to meet anything the enemy throws at us. However, we must *choose* to do this. Remember the old American Express credit card slogan: "Don't leave home without it?" ® When it comes to the armor of God, we probably shouldn't leave bed in the morning without it.

Belt of truth

The belt of truth is essential for every believer. A Roman soldier's belt held all his weapons and allowed him to move about freely. His tunic was tucked into the belt, leaving his legs unimpeded for movement. The world has a very different idea of "truth" than the Word of God. Jesus is "the way, the TRUTH, and the life." (John 14:6) Humans tend to believe in "relative truth"—meaning what they believe becomes their "own truth." Considering what we've learned about faith and belief, we can easily come to understand that trusting in our "own truth" (like Adam and Eve did) can be deadly, as Proverbs 14:12 states. God's Truth is the ONLY Truth, and it is only His truth that leads to life. John 17:17 (NASB) says Jesus prays to the Father, "Sanctify them in the truth; your word is truth." Just as the belt allowed free movement for the soldiers who wore it, those who wear the belt of truth in Christ can move in freedom. John 8:32 (NLT) says, "... and you will know the truth, and the truth will set you free."

Breastplate of righteousness

Jesus imputed His righteousness to us, and that righteousness is attached to truth. It's not *our* righteousness, because as Isaiah 64:6 tells us, our own righteousness is as filthy rags. Rather, we are counted as the righteousness *of God in Christ* based on Christ exchanging our sin for His own righteousness (2 Corinthians 5:21). The breastplate of righteousness covers our vital organs—most specifically, the heart. Understanding that we are righteous in God's eyes—completely accepted, with every trace of sin having been removed—allows us to be at peace. When we experience the peace of God that guards our hearts and minds (Philippians 4:7), our brains return to homeostasis and our minds and bodies can heal. Righteous standing before God means all the root of sin is gone, and when the root is gone, the fruit (guilt, shame, condemnation, sickness, disease) is also gone.

Shoes of the preparation of the gospel of peace

Shoes give us the ability to move about while having our feet protected. Roman soldiers wore thick leather shoes with spikes and hobnails, which gave them stability and kept them from stumbling in the midst of battle. The word "gospel" means "good news," and what Jesus has done for us is the very best news our world has ever received. The gospel is the means by which humanity has experienced peace with God through the sacrifice of Jesus. Romans 10:15 (ESV) says, "And how are they to preach unless they are sent? As it is written, 'How beautiful are the feet of those who preach the good news!'" The preparation of the gospel of peace allows us to take this message—as we are told in the Great Commission—to the rest of the world in order to share with others the good news of all Christ has done for us.

Shield of faith

The shields Roman soldiers used were long, door-shaped, and covered with leather. The soldiers lubricated these shields to keep them flexible so that the arrows that struck them would slide off the surface rather than perforating them and, perhaps, injuring the soldier. I personally like to think of my shield of faith more like an impenetrable bubble shield that surrounds me, kind of like what you'd see in a science fiction movie. It may be invisible, but absolutely nothing can penetrate it, and it is easily regenerated as I focus on the Lord and trust Him. Isaiah 54:17 tells us that no weapon formed against us can prosper when we are in that safe and secure place in the Lord.

Helmet of salvation

A Roman soldier's helmet was made of metal and fitted specifically to the shape of his head. Our own helmets of salvation protect us from the mental assaults of the enemy. Remember how we discovered the tactics the enemy uses and what his voice sounds like earlier? It's imperative that we know who God says we are (identity) and we remember that the Holy Spirit desires to convict us of the righteousness which comes through the gift of salvation; otherwise, we will get caught up in the devil's lies. It's interesting to note that a Roman soldier's helmet was used both for protection and identification. Because of the way the helmets looked, including the red plume, people knew immediately who these soldiers were. Likewise, the helmet of salvation is not only for our protection, but also our identity. We find a similar passage in Isaiah 59:17 (ESV) referring to the breastplate and helmet: "He put on righteousness as a breastplate, and a helmet of salvation on his head; he put on garments of vengeance for clothing, and wrapped himself in zeal as a cloak."

The word "salvation" in this verse is *yeshuah*, which—as discussed in *The Truth About Jesus and Salvation*, is the very name of our Lord Jesus, which means "deliverance," "health," "helping," "salvation," and "welfare." In Ephesians 6:17 we find the Greek word *soteria*, which means "rescue," "safety," "deliver," "health," and "save." The helmet of salvation covers our minds and equips us with healing and deliverance for our mental struggles. We can confess that we are wearing this helmet on our heads—knowing that our brains and minds are healed and delivered.

Sword of the Spirit

The Roman soldier's sword was a short, stabbing or thrusting weapon, more like a dagger than a slashing medieval broadsword. While all his other pieces of armor were for defense, the sword was for offense. When Jesus faced the devil in the wilderness, He met every temptation with the Word of God. In Luke 4 we find Jesus answering every temptation with, "It is written ..." This is our weapon, our sword, as well. 2 Corinthians 10:5 (ESV) says, "We destroy arguments and every lofty opinion raised against the knowledge of God, and take every thought captive to obey Christ ..." Every lie, every temptation, and every attack from the enemy can be defeated with God's Word.

Hebrews 4:12 (NKJV) states, "For the word of God is quick, and powerful, and sharper than any two-edged sword, piercing even to the dividing asunder of soul and spirit, and of the joints and marrow, and is a discerner of the thoughts and intents of the heart." When we speak the Word of God, we are speaking something that is alive, but it must be spoken to be activated. Revelation 12:11 (BSB) says, "And they have conquered him by the blood of the Lamb and by the word of their testimony ..." We defeat the enemy by believing and speaking the Word of God over every thought, lie, situation, and circumstance. When we are geared up with His armor, we are able to defeat the enemy every time.

You have probably gathered from this lesson that it's absolutely imperative that we know and understand how God has revealed who we are through His fruit and whose we are by His armor. What an incredible God we serve to give us everything we need for life and godliness. (2 Peter 1:3)

Truth 13.6 Application

Armor of God Meditation:

Ephesians 6:11 (ESV) tells us, "Put on the whole armor of God, that you may be able to stand against the schemes of the devil." God has given us His armor so that we can stand against the schemes or "wiles of the devil." God knows how our enemy works. He knows that when we forget who we are and whose we are, we will be easy targets. That is the reason He has given us His armor; when we stand in His armor we are able to bring the enemy into captivity when he tries to assault our minds and thoughts. 2 Corinthians 10:5 says, "We demolish arguments and every pretension that sets itself up against the knowledge of God, and we take captive every thought to make it obedient to Christ" (NIV).

Use this outline for a visualization, imagining that you are putting on each article of armor. Go through the physical motions of getting dressed in this armor, if you'd like:

> ➤ "I put on the helmet of salvation—I belong to the Lord." Think about what it means to truly be *His*.

> ➤ "I put on the breastplate of righteousness—He covers me with His righteousness and perfection." There is no sin counted toward you any longer! You are seen just as righteous as Jesus! This breastplate also guards over the peace in your heart.

> ➤ "I put on the belt of truth—God's Word alone is my truth." (Not the doctors' reports – if I had chosen to continue to believe the doctors' reports were going to remain my truth, I would not have healed; the lies on TV; the news from the world—and not even the fears in your mind are Truth. Only the Word of God!)

> ➤ "I put on the shoes of the preparation of the gospel of peace—I stand in the peace of God and take it with me everywhere I go!" When you put those shoes on, you stand and remain in the peace of God, and you bring that peace everywhere when you share the Gospel of Christ.

> ➤ "I put on the shield of faith—it protects me from all the fiery darts of the enemy. It is a protective shield that surrounds me!" Imagine this shield being like a sci-fi kind of shield that creates a bubble around you. Everything the enemy does just bounces off.

> ➤ "I hold the sword of the Spirit—God's Word is the sword and my truth and weapon against the enemy." You activate this sword by speaking the Word out loud.

Chapter 14

YOUR RELATIONSHIP TOGETHER:

The Truth About the Vine and the Branches—Abiding in

Christ

Truth 14.1

This is the final lesson of the *As One* program. Now that you have learned who God is, who you are in Christ, and all the things that your relationship with Him entails, it's important that you continue in them. You are *as one* with Jesus, but you must choose to remain in Him. This is a daily decision—even hourly. From 2 Timothy 3:14 (ESV) we learn, "But as for you, continue in what you have learned and have firmly believed, knowing from whom you learned it…" The word "continue" in this verse is the Greek word *menó*. This word means to "stay, abide, continue, and remain." It also refers to continually living and dwelling in a certain state or place, not a state on the map but a state of mental, emotional, and spiritual being.

The question is, what does it look like to remain *in Him*? What would our lives look like if we offered ourselves completely to Christ to truly be *as one* with Him? I don't just mean being baptized and receiving Him as Savior. What would happen if we were determined to make Him our life? Not just considering Him our Savior, but the Lord of our life? What if we were to be so close to Him that the love of everything not of Him faded away? If we were in total submission? If every act we did was done for His honor and glory—the food and drinks we consumed, the things we did for entertainment, the books and articles we read, the places we went, the things we spent our money on, the conversations we had, the thoughts we focused on, and the words we spoke—what if *everything* about our lives was about Jesus? How would our lives change? How might they look different?

I think many Christians are used to a "fire escape" kind of Christianity, one that allows them to function as they want in the world, but believe they have just enough of Jesus to be "saved". The problem with that mentality is that Jesus wants all of us. Because we are a new creation in Christ, an entirely new creature, we need to leave the old person who died behind; we need to step into our new identity. We are now completely different people, but we cannot be that new creation without Him. Being a part-time Christian is like living part-time without air. This is not about fitting Him into our lives here and there. Our new identity is *in Him*. It's not about a once-a-week "date" with Him at church on Sunday. It's a radical new existence that includes functioning in Him in every way, every moment.

Have you heard of the witness protection program? I did a little digging. The witness protection program has a 100% success rate for those who abide by the rules. Do you know why? The witnesses are moved to a completely new location, receive new identities which include new birth certificates, new driver's licenses, new social security numbers, new names, new backgrounds, sometimes new faces (plastic surgery), new hair, and new style. They go through a thorough orientation. They are mostly criminals, but are forgiven and given a completely new chance for life as a new person.[67]

A life with Christ means that everything about the old person is gone and all things are new. While we may not move to a new state and change our looks when we give our lives to Jesus, sometimes, giving our lives to Jesus may require some pretty drastic changes. Our earthly citizenship changes to a heavenly

---

[67] https://www.mentalfloss.com/article/649685/witness-protection-program-facts

citizenship. We remain in this world when we choose Jesus, but we are no longer citizens of this world. In John 17:16 (ESV) Jesus says, "They are not of the world, just as I am not of the world." Our appetites, desires, priorities, habits, conversations, purposes—all things become new. Every part of our new lives in Him reflects Jesus living His will in and through us. Make it your business to talk with Him often. When issues arise that you need help with, take them to Him first.

First John 2:15-17 tells us, "Do not love the world or the things in the world. If anyone loves the world, the love of the Father is not in him. For all that is in the world—the lust of the flesh, the lust of the eyes, and the pride of life—is not of the Father but is of the world. And the world is passing away, and the lust of it; but he who does the will of God abides forever." First Thessalonians 5:17 (NKJV) tells us to "pray without ceasing ..." Is Paul serious? Is it possible to pray without ceasing? In a sense, I believe it is. While that doesn't mean we talk out loud to God all day long nonstop, it does mean that our inner dialogue should·be with the Holy Spirit. We should constantly filter our thoughts, imaginings, and words through Him.

Consider how you can bring Him into every part of your life. Are there object lessons you might notice in your day-to-day habits? When you are gardening, cleaning house, preparing for work, making food—ask Him to use these things to teach you more about His character. Use the time that you drive to work or do mundane tasks to speak to Him *and* to listen. Take walks with Jesus and talk with Him. In how many ways will you make focusing on Him a habit?

Truth 14.1 Application

I have a grapevine and two apple trees in my yard. There is absolutely no way I can force grapes or apples to grow, however, I can cultivate the soil. I can make certain to water the grapevine and apple trees. I can do whatever is necessary to help the ground and soil around the trees to have good healthy nutrients. The trees and the vine don't strain to bear their fruit; that's what they do. Likewise, we don't have to strain to bear fruit, but we must remain within the vine or part of the tree to bear fruit. What are five ways you have learned in this program that will help you to remain in the vine? Be specific.

_____

_____

_____

_____

_____

_____

Apple trees and grapevines don't produce fruit first thing in the spring. They have to grow the fruit. Because they are apple trees and grapevines, they will produce fruit according to what they are. What are some of the kinds of fruit you can expect to see in your own life as you continue to renew your mind?

_____

_____

_____

_____

_____

_____

If I cut off one of the branches, the vine will not produce fruit, but if the branch remains in the vine, we can expect it to produce fruit, We must remain and abide in the vine, who is Jesus. John 15:5 (ESV) says, "I am the vine; you are the branches. Whoever abides in me and I in him, he it is that bears much fruit, for apart from me you can do nothing."

Truth 14.2

What consumes your mind controls your life. Find ways to keep your focus on Him. Isaiah 26:3 (ESV) "You keep him in perfect peace whose mind is stayed on you, because he trusts in you." This doesn't happen by chance. It has to be a deliberate choice. It has to become your habit. Deuteronomy 6:7 (ESV) says that we need to talk about the Word "when you sit in your house, and when you walk by the way, and when you lie down, and when you rise." Consider for a moment whether there is anything in your life that is hindering your relationship with Him? Is there anything that, when you really evaluate it in light of Jesus living in you, might not belong in this new creation and/or to this new identity that you share with Him? Is there anything He is calling you to change? Is it obvious to people who knew you before you gave your life to Christ and became a new creation that you are an entirely different person? After going through this program, is there anything you need to repent for, (remember that repentance doesn't just mean confession of sin—it means a heart change), or anyone you need to forgive, including yourself? Has the Holy Spirit spoken to your heart about making Him a higher priority? What might that entail?

1 Corinthians 3:16 (NASB) says, "Do you not know that you are a temple of God and that the Spirit of God dwells in you?" Brother Lawrence, a monk who lived in a French monastery in the 1600s, wrote in his book, *The Practice of the Presence of God* (originally published in 1692)[68], that he had no will "but that of God." He endeavored to accomplish God's will in all things. While most of us probably won't find a monastery to join, nor is that necessary because we don't have to *go* somewhere in order to be with God, He is in us. How might we live our lives differently if we choose to submit our own wills so fully to Him that we don't consider ourselves? Sounds radical, doesn't it? But should it sound radical? The world we live in is engrossed in selfishness and self-centeredness: things like taking selfies, speaking "my" truth, seeking validation from others to make ourselves feel better even if our beliefs about self are wrong. True Christianity is about pointing people to Jesus and making Him increase while we decrease until our hearts are so filled with Christ that there's no room for self.

In John 3:30, John the Baptist stated that "He must increase, but I must decrease" (NKJV). Is Jesus your main priority? Is He first in your life? Sometimes even good things may preoccupy our hearts, leaving little space for the Lord. Luke 10:38-42 (NKJV) tells us, "Now it happened as they went that He entered a certain village; and a certain woman named Martha welcomed Him into her house. And she had a sister called Mary, who also sat at Jesus' feet and heard His word. But Martha was distracted with much serving, and she approached Him and said, "Lord, do You not care that my sister has left me to serve alone? Therefore tell her to help me."

And Jesus answered and said to her, "Martha, Martha, you are worried and troubled about many things. But one thing is needed, and Mary has chosen that good part, which will not be taken away from her."

God desires to converse with us, and He delights in us. If we understood and embraced the love He has for us, would there be anything else more important to us than to remain in His presence? Zephaniah 3:17 (NKJV) tells us, "The LORD your God in your midst, The Mighty One, will save; He will rejoice over you with gladness, He will quiet you with His love, He will rejoice over you with singing." Psalm 16:11 (ESV) states, "You make known to me the

---

[68] https://churchleaders.com/pastors/free-resources-pastors/145403-brother-lawrence-free-ebook-the-practice-of-the-presence-of-god.html

path of life; in your presence there is fullness of joy; at your right hand are pleasures forevermore."

Can we possibly comprehend these truths? I believe we can when we choose to quiet our souls in His Presence long enough. If we did that, would we ever desire anything this earth claims it can give us? What could possibly be better than our Creator rejoicing over us with gladness, quieting our hearts with His love, and exulting over us with loud singing? Can you imagine how beautiful your Creator's voice is? We can't find "fullness of joy" anywhere else. Why would we try? Earth's pleasures can't even begin to measure up against even a small drop in the bucket of God's pleasures and goodness toward us. All the busyness and work we feel we must do needs to take a backseat when it comes to spending time with the Lord, because there is nothing more important. God is pursuing us, chasing after us, desiring to capture us in His arms, like a loving Daddy would capture his child, picking her up and swinging her around, embracing her and making her feel safe and secure, letting her know that she is complete in Him. She doesn't have to keep searching for her purpose. She doesn't have to keep striving to be received. In Him, she is *home. He* is her purpose, her completeness.

We can't experience Him without experiencing Him. That may sound circular, but how many of us have looked for some way to feel accepted, forgiven, loved, received, and healed? As if we have to do something for these things instead of just *being* in Him, resting in the understanding that it's already done. Maybe we don't feel worthy of being received and loved by God? But we are—because of *Jesus.* We don't need to *do,* we need to *be*—be with Him. As Psalm 46:10 states. "Be still and know that I am God ..."

Have you ever looked into a pool of water and noticed your reflection? If the water is moving, your reflection is hard to see. Similarly, if you are moving, you aren't going to see a clear reflection. Both you and the water need to be still. Earlier we talked about how we become changed as we behold something or someone. We need to sit in stillness to behold God. As we do this, we will begin to see His reflection in us. We can't experience that if we're too busy or we don't focus on Him purposefully. We must abide in Him. This can't be just a hit and miss relationship. As Rick Renner says, "Inconsistency is a work of the flesh."[69]

Furthermore, Renner, in his *Sparkling Gems from the Greek,* shares this about the word "abide":

---

[69] https://renner.org/article/a-picture-of-who-you-used-to-be/

The word 'continue' in Second Timothy 3:14 is a translation of the Greek word *meno*, which means to *habitually abide* or *stay put*. It describes *a decision from which the one abiding will not budge or move from his spot*. It's the same word that's used over and over in John 15, where Jesus said, 'If ye abide in me, and my words abide in you, ye shall ask what ye will, and it shall be done unto you' (v. 7). Jesus was saying in essence, 'If you *habitually reside* in Me, *refusing to budge and never moving out of Me*—and if My Word *habitually resides* in you, *never budging and never moving out of you* — you shall ask what you will, and it shall be done unto you.' This word *meno* describes a person making the decision, 'This is my spot; I will not move!' That's what Paul was instructing us to do: to *continue*. Paul exhorted us to resolve that *regardless of what was happening around us*, we would not *change our position* where the Word and the will of God were concerned. [70]

As I mentioned, the Holy Spirit begins producing His characteristics in us when we walk in step with Him. What does it mean to walk in step with Him? When you take a walk with someone, you converse with them, get to know them, listen to them, and share your thoughts and heart with them. We do this with the Lord through:

- Reading the Word.
- Prayer/listening to God (without ceasing).
- Spending time in worship, praise, and gratitude (constantly!).
- Meditating on His Word and renewing our minds to His Truth— we're always meditating on *something*—it might as well be His Truth.

Abiding in Him changes us. Earlier, I discussed how Adam and Eve lost their ability to walk with the Lord because their spirits died after they stopped trusting God. Jesus made a way for our spirits to be reborn by becoming one with His Spirit. Even though our spirits were reborn once we became new creations, we still must learn how to operate in faith, which means trusting Him. It's not natural for us to do this in the flesh, because functioning fully out of our five senses keeps us focused on the carnal.

Romans 8:5 (NKJV) says, "For those who live according to the flesh set their minds on the things of the flesh, but those who live according to the Spirit, the things of the Spirit." Being one with Jesus means we must learn to hear the voice of His Spirit. John 10:27 (NKJV) states, "My sheep hear my voice, and I know them, and they follow me." You've learned how to renew your mind by

---

[70] Renner, Rick, *Sparkling Gems from the Greek, Vol.* 1 (Harrison House, 2003) p. 578

getting His Word into your heart and mind, meditating on it, and changing how you speak and think. You've gained even more tools to help you learn how to hear and know the voice of the Lord, including ways to grow your faith and uproot doubt. Each of these lessons has been building upon the others to teach and equip you with the tools to know how to abide in Him.

Truth. 14.2 Application

1. This is only between you and God. You don't need to share your answer with anyone else unless you choose to do so for accountability purposes. Is there anything in your life right now that the Holy Spirit may be telling you to "prune away?" Be specific.

_____

_____

_____

_____

_____

_____

2. Ask the Lord to help you to make a commitment to Him today to follow through and prune that away. Again, if you need help, ask someone to hold you accountable to do this, so you can overcome your hesitancy. Ask the Holy Spirit to help you in this area, as well.

Truth 14.3

Spirit vs Flesh and Relationship vs Legalism

Part of our oneness with Christ requires that we crucify our flesh (or "pick up our cross," as Luke 9:23 states), because our flesh is the "old man." Now that we are joined with Jesus, we are new creations. This new creation or "new man" should look like an entirely new person. Galatians 5:24 (NIV) tells us, "Those who belong to Christ Jesus have crucified the flesh with its passions and desires."

"The flesh" is like a little kid in a grocery store who is screaming for a candy bar when Mom knows that the candy bar isn't the best or most healthy option. The flesh often desires things that are not beneficial for us, or may also be unhelpful for others. The flesh is selfish and self-centered. Being one with

Christ requires that we do what He would do, which often means putting others above ourselves, or using self-control when it comes to things that really aren't good for us.

First Corinthians 10:23 ESV: "'All things are lawful,' but not all things are helpful. 'All things are lawful,' but not all things build up." In making such choices, some things you might ask yourself are: Does it honor Christ? Does it draw me closer to Him? Does it help, bless, or edify another? Would my action or behavior (even if it's lawful) be a stumbling block for me or anyone else?

I've recently begun seeing how and what I consume in a new way—food, drinks, entertainment, etc. First Corinthians 6:19 tells us that our bodies are the temples of the Holy Spirit. Now while it's not necessarily a sin to eat ice cream every day for every meal, it's not beneficial; it probably doesn't provide all of the healthy nutrients my body needs, and it may be loaded with sugar. More importantly, my body is not just mine now that I belong to Christ. I share this body with Him. 1 Corinthians 6:20 (NKJV) says, "For you were bought at a price; therefore glorify God in your body and in your spirit, which are God's."

When I pray over my food now, I consider eating as an act of worship. I not only ask the Lord to bless what I eat for *me*, but I also ask that He bless the food for *His dwelling place*. What I consume affects this body, and this body is Christ's. It's the dwelling place of His Spirit. Can you imagine going into the Old Testament temple where God dwelt and trashing the place? I want to treat my body as God's temple. I certainly don't want to trash it.

Again, this isn't about legalism. It's not about doing these things in order to be saved or to be right with God. We don't want to put ourselves under a dietary law in order to be right with Christ. It's about taking care of ourselves because we are His, and we love Him and want to honor Him. It's an entirely different motivation based on love rather than works, as Paul discusses in the book of Galatians. We can apply this to every area of our lives. What will I choose because I love Him—not because I have to do it in order to be saved, but *because I am saved*. We're not going to be judged on whether we chose to eat ice cream for every meal, so don't let your brain get hung up on that. It's just about a love relationship and choosing to glorify Him in every part of your life. What you choose to eat or drink, or anything else you do, is between you and the Lord. Paul in Colossians 2:16-17 (KJV) says, "Let no man therefore judge you in meat, or in drink, or in respect of an holyday, or of the new moon, or of the sabbath days: Which are a shadow of things to come; but the body is of Christ." Just like the grapevine in my front yard, I have to prune it at least once a week, if not 2-3 times weekly in the summer. Otherwise, the vine will work to produce leaves rather than allowing the sap and nutrients to flow into fruit. We have to choose to prune away the things in our lives that take up space but don't produce fruit. In some ways it's similar to Martha being too busy when she needed to be sitting at the feet of Jesus. Consider the fact that she was working to do things for Him. Doing good things isn't bad, but Jesus wanted the relationship with her more than the work she was doing for Him. The work we do needs to be a fruit of the relationship because of love, not for the purpose of *earning* love.

Far too many of us have learned from the world, and maybe through our upbringing, that in order to be accepted, we must perform and do things perfectly. It's my belief that religion has also taught us that we are only acceptable to God if we are working for Him. God is so much more interested in relationship with us than what we do for Him. Many of us have been taught that in order to secure God's love or salvation we must keep the law perfectly. Our righteous standing with God isn't earned or merited by what we do, but rather what Christ did for us. Perfectionism died on the Cross. Jesus is the only one who is perfect. This is the reason that His righteousness is imparted to us. He wants us to rest in what He has provided because, as I've shared many times throughout this program, it is not possible for us to be perfect. When we try, we are going back to doing what Adam and Eve did —a work of our own flesh rather than trusting the Lord.

Legalism teaches us that our good works and obedience affect our salvation. It focuses on God's laws and our behavior as a means of being right with God. This is impossible, because we cannot do anything to be right with God. Jesus did that work for us. That was the whole purpose of His coming here—to do whatever it took to win us back, including covering our messes with His own life. Our outward works don't do anything for our hearts. God wants our hearts. He wants our love. He isn't waiting for us to mess up so He can punish us. We are fully under the free unmerited love and favor of God; that's the definition of grace. Because of that, there is no condemnation from God toward us, even if we eat ice cream for every meal.

Romans 8:1 (NKJV) says, "There is therefore now no condemnation to those who are in Christ Jesus, who do not walk according to the flesh, but according to the Spirit." There are other things that take up and waste our time and things that we need to prune away altogether; they aren't helpful for us, they don't honor God, and they may keep us so focused on self that we lose sight of what's really important. So much of the world's distractions keep us focused on fear rather than faith. Again, as new creations in Christ, our lives should look very different from the rest of the world because we don't belong here. We are from a heavenly Kingdom.

What it all comes down to is LOVE, friends.

Love honors others above self.

Love puts Christ first because He put us first.

Love receives what He has done and chooses to do whatever will bless and glorify Him, not because we have to in order to be saved, but because *we get to* because we are saved.

Love is a free-will choice to do what honors and blesses others—in this case, Jesus.

Flesh vs Demons

This subject needs to be discussed briefly, as many assume that every bad thing that happens is demonic. While there is absolutely a war between the Kingdom of God and the kingdom of darkness over our souls, not everything negative that happens is a direct attack from the enemy. Many blame the devil when it's often their own flesh that needs to be crucified. Crucifying the flesh, choosing to do what honors God above what we may feel like doing carnally, is part of the sanctification process. We may be able to cast out demons, but it's not possible to cast out our flesh; we have to submit our flesh to God and renew our minds.

When we allow ourselves to function and live out of the flesh, we open ourselves up to the enemy. He often tempts us and if we oblige, then we've taken his bait. It's when we are tempted (with any of his tactics, whether it be sin, sickness, or offense) that we need to resist him.

James 4:7-8 (NKJV) says, "Therefore submit to God. Resist the devil and he will flee from you. Draw near to God and He will draw near to you. Cleanse your hands, you sinners; and purify your hearts, you double-minded."

Many times people will blame the devil when they are suffering from their own actions and behaviors. Sometimes those behaviors have been learned through bad examples they observed from parents or through negative experiences they've had in the past that create triggers. These triggers may lead to emotional pain or coping behaviors they have formed due to some kind of trauma. While in general all of our "yuck" goes back to the Fall of Adam and Eve and original sin, a lot of the bad situations we find ourselves in may be due to our own flesh. That's not to say that we always know what we're doing, or that we even mean to do things that create problems for ourselves. Again, learning how to change and overcome is a part of the mind renewal and sanctification process, and there is always *so much grace* for us. Not only is there grace, but God has a way of taking some of our biggest blunders and turning them around for our good, because He is just so incredibly loving and has a supernatural ability to do so.

Romans 8:28 (ESV) says, "And we know that for those who love God all things work together for good, for those who are called according to his purpose." Ephesians 3:20 (NKJV) says, "Now to Him who is able to do exceedingly abundantly above all that we ask or think, according to the power that works in us...." The more we learn to trust Him, the more we learn to walk by faith rather than by sight. (2 Corinthians 5:7) A fantastic occurrence takes place as we learn to do this: Our faith grows, and we become more like Him. 2 Corinthians 3:18 (ESV) says, "And we all, with unveiled face, beholding the glory of the Lord, are being transformed into the same image from one degree of glory to another. For this comes from the Lord who is the Spirit."

Truth 14.3 Application

1. What was the most important thing you learned from the *Spirit vs Flesh and Relationship vs Legalism* Truth?

_____

_____

_____

_____

_____

2. How does this Truth change the way you look at your relationship with the Lord going forward?

_____

_____

_____

_____

_____

3. Did this lesson teach you that it's never ok to eat ice cream?

_____

_____

_____

_____

_____

Truth 14.4

No Fear

We've discussed that when we receive God's love and we trust Him, perfect Love from Him guards our hearts and casts out all fear. First John 4:18 (ESV) says, "There is no fear in love, but perfect love casts out fear. For fear has to do with punishment, and whoever fears has not been perfected in love." Abiding in Him means we don't succumb to fear of anything. We aren't afraid of the things happening in this world, because being in Jesus means that through His victory we have overcome the world just as He has. In John 16:33 (BSB), we read, "I have told you these things so that in Me you may have peace. In the world you will have tribulation. But take courage; I have overcome the world!"

We don't fear sickness or evil. Luke 10:19 (ESV) says, "Behold, I have given you authority to tread on serpents and scorpions, and over all the power of the enemy, and nothing shall hurt you." Psalm 91:3-7 (NLT) says:

> For he will rescue you from every trap and protect you from deadly disease. He will cover you with his feathers. He will shelter you with his wings. His faithful promises are your armor and protection. Do not be afraid of the terrors of the night, nor the arrow that flies in the day. Do not dread the disease that stalks in darkness, nor the disaster that strikes at midday. Though a thousand fall at your side, though ten thousand are dying around you, these evils will not touch you."

We won't fear the future or of losing our jobs or not having our needs met. Jeremiah 29:11 (ESV) says, "For I know the plans I have for you, declares the LORD, plans for welfare and not for evil, to give you a future and a hope." Philippians 4:19 (NKJV) says, "And my God shall supply all your need according to His riches in glory by Christ Jesus." In Matthew 6:26-32, Jesus tells us we don't need to be anxious about any of our needs being met. He takes care of the birds and the flowers, and we are of much greater value to Him than any bird or flower. He also mentions that worrying isn't going to make anything that we need magically appear. (We know from neuroscience that worry just creates "CAN" chemicals – cortisol, adrenaline, and norepinephrine, which have a negative effect on our brains and bodies.) Instead, we are to seek Him and His righteousness first, abide in Him, and then all of our needs will be met because of that relationship.

When we understand how much He loves us and desires to provide all of our needs—when we TRUST Him to do so, then we truly have no reason to fear. He's got us covered in every possible way. I think it's also common for many of us who have experienced emotional trauma or any kind of legalistic religious teaching to have an unhealthy fear of God. While He is holy and we need to honor Him as such, He is also tender and compassionate, seeing us as His precious children whom He yearns to hold. In Matthew 23:37, Jesus laments over Jerusalem: "How often I have wanted to gather your children together as a hen protects her chicks beneath her wings, but you wouldn't let me." (NLT)

We're even told in Matthew 18:3 that we must become like children in order to enter the Kingdom of Heaven. One of the most endearing qualities of young children is how trusting their hearts are toward their parents. A child may be messy and covered with dirt after playing in mud puddles, but she won't fear that her parents will reject her. She knows they love her and accept her exactly the way she is. Our loving Papa God is the same way, and even more so.

Acts 17:28 (ESV) says, "... for 'In him we live and move and have our being'; as even some of your own poets have said, 'For we are indeed his offspring.'" Imagine living, moving, and having your being in every present moment, whatever you are doing—doing it all in and with Christ. Living in His Presence should be like breathing. Finding yourself saturated in His love and goodness and remaining in an attitude of gratitude and appreciation creates an atmosphere of grace.

In my marriage to my husband, I don't worry about committing adultery. I don't focus on all of the things that I might do wrong. I focus on *him* and my love for him. I enjoy being in his presence and spending time with him. That love drives my behavior, rather than fear driving my behavior. If fear drives our behavior with God, it's a good indication that we are not receiving the love He has for us. It shows that we don't actually know the love God has for us, and the right standing that we have with Him. In John 10:30, Jesus said that He and the Father are One. This is the desire He has for us as His friends, His children, and His bride—to be *As One* with Him. In closing, I want to read the words of Jesus that He prayed for us from John 17:20-26 (BSB):

> [Father],
>
> I am not asking on behalf of them alone, but also on behalf of those who will believe in Me through their message, that all of them may be one, as You, Father, are in Me, and I am in You. May they also be in Us, so that the world may believe that You sent Me.
>
> I have given them the glory You gave Me, so that they may be one as We are one—I in them and You in Me—that they may be perfectly united, so that the world may know that You sent Me and have loved them just as You have loved Me.

Father, I want those You have given Me to be with Me where I am, that they may see the glory You gave Me because You loved Me before the foundation of the world.

Righteous Father, although the world has not known You, I know You, and they know that You sent Me. And I have made Your name known to them and will continue to make it known, so that the love You have for Me may be in them, and I in them."

Truth 14.4 Application:

1. When you are abiding in Christ, what are some of the things you no longer need to fear?

_____

_____

_____

_____

_____

_____

2. Legalism is NOT _____.

3. Over the next few weeks and months, meditate on the Scriptures below. You may choose to do a deep dive/exegesis on them, study them out, write them in a journal, and apply them in the many ways you have learned in this program:

John 15:4 NKJV: "Abide in Me, and I in you. As the branch cannot bear fruit of itself, unless it abides in the vine, neither can you, unless you abide in Me."

Psalm 91:1 NKJV: "He who dwells in the secret place of the Most High Shall abide under the shadow of the Almighty."

1 John 2:24 ESV: "Let what you heard from the beginning abide in you. If what you heard from the beginning abides in you, then you too will abide in the Son and in the Father."

John 15:7 NKJV: "If you abide in Me, and My words abide in you, you will ask what you desire, and it shall be done for you."

John 15:10 NKJV: "If you keep My commandments, you will abide in My love, just as I have kept My Father's commandments and abide in His love."

1 John 2:27 NKJV: "But the anointing which you have received from Him abides in you, and you do not need that anyone teach you; but as the same anointing teaches you concerning all things, and is true, and is not a lie, and just as it has taught you, you will abide in Him."

1 John 4:16 ESV: "So we have come to know and to believe the love that God has for us. God is love, and whoever abides in love abides in God, and God abides in him."

1 John 2:5-6 NKJV: "... But whoever keeps His word, truly the love of God is perfected in him. By this we know that we are in Him. He who says he abides in Him ought himself also to walk just as He walked."

John 15:4-11 ESV:

> Abide in me, and I in you. As the branch cannot bear fruit by itself, unless it abides in the vine, neither can you, unless you abide in me. I am the vine; you are the branches. Whoever abides in me and I in him, he it is that bears much fruit, for apart from me you can do nothing. If anyone does not abide in me he is thrown away like a branch and withers; and the branches are gathered, thrown into the fire, and burned. If you abide in me, and my words abide in you, ask whatever you wish, and it will be done for you. By this my Father is glorified, that you bear much fruit and so prove to be my disciples. As the Father has loved me, so have I loved you. Abide in my love. If you keep my commandments, you will abide in my love, just as I have kept my Father's commandments and abide in his love. These things I have spoken to you, that my joy may be in you, and that your joy may be full."

1 John 3:24 NKJV: "Now he who keeps His commandments abides in Him, and He in him. And by this we know that He abides in us, by the Spirit whom He has given us."

John 15:9 NASB: "Just as the Father has loved Me, I also have loved you; remain in My love."

John 15:5 BSB: "I am the vine and you are the branches. The one who remains in Me, and I in him, will bear much fruit. For apart from Me you can do nothing."

2 Corinthians 5:17 NKJV: "Therefore, if anyone is in Christ, he is a new creation; old things have passed away; behold, all things have become new."

Romans 8:1 NKJV: "There is therefore now no condemnation to those who are in Christ Jesus, who do not walk according to the flesh, but according to the Spirit."

Colossians 3:23-24 NKJV: "And whatever you do, do it heartily, as to the Lord and not to men, knowing that from the Lord you will receive the reward of the inheritance; for you serve the Lord Christ."

1 Corinthians 10:31 NKJV: "Therefore, whether you eat or drink, or whatever you do, do all to the glory of God."

Colossians 3:17 NLT: "And whatever you do or say, do it as a representative of the Lord Jesus, giving thanks through him to God the Father."

2 Corinthians 3:18 NKJV: "But we all, with unveiled face, beholding as in a mirror the glory of the Lord, are being transformed into the same image from glory to glory, just as by the Spirit of the Lord."

It's my prayer for you, dear reader, that this program has enriched not only your intellectual understanding of God, but that you've also encountered Him experientially and have come to realize your true identity as one with Christ. Mind renewal is a life-long process which requires a consistent habit of being in the Word of God and applying its truths daily. It is by beholding Jesus that we become changed. (2 Corinthians 3:18)

To help you in this endeavor, I've created the As One Toolkit for quick reference in the following pages. I pray it continues to bless you as you put these Truths into practice.

Mind Renewal Toolkit

This *Toolkit* can be an invaluable resource as you seek to create long-lasting habits based on lessons which you've studied in this book. Come back and refer to it often. The tools and truths I've shared here are the very tools that helped me heal.

Chapter 1: The Truth About God's Character

1. Speak out loud once a day: *"I was created for a purpose. I was created on purpose. I am at the forefront of God's mind. God created me. I am significant. I was created to overcome and live in victory! I am special in His eyes. God is aware of every part of my being. Thank You, God, for being involved in my conception and birth. Thank You, God, for creating me and re-creating me into a brand-new person TODAY!"*[71]

2. What verses about God's character speak to you in such a way that you will meditate on their truths anytime you need to remember who God is as your personal Papa God and how much He loves you?

3. "I am" statements speak to who and what you are. What "I am" statements do you need to change so that they line up with what God says about you? Examples:
    a. "I am sick" → "I am healed, whole, and well because of Jesus!"
    b. "I am a failure" → "I am an overcomer and have victory in Jesus!"

---

[71] *God Loves Me and I Love Myself!:Overcoming the resistance to loving yourself*© (2016, Mark de Jesus) p. 141-148

    c. "I am guilty" → "I am the righteousness of God in Christ Jesus!"

Chapter 2: The Truth About Jesus and Salvation

1. When you are struggling to believe that your sins are completely washed away by Jesus, how might you meditate on this truth and think about "The Divine Exchange" meditation from Application 2.5 where He washed your hands and purified your heart, giving you clean hands and a brand-new re-created heart? Keep this meditation and truth in mind when the enemy tries to play upon and appeal to your guilt and shame or tries to condemn you.

Chapter 3: The Truth About The Holy Spirit

1. Become aware of your thoughts. Try setting a timer and catching your thoughts every 15, 30, or 60 minutes to be aware of what you are thinking.
2. Download the "Shut Up, Devil!" app on your phone and use it when you're dealing with negative thoughts and emotions.
3. Philippians 4:8 and John 10:10 are excellent verses to filter your thoughts through. If your thought would steal your peace, kill your joy, or destroy your hope in the promises of God, it's NOT a thought from the Holy Spirit. However, if this thought is life-giving and lines up with the promises in the Word, it's a great indication that the Holy Spirit is speaking.
4. Pray in tongues each day. Ask for the Holy Spirit to give you the interpretation or understanding of what you've prayed for.
5. When you have questions that you would like for God to answer, write them in a journal with the date. Ask Him to reveal the answer to you and trust that He will. When the answer comes, write it down in your journal with the date it was answered.

Chapter 4: The Truth About Your True Identity—in Christ

1. Each morning, read at least 10 of the Identity Declarations over yourself. Speak them out loud and speak prayers of gratitude and praise to the Lord that you are truly a new creation in Christ.
2. Write out several of these declarations and post them on your bathroom mirror and other prominent places around your house.

When the enemy comes at you with a negative thought, or you recognize negative core beliefs, write out that belief in a journal in pencil. On the line under it, write out a Bible verse (in ink) that speaks the opposite of this thought or core belief. Repeat the verse throughout your day at least 7 days in a row. When a full week is up, erase the negative belief. (This is true mind renewal!)

Chapter 5: The Truth About Your Authority in Christ

1. No more of the *begging and pleading* kinds of prayers. Now that you know your identity in Christ and all that God has promised to provide for you because you are His child and heir, remember to frame your prayers based on Philippians 4:6-7 ESV: "Do not be anxious about anything, but in everything by prayer and supplication with thanksgiving let your requests be made known to God. And the peace of God, which surpasses all understanding, will guard your hearts and your minds in Christ Jesus."

2. Pray in expectation and faith with thanksgiving.

3. Apply Hebrews 11:1; Luke 10:19; Matthew 16:19 when you pray.

Chapter 6: The Truth About Spirit, Soul, and Body

1. Ephesians 4:20-24 (ESV) states:

   But that is not the way you learned Christ!—assuming that you have heard about him and were taught in him, as the truth is in Jesus, to put off your old self, which belongs to your former manner of life and is corrupt through deceitful desires, and to be renewed in the spirit of your minds, and to put on the new self, created after the likeness of God in true righteousness and holiness.

   Accordingly, you are a new creation in Christ and old behaviors belong to your former manner of life. You must put on the new self that's created after the likeness of God. You do this through mind renewal—changing old beliefs and replacing them with new beliefs. When you are struggling with identity, renew your mind by telling yourself that your spirit is PERFECT, united with Christ, and looks just like His Spirit.

2. Meditate on and say the following when you are struggling in any area. For additional help, do a deep dive into a concordance for each of the verses listed, and put them on note cards to keep with you. Refer back to them often on a daily basis:

   a. I am a partaker of God's divine nature! (2 Peter 1:4)

   b. I am seated with Christ in the heavenlies, and His victory is my victory! (Ephesians 2:6)

   c. I am who God says I am! I am DEAD to sin and that old person! (Romans 6:11)

    d.   I am a new creation WITH Christ—therefore I have the power to overcome all things! (2 Corinthians 5:17; Romans 8:37)

    e.   I am joined unto the Lord and I am one spirit with Him. (1 Corinthians 6:17)

    f.   I have been born of the Spirit! (John 3:6)

    g.   The healing that I need is already in my spirit because the power that raised Christ from the dead is already in me! (Romans 8:11)

Remember to RESIST the devil when he tries to remind you of who you used to be. (James 4:7)

Chapter 7: The Truth About Prayer, Hearing God, and Bible Study

1.   Use Biblehub.com or Biblehub App for Strong's Concordance and deeper studies in the original Hebrew and Greek. (Watch my demonstration video if you need help.) https://youtu.be/PaqWWA_N56s?si=2VC_awbmtQgB95v-

2.   Carve out a specific time and place each day when you are least likely to be interrupted or distracted to be alone and meditate on God's Word.

3.   Create a relaxing space where you can sit with God for at least 10 minutes a day to just pray and relax with Him. Imagine crawling into His lap or sitting under the shadow of His wing. Use YHWH breathing.[72] According to Jewish Rabbis and scholars, the letters YHWH represent breathing sounds, or aspirated consonants. When pronounced without intervening vowels, it sounds like breathing. YH would be the inhale and WH would be the exhale. Inhale "YAH" deeply as you imagine the LOVE of God filling your lungs; exhale "WEH" as you exhale all of your stress. You might want to surround yourself with pillows or a soft, fuzzy blanket that makes you feel safe.

    a.   Start with prayer and ask God to help you with your meditation. You can ask the Lord to draw you closer to Him, open your eyes to His truth, help you apply that truth in your life, and transform you as you meditate on God's Word.

    b.   Choose a small section of Scripture. Think about what the passage means. Study it in depth so that you can understand it in context. Take notes. Ask questions. Memorize the passage. Ask God what He wants to say to you through the text.

---

[72] (https://www.godreports.com/2022/08/when-breathing-speaks-the-name-of-god/)

       c.   Consider how you can apply the passage to your life in practical ways, and ask God to help you follow through in obedience to what He shows you.

4.   For an experience of worship and meditation, spend some time watching/listening to some of Pastor Chris Garcia's videos and meditations on YouTube:

       a.   LET ME SHOW YOU HOW TO HEAR GOD | LEARN HOW TO HEAR: https://www.youtube.com/live/LI-4ki4mXAs?si=L70cpN6cm-ISMxz6

5.   ***"O Hear" Inductive Bible Study***: Find the complete version in the appendix, along with example journal pages.

Chapter 8: The Truth About Faith and Belief – Uprooting Doubt

1.   **See it**: We need to see with our mind what those promises of God look like by vividly imagining His truths.

2.   **Speak it**: Instead of speaking out doubts and complaining, we must learn to speak the Word in agreement over ourselves, our circumstances, and our lives.

3.   **Catch it**: Catch every thought and bring it into obedience to the knowledge of God.

4.   **Pray it**: When tempted to fear or doubt, turn that thought into a prayer of praise and gratitude, thanking God for what you want rather than what you may be feeling or experiencing.

5.   **Think it**: Once you catch those negative thoughts, repeat the truth from the Word of God that counters that negative thought.

6.   **Study it**: Study the Word in depth. The original Hebrew and Greek are rich in application, cutting to the joints and marrow. Make sure you are in the Word daily. "Man does not live by bread alone but by every Word that proceeds from the mouth of the Lord" (Matthew 4:4).

7.   **Watch it**: Steep yourself in the Word and also healing testimonies and teachings that encourage your heart and mind to keep going. If these things can happen for others, they absolutely can happen for you!

8.   **Expect it**: God desires that we expect healing, peace, prosperity. Those in the Bible who followed Jesus did so because they expected Him to heal them. Our attitudes matter a great deal when it comes to receiving.

How to overcome:

1.   Using your imagination to "see" positive outcomes

2.   Say what you want to be your truth in line with Scripture

3. Speaking the Word over yourself and your situation
4. Catching your negative thoughts and changing them
5. Expressing trust in God through praise and gratitude
6. Watching/reading healing testimonies
7. Filling your mind with God's Word
8. Studying out Scripture with a Bible Concordance
9. Don't agree with everything you think (if it doesn't agree with the Word, it's not your truth).
10. Don't assume that what you feel is always your truth (physical or emotional) especially when those feelings are negative..

Chapter 9: The Truth About Mind Renewal

1. Using the Biblehub app or other Bible Concordance, do word studies on 2 Timothy 1:7 and Philippians 4:6-7
2. Directives from Proverbs 4 to cultivate your heart's soil:
    - Be ATTENTIVE to God's Word.
    - Incline your ear to His sayings: LISTEN to Him.
    - Set your mind on it: FOCUS.
    - Make them your truth by MEDITATING on them.
    - CHOOSE GODLY THOUGHTS and defend your heart and mind against anything ungodly.
    - Take care of what is allowed into your heart: GUARD IT.
    - Put away crooked speech. Our WORDS MATTER → WORDS = MATTER
    - No devious talk. (Deceptive talk, profanity, dishonest, slanderous, creating trouble).
    - Remain STEADFAST in the direction that you are going with the Lord. Don't get sidetracked.
    - Be SINGLE-MINDED.
    - DO NOT FLIRT with sin.
3. Meditate on a scripture that speaks to your true identity in Christ, God's love for you, or any others that you feel the Holy Spirit is leading you to focus on. Do so at least 10 minutes per day and plant the truths into your heart.
4. Choose joy! Your attitude matters. When you are having a rough day, choose to elevate your mood. Turn on praise music, dance, sing, watch things that make your heart happy. Choose to smile. Do whatever it takes to get your focus on the goodness of God and choose joy. (Philippians 4:8-9)

5. Each morning write or say 3 positive expectations you have for your day. Anticipate good, positive things. Think about the promises of God that apply to whatever you need for that day. EXPECT the goodness of God and His promises to happen. Praise Him and thank Him all day for those answers before you see them happen. Say, "I declare good things will happen today, in Jesus' name." Declare His promises over your day first thing each morning.

6. Spend some time journaling, specifically writing a letter from you to God about Romans 8:4-8. Consider verses about the tongue and repent in any area that concerns words you've spoken against others or yourself.

Chapter 10: The Truth About "Thinking on These Things" — Dream Big!

1. Create an Imagination Binder:
   Supplies:
   - 3 ring binder
   - Journaling paper
   - Bible
   - List of favorite praise songs

a. Brainstorm how you will imagine these situations and add these ideas to your notebook for quick referencing. Some ideas to get your creative juices flowing:

- Think about *who* you want to be—physically AND emotionally, and *why:* This is especially important. We need to see ourselves healed emotionally as well as physically. We need to see ourselves living out our purpose, experiencing the peace and abundant life God desires for us. Consider the qualities you see in others, especially Jesus. How did He handle things? Journal about how you will choose to handle things in the future, and use those notes to create these new beliefs about yourself in your mind as you imagine seeing yourself functioning in new situations.

- Go back to *Your Identity in Christ* and read over who you are. Spend time imagining scenarios of how that new identity in Christ functions. How do you feel now that you have the mind of Christ? How do you respond to situations and people?

- When you need to have a difficult discussion with someone, journal about how you'd like the discussion to go and how you want to FEEL and RESPOND rather than REACTING. Speak this out as you imagine:

- o *"I am calm."*
- o *"_____ hears my concerns and remains calm as well."*
- o Thank God during this time for the way you remain calm and are able to articulate in a peaceful manner.
- o *"Thank You God that _____ hears me."*
- o *"Thank You God that this meeting is going smoothly."*
- o *"Thank You God that we are able to work things out well through this discussion,"* etc.

b. Use your imagination for everything that you want to change about your life.

- Your physical health—see yourself whole and well. What kind of activities are you doing? Who are you with? How do you feel about it? Be descriptive.
- Your emotional health—you remain joyful, calm, peaceful.
- Your spiritual health—see yourself in a close relationship with Jesus.
- Finances—see and trust that God is providing for all of your needs. God does not want us to lack anything. If you are in need of some kind of provision, begin imagining and seeing that need being fulfilled and thank Him for doing so.
- Your career or ministry—if you are not currently doing what you feel is your calling, begin asking the Holy Spirit to help you imagine what living out that job or ministry might look like.
- Your relationships - imagine conversations, the way you want to respond, etc.

c. Bring God into your creative thinking and imagery.

- Do a short devotion in Scripture—read a chapter in the Bible and journal about it. Create a focused time of using your imagination based on stepping into the past with Jesus (as yourself) and imagine that you are part of His group of followers. Pray before these mental "visuals" and ask the Holy Spirit to reveal God's character to you so that you may see Him as He is. In this chapter is He joyful, loving? Can you see joy on His face and hear it in His voice? How does He look at those He is healing?
- Imagine going for hikes with Jesus. What do you talk about? Take Jesus to the grocery store with you. What foods would

He choose? Think about doing art with Jesus. What would He paint? Sculpt? Would those things come to life?

d.   Have a section in your binder with printed praise music.

- Imagine sitting out under the stars and singing praises to Father God with Jesus. Or singing praise songs to Jesus. You can sing praises during all kinds of creative thinking and times of imagining with the Lord.
- Are you hiking in your creative vision? Sing a song to the Lord about how beautiful His creation is.
- Are you shopping? Sing to Him about His goodness and provision. (Maybe the other shoppers in this creative vision will join in?)
- Are you watching Him heal someone? Is that someone YOU? Sing praises to Him for being your healer!

e.   When using your creative imagery, take time to thank God for what He is doing in your life. If you're seeing yourself healed and living your best life, thank Him for that healing.

- Philippians 4:6-7 (ESV) says, "... do not be anxious about anything, but in everything by prayer and supplication with thanksgiving let your requests be made known to God. And the peace of God, which surpasses all understanding, will guard your hearts and your minds in Christ Jesus."

f.   Thank Him for the answer before you see it. It's His will for you to be well. Thank Him for making that a reality when you are seeing this in your mind and imagination.

- 1 John 5:14-15 (ESV) says, "This is the confidence we have in approaching God: that if we ask anything according to His will He hears us. And if we know that He hears us—whatever we ask—we know that we have what we asked of him."
- Mark 11:24 (ESV) says, "Therefore, I tell you, whatever you ask for in prayer, believe that you have received it, and it will be yours."
- When you thank God while you are seeing these things happen in your mind, it invites Him to work and allows your faith, through the renewing of your mind, to change your circumstances.

g.   Be descriptive in your creative visioning times:

- Use words to explain what things look like in detail.
- How do you want to feel?

- Are there smells? Sounds?
- Really work up your emotions in a positive way to the point that you feel like this is a very real experience. This is how you write new messages upon your heart and change your beliefs. (Remember, the brain doesn't know the difference between what is real and imaginary. You're training your brain to believe what you are seeing in your imagination to be your truth.)
- Imagining positive things and "feeling" them helps your brain create those happy neurotransmitters—Dopamine, Oxytocin, Serotonin, and Endorphins. You're giving yourself a "DOSE" of wellness!

2.   Other ways to use Scripture with your imagination:

   a.   Psalm 23—I love visualizing this entire Psalm and considering how each verse can be applied to my life. I've given a few suggestions of how you might envision these things, but don't limit yourself to what I've shared:

- Vs 1 The LORD is my shepherd; (What does it mean to you that Jesus is your Shepherd? How might you imagine this?)
- I shall not want. (God provides everything that you need! Is there an area that you need for Him to supply? Begin seeing His provision in your imagination!)
- Vs 2 He makes me lie down in green pastures; (Imagine lying under a tree in the warm grass in the middle of summer with Jesus guarding over you. His peace is yours.)
- He leads me beside quiet waters. (You might imagine sitting on a beach next to a lake with Jesus, calm, joyful, relaxed.)
- Vs 3 He restores my soul; (Jesus gives you His peace and removes all of the emotional trauma and pain you've ever experienced. You feel peaceful and light.)
- He guides me in the paths of righteousness for the sake of His name. (Maybe you see yourself walking a road or hiking a beautiful trail with Jesus as you enjoy His company. He is changing and transforming every area of your life.)
- Vs. 4 Even though I walk through the valley of the shadow of death, I will fear no evil, for You are with me; Your rod and Your staff, they comfort me. (Consider whatever trial you might be going through right now. How might you see Jesus changing circumstances and working them out for your good? He is giving you the wisdom and guidance you need.)

- Vs. 5 You prepare a table before me in the presence of my enemies. (What might be on a table that Jesus prepares for you? What kinds of blessings would be included that your enemies would see? Jesus is showing off how He is providing for you!)

- You anoint my head with oil; my cup overflows. (You are the Lord's special guest. He anoints your head and gives you a place of honor. Your cup of blessings never runs dry! Similar to "I shall not want," this verse echoes that in God's blessings and supply for us, there is never any lack. Again, what is an area in your life in which you need His abundance to overtake you? What might that look like?)

- Vs. 6 Surely goodness and mercy will follow me all the days of my life, (All of the goodness that God has for you chases after you. You don't even need to go looking for it. God's provision and goodness comes upon you and overtakes you. What does this look like when you see it in your mind?)

- and I will dwell in the house of the LORD forever. (What does your mind see when you try to imagine the splendor and beauty of heaven? You get to LIVE with God!)

Chapter 11: The Truth About Worship, Praise, and Gratitude—By Beholding We Become

1. Make some time daily to just sit and worship God. If you aren't sure where to begin, watch one of Chris Garcia's YouTube videos: https://www.youtube.com/live/rI3bONsqyOE?si=fjMiQBtNKi1mdsLe

2. Begin by keeping a journal where you write down at least 10 things you are grateful for and your wins. At the end of each day, right before bed, write down all of your wins (catching/reframing negative thoughts, choosing to think greater than you feel, elevating your mood, keeping your mind off symptoms, etc.) and use the rest of the list for a list of thankfulness. For example, if you had only two wins for the day, you would fill in eight other things you were grateful for during that day. These things could be as simple as, "I'm grateful that the sky was blue and sunny today because I got natural vitamin D!" or "I'm grateful for my dishwasher because I don't have to wash dishes by hand." I've heard the statement, "If on Tuesday you only received the things you were grateful for on Monday, what would you have?" Gratitude is important for a number of reasons—it tells your brain that there were

positive things that happened during the day. It helps you sleep and also reminds your brain to look for positive things the following day.

Chapter 12: The Truth About Forgiveness

1. "If he has wronged you at all, or owes you anything, charge that to my account. I, Paul, write this with my own hand: I will repay it—to say nothing of your owing me even your own self." (Philemon 18-19 ESV) Although this is Paul speaking, we can hear this as Jesus speaking to us. Jesus wants us to understand that ALL manner of sin has been forgiven through His death upon the cross, not just *our* sins. We are to charge to His account anything that anyone else has done to us. Any sins that were committed against us went to the cross. Jesus paid the price for the sins of others just as much as He paid the price for our own sins.

    Consider looking at the cross and seeing the sins that were committed against you nailed to there. Those sins—no matter how heinous— were put upon Jesus. Jesus paid the price. Those sins committed against you hung upon that cross in Christ. Pulling them back down from the cross and taking those offenses again is like taking the sin that killed Jesus and making it our own. Why would we choose to hold on to that? What kind of effect do you think that might have?

2. When you consider that any hurts or offenses done against you hurt Jesus FIRST, and that He has already borne those hurts and paid for them, is there any reason for you to hold onto them? The next time someone hurts you, can you see those hurts and offenses placed upon Jesus instead of receiving them as your own? You are one with Christ. What affects you affects Him. Also remember that any offenses YOU commit against others will be similar to you committing those against Jesus. Consider how this might help you release hurts done to you.

3. **Steps to Forgiveness:**
    1. Start by making a list of all of the people you need to forgive, including yourself.
        a. Did you blame yourself? Parents? Anyone who should have protected you?
    2. Write next to each name—emotions and circumstances—be specific.
    3. Write a letter to each person who needs to be forgiven (in order to work through emotions. This letter will not be sent.)

4. Write a letter to yourself from God saying how much He loves you; He never abandoned you; He never wanted you to experience trauma, abuse or sickness from these circumstances.

5. Use your imagination to see yourself with <u>each</u> person who offended or hurt you.

   a. Imagine a SAFE place (maybe a room in a church with many windows or an open place outside), a place where you feel safe to be with the person you need to forgive.

   b. There are two chairs next to each other—one for you, and one for the offender.

   c. Tell the offender all of the things that you wrote about them and how that affected any areas of your life—be specific (e.g. "because it happened in the dark, I've been afraid of the dark, and it's affected my ability to sleep well.")

   d. Tell the offender that you forgive them.
       *Forgiveness does NOT mean you forget or excuse the wrongdoing.
       *Forgiveness is to free the person doing the forgiving from bitterness, resentment, hatred, fear, and other negative feelings.

   e. Tell the offender that you recognize that someone hurt them in their past and they dealt with it by hurting you in return.

   f. See yourself kneeling at the offender's feet and one foot at a time, washing the foot in a basin and then drying the foot with a towel.

   g. Take the dirty water that you can imagine is filled with whatever the offenses were and pour that water down the drain to symbolize forgiveness, letting go of all of the negative feelings you have and all of the awful things that were done to you.

   h. See the offender as a broken child, fragile, and take their hands in yours. Pray and ask God to forgive them for all that they did, and express to God that you forgive them.

    i. Feel a HUGE weight being lifted both physically and emotionally as you hand the offender over to God, and you now walk in freedom.

Chapter 13: The Truth About The Fruit of the Spirit and Armor of God
 1. **Fruit of the Spirit Meditation:**

Once you are filled with the Holy Spirit, you *have* the fruit of the Spirit in you. Think about and meditate on each characteristic of the Fruit and what these look like in your life. Work this into your daily routine. Consider the Scripture references to help you see these characteristics taking root in your life:

Love flows down your head from the crown down to your chin—"God's perfect love flows through me and casts out all fear." (1 John 4:18) Take a moment to consider how you see and hear things differently through a filter of Love.

Joy flows down your neck from the base of your head to your shoulders—"The joy of the Lord is my strength." (Nehemiah 8:10) When God's joy is your strength, what are you able to do differently? Physically? Mentally?

Peace is flowing around your heart and chest—"The peace of God which passes all understanding guards my heart and mind through Christ Jesus." (Philippians 4:7) When you are focusing on the peace of Christ, how will your day be different? How will you look at challenges? Other people? Yourself?

Patience flows down into your stomach and liver—"I am patient with myself and others." (1 Corinthians 13:4-5) What will your relationships look like as you experience patience in them? What will you experience in your heart and mind as you are patient with yourself?

Kindness flows into your belly—"I am kind to myself and others." (1 Corinthians 13:4) How do you choose to express kindness to yourself? And others?

Goodness flows down your shoulders into your arms and hands—"The goodness of God leads me to repentance; it works through my hands, and I bless others." (Romans 2:4) Are there actions that you have done that you might need to repent for as God's goodness speaks to your heart? How might you bless someone else today?

Faithfulness flows down your back—first over your shoulders, between your shoulder blades, mid-back and lower back—"I am filled with the faith of Jesus, and I am faithful to Him and myself." (Galatians 2:16) Did you know that you not only have a measure of faith, but you have THE FAITH of JESUS? What kinds of things can the faith of Jesus do? How might that change your life?

Gentleness flows down your buttocks, hips and thighs to your knees—"A gentle answer turns away wrath; I am gentle with myself and others." (Proverbs 15:1 NIV). Consider how you might begin answering everyone with a gentle answer. Are you gentle with yourself? How does your inner voice sound? How might you change the way you speak to yourself to reveal gentleness and grace in a way that you might speak to your best friend?

Self-control flows from your knees to your toes—"I am self-controlled in every way." (1 Corinthians 10:13) Self-control helps us to make godly choices. By using self-control, how might your choices today look different? Will you exercise? Eat healthfully? Spend quality time with the Lord? Avoid things that may not be beneficial for you physically? Emotionally? Spiritually?

2. **Armor of God Meditation:**

   Ephesians 6:11 ESV: "Put on the whole armor of God, that you may be able to stand against the schemes of the devil."

   God has given us His armor so that we can stand against the "wiles of the devil." God knows how our enemy works. He knows that when we forget WHO we are and WHOSE we are, we will be easy targets. That is the reason He has given us His armor—and when we stand in His armor we are able to bring the enemy into captivity when he tries to assault our minds and thoughts (2 Corinthians 10:5).

Use this outline to imagine that you are putting on each article of armor. Go through the physical motions of getting dressed in this armor, if you'd like:

Helmet: "I put on the helmet of salvation—I belong to the Lord." (Think about what it means to truly be *His*.)

Breastplate: "I put on the breastplate of righteousness—He covers me with His righteousness and perfection." (There is NO SIN counted toward you any longer! You are seen just as righteous as Jesus! This breastplate also guards over the PEACE in your heart.)

Belt: "I put on the belt of truth—God's Word alone is my truth." (Not the doctors' reports, the lies on TV, the news from the world—and not even the fears in your mind are Truth. Only the Word of God!)

Shoes: "I put on the shoes of the preparation of the gospel of peace—I stand in the peace of God, and take it with me everywhere I go!" (When you put those shoes on, you stand and remain in the peace of God, and you bring that peace everywhere when you share the Gospel of Christ.)

Shield: "I put on the shield of faith—it protects me from all the fiery darts of the enemy. It is a protective shield that surrounds me!" (Imagine this shield being like a sci-fi kind of shield that creates a bubble around you. Everything the enemy does just bounces right off!)

Sword: "I hold the sword of the Spirit—God's Word is the sword and my truth and weapon against the enemy." (You activate this sword by speaking the Word out loud.)

Chapter 14: The Truth About the Vine and the Branches—Abiding in Christ

1. Choose to ABIDE in Christ by:
    a. Reading the Word
    b. Prayer/listening to God (without ceasing)
    c. Spending time in worship, praise, and gratitude (constantly!)
    d. Meditating on His Word and renewing your mind to His Truth (we're always meditating on something—it might as well be His Truth!)
2. When a thought or feeling comes that you must do something in order to be loved by God, or in order to receive salvation, remind yourself that Jesus has already done everything for you. Your job is to rest in His finished work.
3. When feeling fearful, recognize that this is your cue to saturate your heart and mind with the truth that God loves you and accepts you.
4. Declutter your life, and choose to prune away anything that may be distracting you and keeping you from spending time with the Lord. Do this on a daily basis.

Meditate on what it means to abide in Christ. Remind yourself of the benefits you receive because you are connected to the Vine. Do this often, especially when you are feeling disconnected.

Appendix 1:

ADDITIONAL RESOURCES

Chapter 1

The Names of God in the Bible *https://www.godisreal.today/names-of-god/*
Names for God   *https://namesforgod.net/*
BibleHub (mentioned in numerous chapters) *https://www.biblehub.org/*

Andrew Wommack Ministries, "Healing University Kit"
https://store.awmi.net/p-1119-healing-university-kit.aspx
What does the Bible teach about the Trinity?
https://www.gotquestions.org/Trinity-Bible.html
The First Fruit Is Love *https://renner.org/article/the-first-fruit-is-love/*

Chapter 3

Winkler, Kyle. *Shut Up, Devil!* (Chosen Books, 2022).
Hagin, Kenneth E. *The Bible Way to Receive the Holy Spirit.* (Kenneth Hagin
Ministries, 1985)
The 7 Benefits of Praying in Tongues Explained
https://andrewsharpe.org/benefits-of-praying-in-tongues-explained/

Caprice Scott

Witter, Connie. *The Struggle is Over! You Have the Mind of Christ!* (Because of Jesus Publishing, 2019)

Chapter 4
Bennett, Barry. *Hearing God.* (Barry Bennett, 2015)

Chapter 5
Wommack, Andrew. *The Believer's Authority: What You Didn't Learn in Church.* (Harrison House, 2009)

Chapter 6
Spirit, Soul, and Body Study Guide by Andrew Wommack
https://www.awmi.net/study-guides/?id=418

Chapter 7
Wommack, Andrew. *Four Basics of Hearing God's Voice.* (Harrison House, 2023)
Chris Garcia: Let Me Show You How To Hear God
https://www.youtube.com/live/LI-4ki4mXAs?si=-LMv_emLUW4FtFoi
6 Bible Study Methods You Need to Know (and Try)
https://www.biblegateway.com/blog/2023/03/6-bible-study-methods-you-need-to-know-and-try/

Other Bible study resources:
➢ *Websters 1828 Dictionary: Free online version:*
   https://webstersdictionary1828.com/
➢ *The American Heritage Dictionary of the English Language. Fifth edition [revised].* (Houghton Mifflin Harcourt, 2016)
➢ Harris, R. Laird, et al, *Theological Wordbook of the Old Testament* (Moody Publishers, 1980)
➢ Connor, Kevin, *Interpreting the Symbols and Types* (Temple Publishing, 1992)
➢ Biblehub.com Tutorial:
   https://youtu.be/PaqWWA_N56s?si=vxALceX3sCpALQLd

Chapter 9

Pastor Mark Cowart and Joseph Z: Howard Pittman Interviewed by Pastor Mark Cowart. The Necessity for the Gospel of Repentance!
https://www.youtube.com/watch?v=rrPKf8WyeEk

Chapter 10

Wommack, Andrew, *The Power of Imagination: Unlocking Your Ability to Receive From God* (Harrison House, 2019)
Caprice's *Walking in the Word* Podcast
https://podcasters.spotify.com/pod/show/caprice-scott/

Chapter 11

Worship VS Praise - Is There Difference?
https://www.sharefaith.com/blog/2013/11/worship-praise-difference/

Chapter 12

What Unforgiveness Does to Your Brain *https://charlesstone.com/what-unforgiveness-does-to-your-brain/*
Dr. Caroline Leaf - On FORGIVENESS and how it affects our bodies
https://www.youtube.com/watch?v=EzR4H4oJbAc
Luskin, Fred, *Forgive for Good* (HarperCollins, 2003)

Chapter 13

Kenyon, E.W. *Identification: A Romance in Redemption* (Kenyon's Gospel Publishing Society, 1968)
Who I Am in Christ *www.whoiaminchrist.net*
Blake, Curry R., *Acknowledging What is in You* (Christian Reality Books, 2011)
Capps, Annette, *Quantum Faith* *http://housechurchministriesforjesus.com/wp-content/uploads/2012/10/BCR_121011_Wholeness-Call-5.pdf*
Wommack, Andrew. *A Better Way to Pray.* (Harrison House, 2007)

Chapter 14

Lawrence, Brother, *The Practice of the Presence of God* (Standard Publications, 2013)

Caprice Scott

List of in Christ, in Him Scriptures to establish your heart in your new creation identity in Christ *https://www.clintbyars.com/blog/2018/1/2/list-of-in-christ-in-him-scriptures*

Appendix 2

"O HEAR" **Inductive Bible Study Helps & Hints**
Open My Eyes and Ears - Invite a Search
Before you begin, pray for the Holy Spirit to open your eyes and ears to God's Word. Invite the Holy Spirit to shine His light into your heart and soul and to give you revelation and understanding.

Highlight and Listen - Note Key Words or Phrases
Read the passage through twice, then go back and highlight words or phrases that stand out to you personally. Remember, being transparent before the Father is the key to being transformed into the image of His Son.

Examine the Passage - Who, What, Where, How, Why, When
Go back and re-read the passage. Write and answer questions that come to you as you read. (Who, what, where, how, and why questions.) Here are a few to get you started:

- Who is the intended audience?
- What is the primary purpose of this passage?
- Why do you think the Holy Spirit had this passage written & included in Scripture?

Write and answer one or two other questions that relate to your examination of this passage. Remember to keep to the facts! Select and look up some key words. Write down a parallel passage. Consider using a Bible Dictionary, concordance or other study helps to deepen your understanding of the meaning in this context (Vine's, Strong's, etc.)

Apply - Moving from Head to Heart - What Does this Mean to Me Personally?

How am I encouraged and strengthened through this passage? What is the Father saying to me personally? Is there an example to follow, a sin to forsake, an error to avoid, a promise to claim, a command to obey?

Respond to the Word - Write a Prayer or Action Plan

A personal response can take many forms.

Write out a prayer that expresses your heart as you respond to His Word. -OR-

Write out an action plan, and/or describe any personal changes in your perspective. Ask God for help. It is a good idea to build in a point of accountability to yourself or someone else. This passage means to me _____ so I can or will _____.

*** On the following pages, you will find an example of Inductive Bible Study worksheets. You may want to make copies of these sheets to use for your daily Bible study time. You might choose to study a certain chapter over a week's time to dig deeply into the Word.

Created by William Rainey Harper and his student Wilbert W. White while at Yale in the late 1800s-early 1900s during the Inductive Bible Study Movement. "One of the most significant contributions to the work of Inductive Bible Study came with the 1952 publication of Robert Traina's seminal book, *The Methodical Bible Study*." (https://www.servantsuniversity.com/a-brief-history-of-the-inductive-bible-study-movement/)

"O HEAR" Bible Study Journal Pages

Date_____ Text_____

Theme_____

    Open My Eyes and Ears - Prayer

    Highlight - Note Key Words or Phrases

    Examine the Passage - Who, What, Where, When, Why, How? (verse by verse when you can)

_____
_____
_____
_____
_____
_____
_____
_____
_____
_____
_____
_____
_____
_____
_____
_____
_____
_____
_____
_____
_____
_____
_____
_____
_____
_____
_____
_____

Continued Examination of Passage answering Who, What, Where, How, Why, When? (verse by verse where you can):

_____
_____
_____
_____
_____
_____
_____
_____
_____
_____
_____
_____
_____
_____
_____
_____
_____
_____
_____
_____
_____
_____
_____
_____
_____
_____
_____
_____
_____
_____
_____
_____
_____
_____
_____

Apply - Moving from Head to Heart - What Does this Mean to Me?

Respond to the Word - Write a Prayer or Action Plan:

Bibliography

Bennett, Barry. *He Healed Them All©*. (Harrison House, 2020)

Capps, Annette, *Quantum Faith©* (Capps Publishing, 2020)

Cordeiro, Wayne, *The Divine Mentor: Growing Your Faith as You Sit at the Feet of the Savior©* (Bethany House, 2008)

DeJesus, Mark, *God Loves Me and I Love Myself!: Overcoming the Resistance to Loving Yourself©* (Turning Hearts Ministries, 2016)

Gonzales, Chad, *Never Be Sick Again: Access Supernatural Health Through Jesus' Resurrection Power©* (Harrison House, 2024)

Gunn, Tricia, *Unveiling Jesus: Beholding Him in His Amazing Grace©* (Patricia Gunn, 2014)

Leaf, Caroline, *Switch on Your Brain: The Key to Peak Happiness, Thinking, and Health©* (Baker Books, 2013)

Ozanich, Steven Ray, *The Great Pain Deception: Faulty Medical Advice is Making Us Worse©* (Silver Cord Records, 2011)

Renner, Rick, *Sparkling Gems from the Greek,* (Harrison House, 2003)

Watson, Thomas, *The Divine Cordial* (Public domain, 1663)

Caprice Scott

Winkler, Kyle, *Shut Up, Devil! Silencing the 10 Lies Behind Every Battle You Face©* (2022, Chosen Books)

Wommack, Andrew. *A Better Way to Pray©* (Harrison House, 2007)

Yandian, Bob, *A New Testament Commentary: Galatians* (Harrison House Publishers, 2016)

Zodhiates, Spiros, *The Complete Word Study Dictionary for a Deeper Understanding of the Word©* (AMG International Publishers, 1992)

Glossary of terms:

- *Amygdala*: The amygdala is the center of the brain that processes emotions. While it has other functions, it is often referred to as the "fear" center because it's the part of the brain that reacts with fear and aggression when we feel unsafe.
  (https://my.clevelandclinic.org/health/body/24894-amygdala)

- *Authority*: God gave the earth to mankind (Psalm 115:16) along with the "power and authority to rule over this earth as if we were the creator. We weren't the Creator, but that's how much dominion he gave us." *The Believer's Authority: What You Didn't Learn in Church©*. Wommack, Andrew. (Harrison House Publishers, 2009. p.45)

- *Baptism of the Holy Spirit*: Baptism of the Holy Spirit is the occurrence of the Holy Spirit coming upon a believer, imparting differing gifts that qualify the believer for service in the body of Christ. (Matthew 7:10-12) The gift of praying in tongues, a heavenly prayer language, is part of this experience when we ask and believe that we receive. (1 Corinthians 14:2)

- *CAN chemicals*: Cortisol, adrenaline, and norepinephrine are the brain and body's stress hormones. These hormones are activated when we are experiencing fearful or stressful situations.

(https://healthsmartva.org/uploads/rteditor/file/3-Adrenaline,%20Cortisol,%20Norepinephrine%20-The%20Three%20Major%20Stress%20Hormones,%20Explained%20.pdf)

- *Concordance:* A Bible concordance is a reference tool in which words from a particular translation of Scripture are arranged alphabetically in a kind of index—often accompanied by words from the immediate context of each use.

- *Condemnation*: When a law has been broken, the guilty party is condemned to receive the penalty for breaking the law. When one chooses not to receive the free gift of salvation, they accept condemnation for their sin by default. Jesus received the condemnation that we deserve, but we must receive Jesus in order to receive the righteousness and freedom from the penalty of sin. (https://www.biblestudytools.com/dictionary/condemnation/)

- *Discipleship*: A disciple is a follower, one who accepts and assists in spreading the doctrines of another. A Christian disciple is a person who follows Jesus Christ and accepts and assists in the spreading of the good news of salvation through Him. Christian discipleship is the process by which disciples grow in the Lord Jesus Christ and are equipped by the indwelling Holy Spirit to overcome the pressures and trials of this present life and become more and more Christlike. (https://www.gotquestions.org/Christian-discipleship.html)

- *Dominion*: Dominion refers to the authority and responsibility given by God to humans to govern, manage, and steward His creation.

- *DOSE chemicals*: Dopamine, oxytocin, serotonin, and endorphins are the major chemicals in our brains that affect our happiness. They are truly the brain's happy chemicals. These chemicals help us experience emotional well-being which also leads to physical healing. (https://www.psychologytoday.com/us/blog/your-neurochemical-self/201212/five-ways-boost-your-natural-happy-chemicals?msockid=03c5e2981d5d6c8409d6f0ee1ce76d89)

- *Doubt*: James 1:6 tells us that doubt hinders our ability to receive from God. Doubt doesn't take God at His Word and therefore doesn't receive from God. It isn't an unwillingness on God's end, it's a broken "receiver" on our end.

- *Forgiveness*: Forgiveness is God not counting our sins against us. This also means we are not continuing to count the sins of others against them. It does not mean we forget what happened or that we allow abusive situations to continue. Forgiveness releases us from anger and resentment towards others which allows our hearts to heal. Forgiveness does not always mean reconciliation between people, but when we receive the forgiveness of God, we are reconciled to Him.

- *Free will*: Free will is the freedom given by God to choose our thoughts, words, and behaviors

- *Justified*: The moment a believer receives Christ as Savior they are justified. This means that they are accepted before God as if they had never sinned at all (Romans 3:24; 5:1)

- *Meditation*: Biblical meditation is choosing to ponder on His Word and reflect upon its truths. It's rehearsing God's truths in one's mind.

- *Mind renewal*: According to Romans 12:2, mind renewal means to learn to see life through the lens of God's Word. As we put His Word into our hearts and minds, we begin to see life through God's perspective and truth. We stop referring to our old past hurts, woundedness, and trauma, and see ourselves as new creations in Christ. This helps us heal as we align our thoughts with God's truth, and we begin to experience His love, peace, and joy. Mind renewal is a daily, moment by moment choice to function from the mind of Christ rather than the flesh. (https://www.biblestudytools.com/bible-study/topical-studies/what-does-the-renewing-of-the-mind-look-like-for-christians.html)

- *Neuroplasticity*: Neuroplasticity is the brain's ability to change. It speaks to the flexibility and adaptability of our brain throughout our life (https://health.clevelandclinic.org/neuroplasticity)

- *Prayer*: Simply put, prayer is a conversation or dialogue we have with God.

- *Repentance*: Repentance in the Bible literally means "the act of changing one's mind." Repentance is not merely feeling sorry or regret for one's sin. Repentance is coming into agreement with God about that sin and choosing to change our direction. (https://www.gotquestions.org/Bible-repentance.html)

- *Revelation:* Revelation from God refers to God's acts of communicating unknown truths and facts about Himself to us. This can occur while we read His Word, meditate on His truths and character, pray, worship, praise, through nature, etc. God has numerous ways of revealing Himself, His purposes, and His ways to us.

- *Righteousness:* Righteousness is not something we can generate. It is a gift from God when we choose to believe that He makes us righteous because of all that Christ has done for us. Christ's perfection is applied to us when we believe Him for this gift.

- *Salvation:* The word salvation means more than just getting to go to heaven. According to Strong's Concordance, the Greek word *soteria* (salvation) includes - welfare, prosperity, deliverance, preservation, salvation, safety, to be saved, rescued.

- *Sin-consciousness:* Sin-consciousness keeps the believer stuck in the mindset that they are still sinners although Christ has made them righteous. While it is possible for a believer to sin (and we do) we are to focus on who God says we are, as His righteous heirs in Christ.

- *Spirit, soul, body:* You are a three-part being: you are a spirit, you have a soul (your mind, will, and emotions), and you live in your body. When you receive Christ as your Savior and are filled with the Holy Spirit, you become one with Him in your spirit. *Never Be Sick Again: Access Supernatural Health Through Jesus' Resurrection Power©*. Gonzales, Chad. (Harrison House Publishers, 2024. p.81)

- *Spirit realm:* The spirit realm is where heavenly angels, fallen angels (demons), and even God exist. They are not confined to our physical existence in the flesh and (for the most part) do not manifest in our physical realm. (https://yrm.org/the-spirit-realm-explained/)

Sources for Deepening Your Walk with God:

- Biblehub Tutorial:
  https://youtu.be/PaqWWA_N56s?si=ALs2Da1TdeZ8leug

- Dr. Kevin Chapman: The Sound Mind Show:
https://youtube.com/playlist?list=PLqXU-GuwMy4KE4ZuvSguQAjprK22coUU6&si=HK8OC1_GujEijasL

- *God Loves Me and I Love Myself! Overcoming the Resistance to Loving Yourself©.* Dejesus, Mark. (Turning Hearts Ministries, 2016)

- *He Healed Them All, Accessing God's Grace for Divine Health and Healing©.* Bennet, Barry. (Harrison House Publishers, 2020)

- Healing is for YOU! Facebook group. Join Caprice Scott's group for daily inspiration, encouragement, healing tips, and community of like-minded believers:
(https://www.facebook.com/groups/healingisforyou)

- *Mastering Our Emotions: Biblical Principles for Emotional Health©.* Chapman, Kevin. (IVP, 2025)

- *Permission to Be Imperfect: How to Strive Less, Stress Less, Sin Less©.* Winkler, Kyle. (Chosen Books, 2024)

- *Shaping Your Future: Releasing Your Destiny Through the Power of the Seed©.* Bennett, Barry. (Harrison House Publishers, 2021)

- *Shut Up, Devil: Silencing the 10 Lies Behind Every Battle You Face©.* Winkler, Kyle. (Chosen Books, 2022)

- Spirit, Soul, and Body by Andrew Wommack:
(https://youtu.be/b5aAGTNWNBA?si=RC2CQI_w8zYyNG-I)

- *Switch on Your Brain: The Key to Peak Happiness, Thinking, and Health©.* Leaf, Caroline. (Baker Books, 2013)

- *The Believer's Authority: What You Didn't Learn in Church©.* Wommack, Andrew. (Harrison House Publishers, 2009)

- *The Power of Identification with Christ.* Hankins, Mark. (MHM Publications, 2008)

- *Two Kinds of Righteousness.* Kenyon, E.W. (Whitaker House, 2019)

- *You've Already Got It! So Quit Trying to Get It©.* Wommack, Andrew. (Harrison House Publishers, 2006)

- *Power of Imagination: Unlocking Your Ability to Receive from God©* Wommack, Andrew. (Harrison House Publishers, 2019)

About
Kharis Publishing:

Kharis Publishing, an imprint of Kharis Media LLC, is a leading Christian and inspirational book publisher based in Aurora, Chicago metropolitan area, Illinois. Kharis' dual mission is to give voice to under-represented writers (including women and first-time authors) and equip orphans in developing countries with literacy tools. That is why, for each book sold, the publisher channels some of the proceeds into providing books and computers for orphanages in developing countries so that these kids may learn to read, dream, and grow. For a limited time, Kharis Publishing is accepting unsolicited queries for nonfiction (Christian, self-help, memoirs, business, health and wellness) from qualified leaders, professionals, pastors, and ministers. Learn more at:
https://kharispublishing.com/